Thirteen Crisis Years

Dedicated to my daughter Hazel Marie Olson, my personal secretary, for her excellent help in research and with the preparation of the manuscript.

Thirteen Crisis Years

1888-1901

From the Minneapolis Meeting to the
Reorganization of the General Conference

A. V. OLSON

Revised Edition
(Formerly published under the title
Through Crisis to Victory)

Review and Herald Publishing Association
Washington, D.C. 20012

Table of Contents

APPENDIXES

A. Ellen G. White Sermons at Minneapolis

Foreword
to First Edition

THROUGH CRISIS TO VICTORY by A. V. Olson is a stimulating historical review of a changing and perilous period in the development of a church movement. The thirteen years between Minneapolis, 1888, and the General Conference session of 1901 were in some ways the most progressive years of the Advent Movement up until that time, but they were fraught with conflict and clashes over organizational ideas and theological views. But it was a period over which Providence could spell out the word *victory*.

While serving as chairman of the board of trustees of the Ellen G. White Estate, a position he held for a number of years, A. V. Olson, through interviews and correspondence, became acutely aware of the misleading conclusions that some Seventh-day Adventists had reached relative to the General Conference held in Minneapolis in the autumn of 1888, and the aftermath of that historic session. It was apparent that not a few had formed opinions based on fragmentary bits of information, and also that at times other major issues of the thirteen years following 1888 were mistakenly confused with the problems of that meeting. Upon his retirement from General Conference administrative responsibilities, and while still serving as chairman of the board of trustees of the White Estate, Elder Olson studied thoroughly the records of the period as they are found in the voluminous files of the White Estate. Available to him were the Ellen G. White manuscript files and relevant articles appearing in the journals of the church, both by Ellen G. White and other authors. Also available were hundreds of letters having a bearing on the issues of the period, written by various denominational workers.

This study led to the conclusion that the 1888 experience was but one of several crisis experiences extending over a period of thirteen years. Painstakingly Elder Olson drew the materials together and formed them into chapters, presenting the historical background for the Minneapolis meeting, the issues relating to church organization, and the problems of our publishing houses,

7

particularly in commercial printing. All of these figure in the background of the interesting history of the Seventh-day Adventist Church from 1888 to 1901.

Assisted by his daughter Hazel in research and stenographic lines, to whom he dedicated this book, Elder Olson had virtually completed his work when, on a Friday afternoon, April 5, 1963, a heart attack suddenly terminated his life.

The White Estate Board has taken the appropriate steps to carry out the intent of the author, to make this information available to the workers of the Seventh-day Adventist Church and church members who may wish to study the history of this period. As was planned from the outset, the volume carries several appendixes, the major one being the Ellen G. White sermons preached at Minneapolis, which inclusion makes these materials in their entirety available for the first time in print.

Another appendix provides information concerning the later experiences of Elders Waggoner and Jones, which will be of interest and of service to the reader.

This volume presents not only a most enlightening historical account but also a great deal of helpful counsel, which makes clear the manner in which the Lord has led us. And we must ever keep in mind that "we have nothing to fear for the future, except as we shall forget the way the Lord has led us, and His teaching in our past history."

Arthur L. White, *Secretary*
ELLEN G. WHITE ESTATE

Washington, D.C.
March, 1966

Foreword
to Second Edition

As study was given to a second edition of this informative book, it was thought that a few changes would improve its usefulness. An Ellen G. White sermon presented at Minneapolis on October 19, 1888, and published a year later in the *Signs of the Times,* which was overlooked in preparing the first edition, has been included in Appendix A. Some footnotes and another important appendix item have been added. Some minor adjustments in wording have, in a few instances, been made. It is believed that this second edition will even more accurately portray the events of the years 1888 to 1901 than did the first edition.

The volume has been given a new title, THIRTEEN CRISIS YEARS, which is, perhaps, a little truer to the text of the book as a whole. The term *victory* used initially may very properly be written over the accomplishments in church reorganization in 1901, which opened the way for a rapid advance of the cause. *Victory* may be written also over the handling of such issues as the proposals of consolidation, the adoption of responsible financial policies, and the elimination of commercial printing in our publishing houses. But in the spiritual areas, such as the response to the messages on righteousness by faith presented at the Minneapolis General Conference and the several years thereafter, there were pluses and minuses. There should have been many more pluses than there were, and the term *victory,* if thought of in the sense of totality, does not create an accurate picture.

Matters of denominational procedures, movements, and policies can be settled by conference and committee actions. In the realm of spiritual concerns, however, acceptance or rejection is an individual matter. Each must decide for himself. Because it is a matter of choice, it cannot be legislated or enforced. At no time in history have all the members of the church been totally committed to the Lord, nor will this be the case until the angels in earth's last harvest separate the wheat from the tares.

9

THIRTEEN CRISIS YEARS

Particularly in the matter of acceptance of the basic provisions of salvation, where the individual in simple trust reaches out to claim the righteousness of Christ as a substitute for his efforts, the decision is a very personal one. It must also be a daily experience on his part. It may be enjoyed today and, by presumption or carelessness, be lost tomorrow. The apostle Paul says, "I die daily." For this reason and because victory could be written over only certain areas of experience of the thirteen years between 1888 and 1901, the title proposed when the manuscript was first submitted to the publishers—*Thirteen Crisis Years*—has now replaced the less accurate title *Through Crisis to Victory.*

Because the Minneapolis Conference is rarely referred to in any other context than the controversy that took place there concerning the presentation of righteousness by faith, the actual accomplishments of the nineteen-day session are almost totally lost sight of. One delegate, William C. White, a member of the General Conference Committee and much involved in the work of the conference, in a letter written as the work of the session drew to a close, described it as quoted on page 46 as "perhaps as profitable a meeting as was ever held."

We must also ever keep in mind that the genuine and simple experiences offered to us by our Lord and Saviour of replacing our filthy garments of self-righteousness with the spotless robe of His righteousness may be blurred or lost sight of in discussions of fine and involved theological points. Nor can one person closely define the steps and the precise course another must personally pursue in order to benefit fully from the Lord's proffered gift of salvation. Satan would confuse minds on this matter, for he knows "his power will be broken" (*Gospel Workers*, p. 161) if people have clear and correct concepts of this vital truth.

A full understanding of the 1888 Minneapolis General Conference session is not essential to gaining the full benefits of the plan of salvation. If so, what shall we say of the large numbers of believers in lands where the gospel must be presented in simple terms, and the third angel's message is progressing by leaps and bounds? Yet, knowledge of what took place at Minneapolis and its aftermath is of great interest. To those who feel it is vital, our concern is that whatever theories are developed should be firmly based, not on suppositions and conjectures, but on soundly documented facts of our history. To this end, the thrilling story and the recital of God's providences that have helped to make us God's remnant church are recounted in this volume, *Thirteen Crisis Years*.

—Arthur L. White

CHAPTER ONE

Preachers of the Law

THE Seventh-day Adventist Church today is an internationally known movement, familiar to Christians and non-Christians. It is looked upon as an aggressive, well-organized evangelical body with a strong sense of mission and a well-established world work. In its early days it was not so. The Advent Movement was regarded with contempt by the popular churches and the world in general. Its adherents—inconspicuous, few in number, and unorganized—were held to be deluded enthusiasts with queer doctrines to preach.

The early believers were usually poor in worldly goods and widely scattered. Its ministers were not seminary trained, and they preached to the "little flock" in modest homes or schoolhouses in countryside, villages, or cities. Church buildings and institutions were nonexistent. The tiny movement was expected to disappear from the scene of action, and its work to come to nought.

But the movement grew, becoming in time a vigorous body spreading itself across America and over the seas into other lands, organizing churches, erecting chapels, developing publishing houses, establishing schools, and building medical institutions. And as this growth and expansion occurred, many of the ministers of other denominations became uneasy. Conscious that Seventh-day Adventists were really beginning to make an impact upon the world and the members of their own churches, they became alarmed and moved in to save their flocks from this strange but convincing new doctrine. Danger signals were hoisted. From pulpit and press, warnings were sounded by the alarmed clergy. Tracts, pamphlets, and books were published denouncing the doctrines of the Seventh-day Adventists. The Sabbath became the special object of attack, and in order to counter the Bible evidence for seventh-day observance, Protestant preachers produced the most fantastic arguments to prove that God had changed, modified, or abolished the moral law of ten commandments. This they did in spite of the fact that their own creeds or confessions of faith made crystal clear that the law of ten commandments is as unchangeable and eternal as its Author, and that it is binding upon all men in all ages.

Seventh-day Adventist ministers and writers constantly were called upon to meet these spurious arguments and misrepresentations. At times their evangelists were challenged to debate the issues with these antinomians. Many of them became expert in the debater's arena, and seldom lost a battle.

Because of this intense warfare against the law and the Sabbath, Adventist preachers were forced to devote time, thought, and effort to controversial subjects. The vital, life-giving doctrines of the gospel and the cross of Christ—conversion, justification, sanctification, righteousness by faith—were taken for granted in the main without denying or questioning their necessity and importance. After all, these were not the issues at stake.

It is easily understood that Seventh-day Adventist writers and editors of the first few decades of the movement also gave a preponderance of space to the discussion of the law and the Sabbath. For the first few decades, nearly every issue of the church papers carried articles dealing with the various facets of law keeping, Sabbath observance, the covenants, et cetera.

The arguments produced, from the pulpit and through the press, were founded on the Word of God. They were

13

sound. No one doubted that Seventh-day Adventist evangelists were able defenders of the moral law. In time few dared to meet them in debate. They were respected for their knowledge of the Bible.

It was true then, however, as it is true now, that debates do not produce the best results, and they often have a detrimental influence upon the debater, his opponent, the audience, and the cause he represents. In 1871 Ellen G. White denounced this practice in forceful language: "These discussions," she wrote, "either oral or written, result in more harm than good" (*Testimonies*, vol. 3, p. 213). And with true insight she observed that—

"those who love to engage in discussion generally lose their spirituality. They do not trust in God as they should. They have the theory of the truth prepared to whip an opponent. The feelings of their own unsanctified hearts have prepared many sharp, close things to use as a snap to their whip to irritate and provoke their opponent. The spirit of Christ has no part in this."—*Ibid.*, p. 215.*

As the result of the constant emphasis upon the law and the Sabbath in lectures, sermons, and debates, Adventist preachers became known as legalists, and were accused of believing in salvation through works rather than through faith in Christ's work for them. It was a common charge that the Adventists did not really believe in Christ and His work of grace.

Now while it was grossly untrue to say that the early Adventist preacher disbelieved in the gospel and the precious

---

* Arthur W. Spalding, educator and historian, wrote of the Seventh-day Adventist Church of that day: "Their ministers engaged in debating with their opponents, and they triumphed over them on the question of the perpetuity of the law. To their credit be it said they did not often seek debate, for not only were they mindful of the warnings by Mrs. White against its influence on them, but in themselves they sensed the threat of polemics to the Spirit of Christ. But they were frequently challenged, and they did not fear to fight. The regularity of their triumphs begot in some of them, as they were warned it would, a spirit of self-sufficiency and personal prowess that was the ruination of their Christianity. Some of their great debaters passed out from their ranks. Case was an example. Moses Hull was another, an able and eager debater. Snook and his second, Brinkerhoff, were ready to take on all comers. Canright gloried in polemics. And it came to be the pride of many lay members that their champions were unbeatable on Bible grounds. It was likewise a byword in the religious world: 'No one loves a fight,' it was said, 'like a Seven Day Advent, except a Campbellite.' "—*Origin and History of Seventh-day Adventists*, vol. 2, p. 288.

light of the love and mercy of God, it was exceedingly difficult to detect such faith in Christ while listening to his vigorous defense of the moral law. There was little room in his preaching for the precious light of the love and righteousness of Christ—the Giver and Fulfiller of the law of God, the Lord of the Sabbath, and the Revealer of the character of God the Father. Alas, it must be said in truth that some Adventist ministers failed to emphasize that by living faith in Christ and His atoning sacrifice, the very righteousness of God is available to the repentant, believing sinner. Because they neglected to set forth this bright and appealing light of truth, all too often many lost it from their own sight and experience. And as a result, God's truth was at times robbed of its converting power.

Referring to these sad facts, in a sermon preached at Otsego, Michigan, on October 10, 1890, Ellen White remarked:

"In presenting the binding claims of the law, many have failed to portray the infinite love of Christ. Those who have so great truths, so weighty reforms to present to the people, have not had a realization of the value of the atoning Sacrifice as an expression of God's great love to man. Love for Jesus, and Jesus' love for sinners, have been dropped out of the religious experience of those who have been commissioned to preach the gospel, and self has been exalted instead of the Redeemer of mankind. . . .

"Many sermons preached upon the claims of the law have been without Christ, and this lack has made the truth inefficient in converting souls."—*Review and Herald*, Feb. 3, 1891, p. 66; in *Selected Messages*, book 1, pp. 371, 372.

In the same sermon Mrs. White said:

"The law is to be presented to its transgressors, not as something apart from God, but rather as an exponent of His mind and character. As the sunlight cannot be separated from the sun, so God's law cannot be rightly presented to man apart from the divine Author. The messenger should be able to say, 'In the law is God's will; come, see for yourselves that the law is what Paul declared it to be—"holy, and just, and good." ' It reproves sin, it

15

condemns the sinner, but it shows him his need of Christ, with whom is plenteous mercy and goodness and truth. Though the law cannot remit the penalty for sin, but charges the sinner with all his debt, Christ has promised abundant pardon to all who repent, and believe in His mercy. The love of God is extended in abundance to the repenting, believing soul. The brand of sin upon the soul can be effaced only through the blood of the atoning Sacrifice. No less an offering was required than the sacrifice of Him who was equal with the Father. The work of Christ—His life, humiliation, death, and intercession for lost man—magnifies the law, and makes it honorable."—*Selected Messages,* book 1, p. 371.

And Mrs. White emphasized the wonderful grace of God:

"Without the grace of Christ it is impossible to take one step in obedience to the law of God. Then how necessary that the sinner hear of the love and power of his Redeemer and Friend! While the ambassador for Christ should plainly declare the claims of the law, he should make it understood that none can be justified without the atoning sacrifice of Christ. Without Christ there can be only condemnation and a fearful looking for of fiery indignation, and final separation from the presence of God. But he whose eyes have been opened to see the love of Christ, will behold the character of God as full of love and compassion. God will not appear as a tyrannical, relentless being, but as a father longing to embrace his repenting son. The sinner will cry with the psalmist, 'Like as a father pitieth his children, so the Lord pitieth them that fear him' (Ps. 103:13). All despair is swept from the soul when Christ is seen in His true character."—*Ibid.,* p. 372.

Seventh-day Adventist ministers were not incorrect in defending the law of God, but they should have presented it in the setting of such Christ-filled texts as Romans 8:3, 4: "God sending his own Son in the likeness of sinful flesh, and for sin, condemned sin in the flesh: that the righteousness of the law might be fulfilled in us." The law of God should have been magnified as an expression of God's love—a way of righteousness and life for repentant sinners who believe in Christ as the perfect expression and embodiment of righteousness.

But Christ the Lord of the Sabbath (Mark 2:28; Luke 6:

5) should have been the center of their presentations. Indeed, as affirmed by Sister White in an article printed in the *Review and Herald* of March 20, 1894, page 177:

"The third angel's message calls for the presentation of the Sabbath of the fourth commandment, and this truth must be brought before the world; but the great center of attraction, Jesus Christ, must not be left out of the third angel's message.

"By many who have been engaged in the work for this time, Christ has been made secondary, and theories and arguments have had first place. The glory of God that was revealed to Moses in regard to the divine character has not been made prominent. . . .

"A veil has seemed to be before the eyes of many who have labored in the cause, so that when they presented the law, they have not had views of Jesus, and have not proclaimed the fact that, where sin abounded, grace doth much more abound. . . .

"What a loss it is to the soul who understands the strong claims of the law, and who yet fails to understand the grace of Christ which doth much more abound! . . . It is no wonder that hearts have not been melted by the truth, when it has been presented in a cold and lifeless manner. No wonder faith has staggered at the promises of God, when ministers and workers have failed to present Jesus in His relation to the law of God."—Reprinted in *Selected Messages*, book 1, pp. 383, 384.

If there had been a preaching of "Jesus in His relation to the law of God," the charges of legalism would not have been hurled against the early Adventist ministers. Had there been a preaching of the law and the Sabbath of God with an accompanying emphasis upon "the love of God, which is in Christ Jesus our Lord" (Rom. 8:39), and Christ, "the end of the law for righteousness to every one that believeth" (chap. 10:4); "a propitiation through faith in his blood" (chap. 3:25); "the propitiation for our sins: and not for our's only, but also for *the sins of* the whole world" (1 John 2:2); the Light of the world would have shone forth in clear and distinct rays everywhere.

By preaching the law apart from Christ, many of our ministers were found to be walking contrary to Paul's advice to Titus to "avoid . . . strivings about the law; for they are unprofitable and vain" (Titus 3:9), and following the example of Paul, they should have preached, saying: "Now the righteousness of God without the law is manifested, being witnessed by the law and the prophets; even the righteousness of God *which is* by faith of Jesus Christ unto all and upon all them that believe" (Rom. 3:21, 22).

The situation in the late 1880's was summarized by A. W. Spalding in these words:

"Seventh-day Adventists were the advocates of the immutability of the law of God, the whole law, and particularly, because of its being flouted, that part of the law which revealed the Sabbath. They engaged in battle in its behalf; they were beset on every side by their foes. Like the Dauphin at Poitiers, they cried out to their father, between thrust and parry: 'Have a care on your right, sir! Have a care on your left!' As Samuel Rhodes wrote to James White, 'Be of good cheer, my dear tried brother, and in Jesus' name press the battle to the gate!'

"Without a doubt the fathers of the Second Advent cause believed in the atoning grace of Christ as the sole means of salvation. It was acknowledged by Andrews, Waggoner, Smith, Loughborough, Cottrell, James White. And perhaps every member said amen. Yet, because in the minds of most the doctrine was assumed as the basic truth rather than emphasized as the dominant truth, it was in great measure lost sight of. The trend was to legalism."— *Op. cit.,* vol. 2, p. 286.

CHAPTER TWO

Believers in Christ

SEVENTH-DAY ADVENTISTS were early accused of being legalists, of believing and teaching salvation by works, and of not believing in Christ as the only Saviour from sin. But this charge was not true.

From the very beginning Seventh-day Adventists have been firm believers in Christ. Their very name—Seventh-day Adventist—testifies to their faith in Christ, for it was chosen by them because of their ardent belief in the Bible doctrine of the second advent of Christ. And this belief presupposes belief in His first advent, for there could be no second coming unless there had been a first. And it was His first advent that secured for all who accept Him the blessings of redemption through His sacrifice.

An Adventist minister and author, George C. Tenney, in 1880 wrote as follows on the question of the image of Seventh-day Adventist teaching, showing how Christ was the central theme of every doctrine we held:

"While we are presenting to the people the peculiar views held by S. D. Adventists, objectors are ever raising the inquiry, 'Why don't you preach Christ?' Certainly Christ is the great central character in every Bible doctrine, and a religion without Christ is not the religion of the Bible. Nor can we lay other foundation than that which is laid, which is Jesus Christ. Therefore, if the doctrines we present do not exalt Christ, they are worthy of censure, and the objection is a pertinent one.

"A glance at the different points of present truth will settle the question.

"We present first the prophecies. All lines of prophecy converge, and the grand terminal point is the setting up of the kingdom of Heaven. Of this kingdom Christ is the glorious and eternal King.

"We teach concerning the earth redeemed and restored to its Eden beauty. Christ is the redeemer and restorer of all things.

"The subject of the sanctuary presents Christ as our atoning sacrifice, our faithful high priest, and our advocate with the Father.

"The second advent is a doctrine made prominent by the Saviour and the apostles, and one that brings to view the consummation of the Christian's hope, the brightest point in all the experience of God's people. It gives release from sin and death, pain and sorrow; and ushers in everlasting peace and joy. This blessed hope rests upon Christ.

"Seventh-day Adventists teach the law of God as the rule of that perfect righteousness of which Christ was the living expositor. He kept His Father's commandments. He magnified the law. He declared Himself Lord of the Sabbath, and we strive to uphold that institution and maintain it against the usurpation of an anti-Christian power.

"The third angel's message is the forerunner of the second advent of Christ; and it proclaims not only the commandments of God, but also the faith of Jesus.

"Denying the natural inherent immortality of man, we teach that eternal life is the gift of God through Christ alone. Thus all our hopes for immortality depend upon Him.

"The testimony of Christ to His church finds expression, as the angel teaches and as we believe, in the spirit of prophecy.

"Thus the present truth presents Christ, not only humiliated and crucified, but risen and glorified. It holds up Christ as our exemplar while upon earth, our advocate above, and our approaching king in the world to come. It points to Christ as the only means of escape from eternal death, and to His second coming as the blessed hope of the people of God in all ages."—*Review and Herald,* Sept. 16, 1880, pp. 200, 201.

Yet, it was possible, as it has always been and will always be, to accept the theory of certain of the vital truths of Christianity without experiencing the power of these truths in personal life.

A perusal of Seventh-day Adventist publications of the

early decades of their denominational history gives abundant evidence that they believed then, as they do today, in salvation through faith in Christ. True, some of the pioneers coming as they did from religious groups that held Arian views, did not see fully, as is generally accepted today by Seventh-day Adventists, the eternal pre-existence of Christ. Ellen G. White was ever clear on this. And it was her writings in the 1890's, including *The Desire of Ages,* which clarified this important matter in the minds of Seventh-day Adventists.

Mrs. White—who was generally recognized by Adventists, and by many outside the movement, as the most authoritative writer on Bible themes—made plain in her earliest books published in the 1860's and 1870's that aside from Christ there is no salvation from sin and through Him there is plenteous redemption.

During the year 1864, there appeared volumes three and four of a four-volume set known as *Spiritual Gifts.* In volume three Mrs. White made clear that Christ has made salvation from sin possible:

"All heaven mourned on account of the disobedience and fall of Adam and Eve, which brought the wrath of God upon the whole human race. They were cut off from communing with God, and were plunged in hopeless misery. The law of God could not be changed to meet man's necessity, for in God's arrangement it was never to lose its force, or give up the smallest part of its claims.

"The Son of God pities fallen man. He knows that the law of His Father is as unchanging as Himself. He can only see one way of escape for the transgressor. He offers Himself to His Father as a sacrifice for man, to take their guilt and punishment upon Himself, and redeem them from death by dying in their place, and thus pay the ransom. The Father consents to give His dearly beloved Son to save the fallen race; and through His merits and intercession promises to receive man again into His favor, and to restore holiness to as many as should be willing to accept the atonement thus mercifully offered, and obey His law."—Pages 46, 47.

"Angels held communication with Adam after his fall, and

21

informed him of the plan of salvation, and that the human race was not beyond redemption. Although a fearful separation had taken place between God and man, yet provision had been made through the offering of His beloved Son by which man might be saved. But their only hope was through a life of humble repentance, and faith in the provision made. All those who could thus accept Christ as their only Saviour, should be again brought into favor with God through the merits of His Son."—*Ibid.*, p. 52.

During the years 1877 and 1878 two Ellen G. White volumes appeared known as volumes two and three of a four-volume set published under the general title *The Spirit of Prophecy*. All of volume 2 and part of volume 3 are devoted to the life and works of Jesus. From beginning to end, the author presents Christ as man's only hope of salvation from sin and eternal death. Writing of the Saviour as He hung upon the cross, she said:

"As man's substitute and surety, the iniquity of men was laid upon Christ; He was counted a transgressor that He might redeem them from the curse of the law. The guilt of every descendant of Adam of every age was pressing upon His heart; and the wrath of God, and the terrible manifestation of His displeasure because of iniquity, filled the soul of His Son with consternation. . . . He who stilled the angry waves by His word, and walked the foam-capped billows, who made devils tremble, and disease flee from His touch, who raised the dead to life and opened the eyes of the blind,— offers Himself upon the cross as the last sacrifice for man. He, the sin-bearer, endures judicial punishment for iniquity, and becomes sin itself for man."—*The Spirit of Prophecy*, vol. 3, pp. 162, 163.

For many years nearly every issue of both the *Review and Herald* and *The Signs of the Times* carried an article from the pen of Ellen G. White, and these articles never failed to point their readers to Jesus, the blessed Redeemer of lost sinners. A series of her articles entitled "The Sufferings of Christ" appeared in 1879 in *The Signs of the Times** in the issues of

---

* Appeared originally in Testimony No. 17, 1869 (See *Testimonies*, vol. 2, pp. 200-215).

August 7, 14, 21, and 28. These were repeatedly reproduced in tract form, and those who have read them agree that they are among the most inspiring messages ever written on the subject of salvation through Christ.

Turning to other authors and to contributors to the journals of the church, we find that although articles on the law and Sabbath predominated, there were many studies during these early years dealing with Christ as Saviour, the plan of salvation, the law and the gospel, justification by faith, sanctification, life only in Christ, and the second coming of Jesus. The reader will understand that the space limitations of this chapter, with due consideration for the proportions of this volume, allow for no more than a bare sampling of such from ministers and layman.

James White, one of the founders of the Advent Movement, and the first editor of the *Review and Herald,* church paper of the denomination, early expressed his belief in salvation through Christ as follows:

"The gospel arrangement is plain. God's law convicts of sin, and shows the sinner exposed to the wrath of God, and leads him to Christ, where justification for past offenses can be found alone through faith in His blood. The law of God has no power to pardon past offenses, its attribute being justice, therefore the convicted transgressor must flee to Jesus."—*Review and Herald,* June 10, 1852, p. 24.

In the next decade, in a volume published in 1868, he wrote:

"Here let it be distinctly understood that there is no salvation in the law, that is, there is no redeeming quality in law. Redemption is through the blood of Christ. The sinner may cease to break the commandments of God, and strive with all his powers to keep them, but this will not atone for his sins, and redeem him from his present condition in consequence of past transgression. Notwithstanding all his efforts to keep the law of God, he must be lost without faith in the atoning blood of Jesus. And this was as true in the time of Adam, of Abel, Enoch, Noah, Abraham, Moses, and the

23

Jews, as since Jesus died upon the cross. No man can be saved without Christ. On the other hand, faith in Jesus Christ, while refusing obedience to the law of the Father, is presumption. An effort to obtain friendship with the Son while living in rebellion against the Father, is Heaven-daring."—*Life Incidents in Connection With the Great Advent,* p. 354 (1868).

From time to time he expounded on this as he did in 1877, close to the time of his death:

"The perpetuity of the law of God, transgressed, makes the death of Christ a vital and perpetual truth in the system of redemption to be set forth in the gospel of the Son of God as long as human probation shall last. . . .

"But the glorious gospel of the Son of God presents Christ as now pleading the merits of his blood which was shed for our sins. This fact constitutes the highest evidence of the perpetuity of the law of God. It gives force to the grand truth, lying at the foundation of redemption, to be perpetuated in the gospel message to the end, as uttered by John in these words: 'If any man sin, we have an advocate with the Father, Jesus Christ the righteous.' 1 John 2:1. . . .

"Away with the idea that the law of God alone can save the sinner, however carefully he may observe all its precepts. . . . There is no redeeming power in law. If it were the province of law to redeem the transgressor of law, then Christ need not have died for our sins. . . . But away, *away* with the heresy that men may be saved by Christ and the gospel while trampling the law of God under their feet. God gave Christ to the world because his law was as changeless and enduring as his eternal Self. And there was no other way to meet the demands of that law, and at the same time save the sinner, than that Christ should die, the just for the unjust."—*The Redeemer and Redeemed; or the Plan of Redemption Through Christ,* pp. 5-7 (Pacific Press, 1877).

Uriah Smith—editor of the *Review and Herald* during most of the second half of the nineteenth century and until his sudden death on March 6, 1903, and the author of several helpful books—again and again expressed in his writings his faith in his blessed Saviour. Commenting, in his 1865 edition of his *Thoughts, Critical and Practical, on the Book of Reve-*

24

lation,* on verses eleven and twelve of the fifth chapter of Revelation, he first calls attention to the songs of praise arising from the myriads of angels around the throne of God in honor of the Lamb that was slain, and then breaks forth in words of admiration and adoration, saying:

"Fitting assemblage for such a place! Fitting song of adoration to be raised to Him who by the shedding of His blood became a ransom for many, and who as our great High Priest, still pleads its merits in the sanctuary above in our behalf. And here, before such an august assemblage must our characters soon come up in a final review. What shall fit us for the fiery ordeal? And what shall enable us to rise and stand at last with the sinless throng above? Oh, infinite blood of Christ! which can cleanse us from all our pollutions and make us meet to tread the holy hill of Zion! Oh, infinite grace of God! which can prepare us to endure the glory, and give us boldness to enter into His presence, even with exceeding joy."—Page 89. †

In the *Review and Herald* of February 27, 1883, F. Peabody builds his faith upon Christ. After quoting Acts 4:12, where Peter declares that "there is none other name under heaven given among men, whereby we must be saved," the writer voiced his personal conviction that only in Christ can we find salvation as follows:

"What is He to us? Just what He has always been to rebellious man 'the only name under heaven, given among men, whereby we must be saved.' Ever since rebellion began among men, Christ has been the one, and the only one, in whom was salvation. . . .

"Your Saviour is my Saviour. The rich, the poor, the high, the low, must alike look in one direction. No privileged characters here. The proud and haughty must come down. All are rebels to the government of Heaven, and need to be sought with terms of reconciliation. All must find mercy here. . . .

"Thou Lamb of God, we would ask for no other name. We will

---

* Uriah Smith later coupled this with his *Thoughts, Critical and Practical, on the Book of Daniel* in a book entitled *Thoughts, Critical and Practical, on the Books of Daniel and the Revelation*, which still later was entitled *Daniel and the Revelation*.
† In the 1884 edition of Uriah Smith's book *Thoughts, Critical and Practical, on the Books of Daniel and the Revelation*, this passage appears with very slight modifications, on page 407.

trust all in thy hands. Though the last enemy overtake us, we know that in thine own good time thou wilt enter his dark domains and rescue us. O Immanuel, if we leave thee, to whom shall we go?"—Page 133.

Seven months after the foregoing appeared in the *Review and Herald*, M. C. Wilcox, later editor of *The Signs of the Times*, voiced his belief in Christ in positive words:

"Here we have the plan of salvation in brief. All have sinned and come short—worthy of death. Christ the Creator of countless worlds, a Being above law, perfect in holiness, offers to die. He died for his people, or those who will prove faithful (1 Thess. 5:10); he died also for the ungoldly (Rom. 5:6).

"He not being amenable to law, and having no sins for which to answer, can offer himself a substitute for fallen man. Upon him were laid our sins (Isa. 53; 2 Cor. 6:21). It was a free offering— he 'gave himself' (Titus 2:14). God not only accepted that offering, but freely gave his Son (John 3:16; Rom. 8:32).

"Through this offering forgiveness is granted on conditions. By coming to God with sincere sorrow for our sins, and the determination to do wrong no more, by faith in Christ forgiveness is granted us. God for Christ's sake forgives our sins (Eph. 4:32). The repentance, however, must be genuine, or forgiveness will not be granted. It will only be found when it is sought for with *all* the heart, when sin appears exceedingly sinful; every known sin is cherished no longer, and so far as possible, restoration is made (Jer. 29:13; Eze. 33:14-16). Christ's perfect righteousness covers our unrighteousness; His character is imparted to us, and our sins are 'passed over' (Rom. 4:7, 8). Our names are now written in the 'book of life.' "—*Review and Herald*, Sept. 25, 1883, p. 610.

Four years later, a frequent contributor, Joseph Clarke, wrote for the *Review:*

"Christ became poor, that we through His poverty might be made rich. Would to God that His example might stimulate all, both rich and poor, to follow Him in all things. God is liberal. The air we breathe, the light we enjoy from the sun, moon, and stars, the genial warmth of summer, the breezes that cool the heated atmosphere,—all these are free. The water we drink is given in unlimited supply. But last of all, and most wonderful of all, is the free gift of God's dear Son, and the offer of eternal life to all who will avail themselves of the plan of salvation."—May 3, 1887, p. 275.

These, and many similar statements that could be cited, constitute so many exhibits which show that Seventh-day Adventists, in the early decades of their history, as well as today, believed in salvation only through faith in Christ. They never at any time taught that man can be saved by his own works. They always insisted that obedience to the law of God comes as a result of faith in Christ and the working of God's grace, that it is the fruitage of true faith in Him and love for Him.

Why, then, were the Adventists of that era accused of being legalists? Why was it said that they did not believe in Christ? Why was the charge directed against them of believing and teaching salvation by works? It was because many early Seventh-day Adventist preachers in their public ministry placed their principal emphasis on the law and the Sabbath instead of on Christ. It was because love for Jesus and love for sinners was inadvertently dropped out of the preaching and religious experience of many who had been commissioned to declare the gospel, but had not "had a realization of the value of the atoning Sacrifice as an expression of God's great love to man" (*Selected Messages,* book 1, p. 371).

And it was also because to many the light of righteousness by faith in Christ shining from the pages of God's Word and from the Spirit of Prophecy writings had grown dim through a neglect of prayer and communion, while the law and the Sabbath of the fourth commandment were brought to the front and emphasized apart from Christ, the only Saviour!

Without knowing it, the preachers drifted into legalism. As L. H. Christian wrote, the "leaders held fast to the doctrines of the message and . . . new converts were won," yet "there was a marked spiritual dearth."

27

CHAPTER THREE

The Call to Revival

IN BIBLE times, when lukewarm conditions developed in the church, God sent prophets with burning messages calling for revival and reformation. So among the Adventists of those early times God worked to right every wrong and to bring His people into a vital relationship with Christ. Through Ellen G. White the Lord sent earnest messages to the people of His remnant church. These messages pointed out their lukewarm condition, the reasons responsible for it, and called for a change. They contained earnest appeals to put first things first—to make Christ the center of all their living and preaching and activity.

Referring several years later to the situation that had developed, Mrs. White showed how serious it was and said:

"As a people, we have preached the law until we are as dry as the hills of Gilboa that had neither dew nor rain."—*Review and Herald*, March 11, 1890, p. 146.

"The trouble with our work has been that we have been content to present a cold theory of the truth."—*Ibid.*, May 28, 1889, p. 338.

"Spiritual things have not been discerned. Appearance and machinery have been exalted as of power, while the virtue of true goodness, noble piety, and heart-holiness, have been made a secondary consideration. That which should have been first has been made last and of least importance."—*Ibid.*, Feb. 27, 1894, p. 130.

Cold, theoretical preaching can neither produce nor maintain spiritual power and fervor in the church. Under the influence of such preaching, spiritual life tends to wither and die. Cold formality takes its place.

As early as 1879 Mrs. White wrote:

"A great and solemn truth has been entrusted to us, for which we are responsible. Too often this truth is presented in cold theory. Sermon after sermon upon doctrinal points is delivered to people who come and go, some of whom will never have another as favorable opportunity of being convicted and converted to Christ. Golden opportunities are lost by delivering elaborate discourses, which display self but do not magnify Christ. A theory of the truth without vital godliness cannot remove the moral darkness which envelops the soul."—*Testimonies,* vol. 4, pp. 313, 314.

In the following year, 1880, Mrs. White expressed the burden of her own heart and the plan of God for His people as follows:

"I long to see our ministers dwell more upon the cross of Christ, their own hearts, meanwhile, softened and subdued by the Saviour's matchless love, which prompted that infinite sacrifice. If, in connection with the theory of the truth, our ministers would dwell more upon practical godliness, speaking from a heart imbued with the spirit of truth, we should see many more souls flocking to the standard of truth; their hearts would be touched by the pleadings of the cross of Christ, the infinite generosity and pity of Jesus in suffering for man. These vital subjects, in connection with the doctrinal points of our faith, would effect much good among the people."—*Ibid.,* pp. 374, 375.

In an appeal to be read to Seventh-day Adventists as they assembled in camp meetings during the summer of 1882, the messenger of the Lord declared:

"God has made ample provision that we may stand perfect in His grace, wanting in nothing, waiting for the appearing of our Lord. Are you ready? Have you the wedding garment on? That garment will never cover deceit, impurity, corruption, or hypocrisy. . . .

"God spared not His own Son, but delivered Him to death for our offenses and raised Him again for our justification. Through Christ we may present our petitions at the throne of grace.

Through Him, unworthy as we are, we may obtain all spiritual blessings. Do we come to Him, that we may have life?"—*Ibid.,* vol. 5, pp. 220, 221.

"Will we put forth most earnest efforts to form this alliance with Christ, through which alone these blessings are attained? Will we break off our sins by righteousness and our iniquities by turning unto the Lord?"—*Ibid.,* p. 231.

She continued to speak along this line. During 1887, the year preceding the memorable meeting in Minneapolis, Minnesota, and on into 1888, her messages followed one another in quick succession through the columns of the *Review and Herald.*

Arthur W. Spalding, impressed by these calls to revival, observed that—

"it was the constant office of the Spirit of prophecy . . . to elevate; to save; to cry, 'Look to Jesus'; to bring souls out of their sin, out of their complacency, out of their self-righteousness; to bow at the feet of the Master of life and receive His power to live."—*Origin and History,* vol. 2, p. 285.

That the reader may get a clear picture of the situation, and sense the burden of the Spirit of Prophecy messages, we quote in chronological order a number of representative paragraphs that described the condition and need that called for a change:

Profession Not Enough: "The observance of external forms will never meet the great want of the human soul. A mere profession of Christ is not enough to prepare one to stand the test of the judgment."—ELLEN G. WHITE, in *Review and Herald,* Jan. 25, 1887, p. 491.

Too Much Formality: "There is too much formality in the church. Souls are perishing for light and knowledge. We should be so connected with the Source of light that we can be channels of light to the world."—*Ibid.,* Feb. 15, 1887, p. 97.

Like the Pretentious Fig Tree: "Those who profess to be guided by the Word of God, may be familiar with the evidences of their faith, and yet be like the pretentious fig tree, which flaunted its foliage in the face of the world, but when searched by the Master, was found destitute of fruit."—*Ibid.*

A Revival of True Godliness: "A revival of true godliness among us is the greatest and most urgent of all our needs. To seek this should be our first work. There must be earnest effort to obtain the blessing of the Lord, not because God is not willing to bestow His blessing upon us, but because we are unprepared to receive it. . . .

"There are persons in the church who are not converted, and who will not unite in earnest, prevailing prayer. We must enter upon the work individually. We must pray more, and talk less. Iniquity abounds, and the people must be taught not to be satisfied with a form of godliness without the spirit and power. . . .

"We have far more to fear from within than from without. The hindrances to strength and success are far greater from the church itself than from the world. . . .

"There is nothing that Satan fears so much as that the people of God shall clear the way by removing every hindrance, so that the Lord can pour out His Spirit upon a languishing church and an impenitent congregation. If Satan had his way, there would never be another awakening, great or small, to the end of time.

"But we are not ignorant of his devices. It is possible to resist his power. When the way is prepared for the Spirit of God, the blessing will come. Satan can no more hinder a shower of blessing from descending upon God's people than he can close the windows of heaven that rain cannot come upon the earth. Wicked men and devils cannot hinder the work of God, or shut out His presence from the assemblies of His people, if they will, with subdued, contrite hearts, confess and put away their sins, and in faith claim His promises. Every temptation, every opposing influence, whether open or secret, may be successfully resisted, 'not by might, nor by power, but by my Spirit, saith the Lord of hosts.' . . .

"What is our condition in this fearful and solemn time? Alas, what pride is prevailing in the church, what hypocrisy, what deception, what love of dress, frivolity, and amusement, what desire for the supremacy! All these sins have clouded the mind, so that eternal things have not been discerned."—*Ibid.*, March 22, 1887, pp. 177, 178.

As 1887 was about to close, this message from the pen of Ellen G. White appeared in the *Review and Herald:*

Pretended or Real Connection With Christ: "There is a wide difference between a pretended union and a real connection with Christ by faith. A profession of religion places men in the church, but this does not prove that they have a vital connection with the living Vine. . . .

"When this intimacy of connection and communion is formed, our sins are laid upon Christ, His righteousness is imputed to us. He was made sin for us, that we might be made the righteousness of God in Him. . . .

"The power of evil is so identified with human nature that no man can overcome except by union with Christ. Through this union we receive moral and spiritual power. If we have the Spirit of Christ, we shall bring forth the fruit of righteousness—fruit that will honor and bless men, and glorify God. . . .

"A union with Christ by living faith is enduring; every other union must perish. Christ first chose us, paying an infinite price for our redemption; and the true believer chooses Christ as first and last, and best in everything. But this union costs us something. It is a relation of utter dependence, to be entered into by a proud being. All who form this union must feel their need of the atoning blood of Christ. They must have a change of heart. They must submit their own will to the will of God. There will be a struggle with outward and internal obstacles. There must be a painful work of detachment, as well as a work of attachment. Pride, selfishness, vanity, worldliness—sin in all its forms—must be overcome, if we would enter into a union with Christ. The reason why many find the Christian life so deplorably hard, why they are so fickle, so variable, is, they try to attach themselves to Christ without first detaching themselves from these cherished idols."—*Ibid.,* Dec. 13, 1887, p. 769.

The positive remedial messages continued into the following year, the year of the Minneapolis meeting, with even greater urgency. Note the following:

The Presence of Jesus Needed: "Without the presence of Jesus in the heart, religious service is only dead, cold formalism. The longing desire for communion with God soon ceases when the Spirit of God is grieved from us; but when Christ is in us the hope of glory, we are constantly directed to think and act in reference to the glory of God."—*Ibid.,* April 17, 1888, p. 242.

The Solemn Question: "The solemn question should come home to every member of our churches, How are we standing before God, as the professed followers of Jesus Christ? Is our light shining forth to the world in clear, steady rays? Have we, as a people solemnly dedicated to God, preserved our union with the Source of all light? Are not the symptoms of decay and declension painfully visible in the midst of the Christian churches of today? Spiritual death has come upon the people that should be manifesting life and zeal, purity and consecration, by the most earnest devotion to the cause of truth. The facts concerning the real condition of the professed people of God speak more loudly than their profession, and make it evident that some power has cut the cable that anchored them to the Eternal Rock, and that they are drifting away to sea, without chart or compass."—*Ibid.*, July 24, 1888, p. 465.

Arguments Not Enough: "It is not enough to be familiar with the arguments of the truth alone. You must meet the people through the life that is in Jesus. Your work will be made wholly successful if Jesus is abiding with you; for He has said, 'Without me, ye can do nothing.'

"Jesus stands knocking—knocking at the door of your hearts —and yet, for all this, some say continually, 'I cannot find Him.' Why not? He says, 'I stand here knocking. Why do you not open the door, and say, Come in, dear Lord?' I am so glad for these simple directions as to the way to find Jesus. If it were not for them, I should not know how to find Him whose presence I desire so much. Open the door now, and empty the soul temple of the buyers and sellers, and invite the Lord to come in. Say to Him, 'I will love Thee with all my soul. . . . I will obey the law of God.' Then you will feel the peaceful presence of Jesus."—*Ibid.*, Aug. 28, 1888, p. 546.

The General Conference session for the year 1888 was called to meet in Minneapolis, Minnesota. As the date for the opening of this session approached, a ringing message came from the servant of the Lord. It was as a capsheaf to all the messages that had been coming from her pen during the preceding months. She wrote:

"What is the work of the minister[s] of the gospel? It is to rightly divide the word of truth; not to invent a new gospel, but to rightly divide the gospel already committed to them. They cannot rely upon old sermons to present to their congregations; for these set discourses may not be appropriate to meet the occasion, or the wants of the people. There are subjects that are sadly neglected, that should be largely dwelt upon. The burden of our message should be the mission and life of Jesus Christ. Let there be a dwelling upon the humiliation, self-denial, meekness, and lowliness of Christ, that proud and selfish hearts may see the difference between themselves and the Pattern, and may be humbled.

"Show to your hearers Jesus in His condescension to save fallen man. Show them that He who was their surety had to take human nature, and carry it through the darkness and the fearfulness of the malediction of His Father, because of man's transgression of His law; for the Saviour was found in fashion as a man. Describe, if human language can, the humiliation of the Son of God, and think not that you have reached the climax, when you see Him exchanging the throne of light and glory which He had with the Father, for humanity.

"He came forth from heaven to earth; and while on earth, He bore the curse of God as surety for the fallen race. He was not obliged to do this. He chose to bear the wrath of God, which man had incurred through disobedience to the divine law. He chose to endure the cruel mockings, the deridings, the scourging, and the crucifixion. 'And being made in fashion as a man, he humbled himself, and became obedient unto death'; but the manner of His death was an astonishment to the universe; for it was even the death of the cross.

"Christ was not insensible to ignominy and disgrace. He felt it all most bitterly. He felt it as much more deeply and acutely than we can feel suffering, as His nature was more exalted, and pure, and holy than that of the sinful race for whom He suffered. He was the majesty of heaven, He was equal with the Father, He was the commander of the hosts of angels, yet He died for man the death that was, above all others, clothed with ignominy and reproach. O that the haughty hearts of men might realize this! O that they might enter into the meaning of redemption, and seek to learn the meekness and lowliness of Jesus!"—*Ibid.*, Sept. 11, 1888, p. 578.

The extracts just quoted constitute only a fraction of the messages of appeal sent by the Lord through His messenger,

Ellen G. White, before the Minneapolis meeting. Through these messages God gave His people a clear picture of the sad, backslidden state of the church. They also indicated the remedy. The testimonies given appealed to workers and members to turn their eyes upon Jesus; to make Him first in their preaching, teaching, and living; and to exchange their unrighteousness for the righteousness of Christ. Thus before the Minneapolis meetings the call to receive the righteousness of Christ by faith and to preach it in Seventh-day Adventist churches and to the world in general was clearly sounded by the servant of the Lord. And who can know the influence of these preparatory messages? God was speaking to His people and helping them to understand their true spiritual poverty and their need of the heavenly treasure.

CHAPTER FOUR

The Session at Minneapolis

THE GENERAL CONFERENCE session of 1888 has gone down in the history of Seventh-day Adventists as one of the most important and controversial sessions ever held. The vital subject of righteousness by faith presented by two young ministers—E. J. Waggoner and A. T. Jones, editors of *The Signs of the Times*—provoked discussions marked by misunderstanding and perplexity on the one hand and a settled feeling of gratitude for God's providential leadings on the other.

When this historic twenty-seventh annual session of the General Conference convened in Minneapolis, Minnesota, October 17 to November 4, 1888, I was a boy four years old, living with my parents in Minnesota. Twenty-two years later I became the pastor of the church in which this great series of meetings was held. This church, on the corner of Lake Street and Fourth Avenue, was in 1888 one of the largest church buildings, if not the largest, owned by Seventh-day Adventists outside of Battle Creek, Michigan.

According to the minutes of that history-making session, as recorded in the *General Conference Bulletin* for that year, the opening service was attended by eighty-two delegates from North America and three from overseas, making a total of eighty-five, representing a world membership of 26,968, as reported to the session. Five additional delegates were seated on October 26.

The nineteen-day session followed a week-long Bible institute. The topics proposed for institute discussion included, "A Historical

View of the Ten Kingdoms," "The Divinity of Christ," "The Healing of the Deadly Wound," "Justification by Faith," "How Far Should We Go in Trying to Use the Wisdom of the Serpent," and "Predestination," (*Review and Herald,* Oct. 16, 1888, p. 648). It is possible, and even probable, that not all these topics were actually taken up, however. Near the close of the institute Elder E. J. Waggoner began a series of studies on the law in Galatians, which merged into a presentation of righteousness by faith. These continued at the Bible study hour through the first week of the General Conference session.

The session itself was quite routine but constructive. Reports were received. The various associations, such as Sabbath School, Health and Temperance, Tract and Missionary, held meetings. Fields of labor were assigned, the advancement of the cause was planned, and officers and committees elected. Since General Conference president George I. Butler could not be present because of ill health, Elder S. N. Haskell presided through both the Biblical institute and the session.

In the election that took place during the session, some changes in leadership were made. G. I. Butler, who had served as president of the General Conference for a total of eleven years (1871-1874 and 1880-1888), and who was absent from the session because of ill-health, was not re-elected. The new slate of officers chosen and the General Conference Committee elected as compared with the old, read as follows:

	New Slate *	*Old Slate* †
President:	O. A. Olsen	George I. Butler
Secretary:	D. T. Jones	Uriah Smith
Treasurer:	Harmon Lindsay	A. R. Henry

---

* This is not the list as first submitted by the nominating committee on October 31, 1888, but as it stood at the end of the session. See the 1889 *Yearbook*, pp. 25, 62.
† This list is taken from the *Review and Herald* of Dec. 6, 1887, p. 760. See also *Yearbook* of 1888, p. 11.

Executive Committee:	O. A. Olsen	George I. Butler
	S. N. Haskell	S. N. Haskell
	R. M. Kilgore	R. M. Kilgore
	E. W. Farnsworth	O. A. Olsen
	Dan T. Jones	Uriah Smith
	R. A. Underwood	R. A. Underwood
	W. C. White	W. C. White

Unfortunately no *General Conference Bulletin* reports exist of the Bible studies given at the session.

In the *General Conference Bulletin* of October 26, 1888, on page 3, in a report dated Wednesday, October 25, 1888, brief mention is made of studies presented by Elder E. J. Waggoner:

"A series of instructive lectures has been given on 'Justification by Faith' by Eld. E. J. Waggoner. The closing one was given this morning. With the foundation principles all are agreed, but there are some differences in regard to the interpretation of several passages. The lectures have tended to a more thorough investigation of the truth, and it is hoped that the unity of the faith will be reached on this important question."

The practice of recording all the Bible studies presented at our General Conference sessions was not adopted until 1891. However, we are not without knowledge regarding the contents of some of these sermons, for we have statements made concerning them from the pen of Ellen G. White and other persons, and fair judgment may be made from the later published works of Elders Waggoner and Jones.

The real burden of the message on righteousness by faith as presented by them, but primarily by Elder Waggoner, at the Minneapolis session was to affirm the truth that the only way righteousness can be obtained is through a living faith in the Lamb of God, whose blood was shed on Calvary's cross as a propitiation for the sins of the world. No one can enter the kingdom of God without being clad in the spotless robe of

Christ's righteousness. This robe can neither be purchased with silver and gold nor earned by good works. This message was a clarion call to make Christ and His righteousness the center of all our living and our preaching. It placed special emphasis on righteousness by faith as a real personal experience rather than a mere theory.

Seven years after the General Conference session of 1888, in a letter written May 1, 1895, from Hobart, Tasmania, to O. A. Olsen, then president of the General Conference, Sister White made the following significant statement regarding the message presented by Elders Waggoner and Jones at the meetings in Minneapolis:

"The Lord in His great mercy sent a most precious message to His people through Elders Waggoner and Jones. This message was to bring more prominently before the world the uplifted Saviour, the sacrifice for the sins of the whole world. It presented justification through faith in the Surety; it invited the people to receive the righteousness of Christ, which is made manifest in obedience to all the commandments of God. Many had lost sight of Jesus. They needed to have their eyes directed to His divine person, His merits, and His changeless love for the human family. All power is given into His hands, that He may dispense rich gifts unto men, imparting the priceless gift of His own righteousness to the helpless human agent. This is the message that God commanded to be given to the world. It is the third angel's message, which is to be proclaimed with a loud voice, and attended with the outpouring of His Spirit in a large measure. . . .

"The efficacy of the blood of Christ was to be presented to the people with freshness and power, that their faith might lay hold upon its merits. . . .

"Unless he makes it his life business to behold the uplifted Saviour, and by faith to accept the merits which it is his privilege to claim, the sinner can no more be saved than Peter could walk upon the water unless he kept his eyes fixed steadily upon Jesus. Now it has been Satan's determined purpose to eclipse the view of Jesus, and lead men to look to man, and trust to man, and be educated to expect help from man. For years the church has been looking to man, and expecting much from man, but not looking to Jesus, in whom our hopes of eternal life are centered. Therefore God gave to His servants a testimony that presented the truth as it is in Jesus, which is the third angel's message in clear, distinct lines."—Letter 57, 1895; in *Testimonies to Ministers*, pp. 91-93.

The message on righteousness by faith, which should have been joyfully received by all present at the Minneapolis session, was welcomed by many of the delegates, but not by all. Some were opposed to it, and still others adopted a neutral position.

Unfortunately, the impression exists in some minds today that the General Conference session in 1888 officially rejected the message of righteousness by faith presented to it. This is a serious mistake. No action whatever was taken by vote of the delegates to accept it or to reject it. Its acceptance or rejection by the people present at the session was an individual matter. And the acceptance or rejection of this teaching is still an individual matter.

That the message of righteousness by faith preached at the session was accepted differently by those attending is obvious from the following remarks by A. T. Jones himself, made five years later in a talk given by him at the General Conference session held in Battle Creek in 1893. After referring specifically to the Minneapolis session and the message of righteousness presented there, he said, on Tuesday, February 7:

"I know that some there accepted it; others rejected it entirely. . . . Others tried to stand half way between, and get it that way."—*General Conference Bulletin*, 1893, p. 185.

In a Bible study that Elder Jones gave a few days later (Monday, February 13) at the same session, he elaborated on the same point. Alluding first to the foregoing declaration, that he had made just a few days before, he said:

"There is a thought again that we had the other night [Tuesday, February 7, 1893], that when it was presented four years ago* and all along since, some accepted it just as it was given, and were glad of the news that God had righteousness that would pass the judgment, and would stand accepted in His sight. A righteousness that is a good deal better than anything that people could manufacture by years and years of hard work.

"People had worn out their souls almost, trying to manufacture a sufficient degree of righteousness to stand through the time of trouble, and meet the Saviour in peace when he comes; but they had not accomplished it. These were so glad to find out that God had already manufactured a robe of righteousness and offered it as a free gift to every one that would take it, that would answer now, and in the time of the plagues, and in the time of judgment, and to all eternity, that they received it gladly just as God gave it, and heartily thanked the Lord for it.

"Others would not have anything to do with it at all; but rejected the whole thing. Others seemed to take a middle position. They did not fully accept it, neither did they openly reject it. They thought to take a middle position, and go along with the crowd, if the crowd went that way. And *that* is the way they hoped to receive the righteousness of Christ and the message of the righteousness of God. Others deliberately discounted the message about fifty per cent, and counted *that* the righteousness of God. And so, all the way between open and free deliberate surrender and acceptance of it, to open, deliberate, and positive rejection of it—all the way between—the compromisers have been scattered ever since; and those who have taken that compromising position are no better prepared tonight to discern what is the message of the righteousness of Christ than they were four years ago.—*Ibid.*, pp. 243, 244.

These two statements made by A. T. Jones at the General Conference session of 1893, held at Battle Creek, Michigan, show clearly that the message of righteousness by faith presented at the General Conference session of 1888 brought forth diverse responses, and that those who heard it were divided into three groups: (1) those who gladly accepted the message, (2) those who opposed it, and (3) those who, neither

---

* Elder Jones meant "over" "four years ago," for the Minneapolis session, to which he here refers, was held from October 17 to November 4, 1888.

accepting nor rejecting it, preferred to remain neutral or undecided.

Commenting on the reception of the message presented at the General Conference session of 1888, A. G. Daniells—who was then a successful young worker in New Zealand, but who thirteen years later (1901) became president of the General Conference, and who continued to be president for twenty-one years—observes in his book *Christ Our Righteousness:*

"The message was not received alike by all who attended the Conference; in fact, there was serious difference of opinion concerning it among the leaders. This division of opinion may be classified as follows:

"*Class 1.*—Those who saw great light in it and gladly accepted it. . . .

"*Class 2.*—There were some, however, who felt uncertain about the 'new teaching,' as they termed it. They seemed unable to grasp it. . . .

"*Class 3.*—But there were others who were decidedly opposed to the presentation of the message."—Edition of 1926, pp. 56, 57; ed. of 1941, pp. 41, 42.

Those who at Minneapolis received the needed message of righteousness by faith found in it a source of joy and blessing. At times they spoke of this as did Elder A. O. Tait in his letter to W. C. White, written from Battle Creek, October 7, 1895:

"I found that doctrine just the food that my poor soul needed there at Minneapolis, and I was converted at that meeting, and have been rejoicing in the light of it ever since."

Some of those who spurned the message, yielded to feelings and expressions of bitter criticism, sarcasm, and animosity for the men who had presented it. This is impressively revealed in the following statement by Mrs. White in a letter to Elder Olsen, written May 1, 1895, and quoted earlier:

"God gave to His messengers just what the people needed. Those who received the message were greatly blessed, for they saw the bright rays of the Sun of Righteousness, and life and hope sprang up in their hearts. They were beholding Christ. . . .

"But there are those who despised the men and the message they bore. They have taunted them with being fanatics, extremists, and enthusiasts."—*Testimonies to Ministers,* pp. 95-97.

Instead of following the example of the noble Bereans, who "received the word with all readiness of mind, and searched the scriptures daily, whether those things were so" (Acts 17:11), the delegates at the General Conference session became divided into opposing camps, which sought to settle their differences by heated arguments and debates. Soon the atmosphere became charged, and feelings ran high.

This most regrettable experience was referred to by Mrs. White in a letter that she wrote on November 19, 1902:

" 'I have been instructed that the terrible experience at the Minneapolis Conference is one of the saddest chapters in the history of the believers in present truth.' "—Letter 179, 1902.

She elaborated upon this sad chapter in the history of Seventh-day Adventists in a letter written from Australia to her nephew Frank Belden and his wife:

"Never before have I seen among our people such firm self-complacency and unwillingness to accept and acknowledge light as was manifested at Minneapolis. I have been shown that not one of the company who cherished the spirit manifested at that meeting would again have clear light to discern the preciousness of the truth sent them from Heaven until they humbled their pride and confessed that they were not actuated by the Spirit of God, but that their minds and hearts were filled with prejudice. The Lord desired to come near to them, to bless them and heal them of their backslidings, but they would not hearken. They were actuated by the same spirit that inspired Korah, Dathan, and Abiram. . . .

"When I purposed to leave Minneapolis, the Angel of the Lord stood by me and said: 'Not so; God has a work for you to do in this place. The people are acting over the rebellion of Korah, Dathan, and Abiram. I have placed you in your proper position, which those who are not in the light will not acknowledge; they will not heed your testimony; but I will be with you; My grace and power shall sustain you. It is not you they are despising, but the messengers and the message I sent to My people. They have shown contempt for the word of the Lord. Satan has blinded their eyes and perverted their judgment; and unless every soul shall repent of this their sin, this unsanctified independence that is doing insult to the Spirit of God, they will walk in darkness. I will remove the candlestick out of his place except they repent and be converted, that I should heal them. They have obscured their spiritual eyesight. They would not that God should manifest His Spirit and His power, for they have a spirit of mockery and disgust at My word. Lightness, trifling, jesting, and joking are daily practiced. They have not set their hearts to seek Me. They walk in the sparks of their own kindling, and unless they repent, they shall lie down in sorrow. Thus saith the Lord: "Stand at your post of duty; for I am with thee, and will not leave thee nor forsake thee." '

"These words from God I have not dared to disregard."—Letter 2a, 1892.

In spite of the tensions, conflicts, and disappointments, the Minneapolis meeting was a victory in many respects. The hearts of all present were greatly cheered by the reports that came from Europe, Australia, New Zealand, the South Sea Islands, and South Africa—most of them new mission fields—bringing words of hope and of progress in souls won to the third angel's message. As the delegates lifted up their eyes and beheld these great, ripening fields their hearts were moved with compassion. Plans were laid to send forth more laborers to help gather in the golden grain. There were also seasons of refreshing for all who opened their hearts. Referring to these, in a letter written seven years later (May 1, 1895), Mrs. White said:

"Again and again the Spirit of the Lord came into the meeting [at Minneapolis] with convincing power, notwithstanding the unbelief manifested by some present."—Letter 51a, 1895.

"Unbelief," wrote Mrs. White, was "manifest by *some* present." (Italics supplied.) But not by all. Seasons of spiritual refreshing were occasioned by the many soul-stirring sermons preached by Mrs. White during the course of the session itself and during the General Conference institute, or workers' meeting, which immediately preceded it.* One of these sermons, "Tell of God's Love and Power," in which she dealt with Christless preachers (given on Sabbath, October 13), made a profound impression upon the entire group assembled at the institute. (See Appendix A, page 252.) This is apparent in a statement from the pen of Uriah Smith, the secretary of the session as well as the editor of the *Review and Herald*, which reads:

"Sabbath, October 13, was a memorable day on account of the refreshing received from the Lord. Sister White spoke in the afternoon with great freedom and power. From the text 'Behold, what manner of love the Father hath bestowed upon us, that we should be called the sons of God,' most precious lessons were drawn of the great goodness of God to us, and how we should receive his love, and what he is willing to do for us, and what returns we should make to him for his manifold mercies to us. Hearts were melted by the sweet influence of the meeting, and it was indeed good to be there. After the discourse, sixty-two earnest testimonies were borne in quick succession, the burden of which was thanksgiving and praise for the mercies and goodness of the Lord."— *Review and Herald*, Oct. 23, 1888, p. 664.

The sermons and talks presented by Mrs. White through both institute and conference were marked by deep spiritual fervor and the power of the Holy Spirit. The spiritual refreshing brought to the Minneapolis session through her ministry was again attested to by Uriah Smith as he reported for the *Review and Herald* the proceedings of Wednesday, October 25, the eighth day of the session:

"Among the most interesting and important meetings, are the early morning devotional meetings. The exhortations of Sr.

---

* This institute was held in Minneapolis during October 10-17. (See *Review and Herald*, Oct. 16, 1888, and Oct. 23, 1888.) Much of the conflict over the question of righteousness by faith took place in this gathering. The eight sermons preached by Mrs. White during this institute and the conference session following it appear in Appendix A.

White have been most cheering, as she has presented the love of Christ and His willingness to help. That He is waiting to pour out of His Spirit upon His people in abundant measure. One important thing in the cause of Christ is to be connected with Christ."—*General Conference Bulletin*, Oct. 26, 1888, p. 3.

The over-all spirit and work of the Minneapolis conference is reflected in a statement written just two days before the session closed, by W. C. White, a son of Ellen G. White. William C. White had carried heavy responsibilities during the meeting, had been re-elected to the General Conference Committee, and was asked to serve as acting president of the General Conference during the interim between the session and the arrival from Europe, several months later, of O. A. Olsen, the newly elected president. Elder White wrote:

"We are just at the close of another General Conference, and in a few days the delegates will be scattered to their respective fields, and another year's work begun.

"This has been a very interesting conference, and although not accompanied with all that peace and harmony that sometimes has been manifest, it is perhaps as profitable a meeting as was ever held, for many important principles were made prominent, and some conclusions arrived at, that will be of great value, as they may influence our future work. Many go forth from this meeting determined to study the Bible as never before, and this will result in clearer preaching.

"As you have no doubt noticed in the *Bulletin*, many advance steps have been taken as to our foreign missions, also some good moves for the advancement of the work in the South."—Letter to Smith Sharp, written from Minneapolis, Minnesota, Nov. 2, 1888.

The emphasis of this letter is on the encouraging aspects of the Minneapolis session, and only a brief allusion is made to the unfortunate experience that marked this important meeting. The reference to this particular characteristic is ampler in the following lines, written almost three weeks later by W. C. White to a close associate, J. N. Loughborough. Even this is brightened by an expression of good cheer:

"The conference is over and instead of my being ready to come home to California, I am tied here for several weeks, if not for several months.

"You have no doubt formed quite an idea of how our conference went off from the *Bulletins* and the *Review*. Some things you would read between the lines that were quite as interesting if not in all respects as encouraging as what was printed. The delegates went home from the conference with a great variety of sentiments. Some felt that it had been the greatest blessing of their lives; others, that it marked the beginning of a period of darkness, and that the evil effects of what had been done at the conference could never be effaced. As for myself, I am content to take the Scripture statement, 'For we know that all things work together for good to those who love God.'"—Written from Battle Creek, Michigan, Nov. 20, 1888.

The Conference closed at noon, Sunday, November 4. How enlightening any letter written by delegates on that day would be! As it happened Ellen G. White wrote a letter to Mary White, her daughter-in-law, that afternoon. With the Conference over and her work done, she writes this family letter in a free and easy way. Nonetheless, its careful reading is quite illuminating, offering a number of insights. Its essential parts make a fitting conclusion to the account of the session at Minneapolis. It bears no pessimistic overtones:

Our meeting is closed. I have on last Sabbath given my last discourse. There seemed for the first time to be considerable feeling in the congregation. I called them forward for prayers although the church was densely packed. Quite a number came forward. The Lord gave me the spirit of supplication and His blessing came upon me.

I did not go out to meeting this morning. This has been a most laborious meeting, for Willie and I have had to watch at every point lest there should be moves made, resolutions passed, that would prove detrimental to the future work.

I have spoken nearly twenty times with great freedom and we believe that this meeting will result in great good. We know not the future but we feel that Jesus stands at the helm and we shall not be shipwrecked. My courage and faith have been good and have not failed me, notwithstanding we have had the hardest and most incomprehensible tug of war we have ever had among our people. The matter cannot be explained by pen unless I should write many, many pages; so I had better not undertake the job.

THIRTEEN CRISIS YEARS

Elder Olsen is to be president of the General Conference and Brother Dan Jones of Kansas is to help him. Elder Haskell will serve until Brother Olsen shall come from Europe.* I cannot tell what the future may reveal, but we shall remain for about four weeks in Battle Creek and get out a testimony that should come out just now without delay. Then we can see how matters move at the great center of the work. We are determined to do all we can in the fear of God to help our people in this emergency.

A sick man's mind has had a controlling power over the General Conference Committee and the ministers have been the shadow and echo of Elder Butler about as long as it is healthy and for the good of the cause. Envy, evil surmisings, jealousies have been working like leaven until the whole lump seemed to be leavened. . . .

Today, Sunday, I have not attended meeting, but have had to visit considerably. I am grateful to God for the strength and freedom and power of His Spirit in bearing my testimony although it has made the least inpression upon many minds than at any period before in my history. Satan has seemed to have power to hinder my work in a wonderful degree, but I tremble to think what would have been in this meeting if we had not been here. God would have worked in some way to prevent this spirit brought to the meeting, having a controlling power. But we are not the least discouraged. We trust in the Lord God of Israel. The truth will triumph and we mean to triumph with it.

We think of you all at home and would be pleased to be with you, but our wishes are not to be consulted. The Lord is our Leader, let Him direct our course and we will follow where He leads the way.—Letter 82, 1888.

If only all who were in attendance at the Minneapolis gathering had accepted without reserve the message sent them by God on the subject of righteousness by faith, the General Conference session of 1888 would have gone down in the annals of Adventism as the greatest and most glorious session up to that time. Unfortunately this was not the case.

---

*At a meeting of the General Conference Committee held in Battle Creek after the delegates returned from Minneapolis, Elder Haskell was released and Elder W. C. White was asked to serve as acting president.

CHAPTER FIVE

Voices of Opposition

THE OPPOSITION that developed at the Minneapolis General Conference session of 1888 against the message of righteousness by faith preached by E. J. Waggoner and A. T. Jones sprang from the weaknesses of human nature. One of these was prejudice.

It often happens that when a speaker presents some apparently new thought or theme, prejudice on the part of his hearers makes them unable to properly weigh the evidences set forth in its favor. So it was in Minneapolis. Some who heard E. J. Waggoner and A. T. Jones thought they were too young to have such a prominent part in the hours set apart for the study of the Bible, and some felt that the manners and language of one of the young speakers were objectionable.*

Of course, these prejudiced opinions concerning these two men were not a valid reason for opposing or rejecting the message of righteousness by faith presented by them. A doctrine should be judged on its own merits, and those to whom it is presented should examine it, with God's help, in such a way as to ascertain if it is supported by the Word of God.

In addition to prejudice, there were three matters that weighed heavily in the balance of opinions at Minneapolis

---

* NOTE: "The conflict," wrote Arthur W. Spalding, ". . . involved personalities quite as much as preaching. Jones, and especially Waggoner, were young men, and their voices, with the note of authority in them, were resented by not a few of the older men. . . .
"Jones was aggressive, and at times obstreperous, and he gave just cause for resentment, yet most of his hearers could forgive occasional crudities in view of his evident sincerity and his forceful presentation."—SPALDING, *Origin and History*, vol. 2, pp. 292, 293.
E. J. Waggoner was 33 years of age and A. T. Jones was 38.

with regard to the message of righteousness by faith as there presented. These we shall now consider.

I. *The Implication That It Was New Light*

The opposers of the message of righteousness by faith preached by E. J. Waggoner and A. T. Jones regarded this message as a veiled accusation against themselves, their belief, and their preaching. They felt that even though the speakers had not stated it in so many words, the implication of their presentations was that righteousness by faith was something new, something that our ministers had never understood, believed, or preached. This, their opponents averred, was entirely wrong. They maintained that Seventh-day Adventists had always believed in righteousness by faith.

Technically, this was true. An examination of the Seventh-day Adventist publications of the times that we are considering reveals statements that support their contention.

Just four years before the Minneapolis meeting George I. Butler, then president of the General Conference, wrote in clear, positive language concerning righteousness by faith:

"Paul failed in every effort to keep the law in his own strength; and so will every one of us. What did he do? Did he give up in despair? By no means. After crying out, 'O wretched man that I am!' he looks to Jesus Christ, and finds help and deliverance. He then exclaims, 'There is therefore now no condemnation to them who are in Christ Jesus, who walk not after the flesh but after the Spirit; for the law of the Spirit of life in Christ Jesus hath made me free from the law of sin and death. For what the law could not do, in that it was weak through the flesh, God sending his own Son in the likeness of sinful flesh, and for sin [by sacrifice for sin, *margin*], condemned sin in the flesh; that the righteousness of the law might be fulfilled in us [the precept of the law fulfilled by us— *Whiting*] who walk not after the flesh, but after the Spirit.'

"Paul utterly failed in keeping the law before in his own strength. His garment of right doing was properly represented by filthy rags; but now he has found life in Christ, and the precepts of the law he keeps through the strength which Christ imparts. He is now found not having his own righteousness, 'which is of the law; but that [righteousness] which is through the faith of Christ, the righteousness which is of God by faith.'

"Christ's strength imparted to Paul through faith, gave him victory over his besetments, and he was now clothed with Christ's righteousness, that is, righteousness or right doing, which he was enabled by the strength of Christ to obtain. Christ, then, has strength to impart which will enable us to keep the law in the spirit and the letter; but this strength can never be obtained till with brokenness of heart and a sense of our own weakness, we fall upon Him, and then by faith draw His blessing down.

"God forbid that any of us should appear before the judgment bar having 'our own righteousness, which is by the law;' that is, being satisfied with our own efforts to keep the law without the help of Christ's Spirit; but may we all appear before Him, having that righteousness which comes by faith in Christ, giving us strength to carry out its sacred principles, and live up to all its requirements. This power comes alone through conversion and living faith."— *Review and Herald*, Sept. 23, 1884, pp. 616, 617.

As early as 1852, James White, sturdy leader and able writer, expressed his belief in justification by faith as follows:

"Those who represent Sabbathkeepers as going away from Jesus, the only source of justification, and rejecting His atoning blood, and seeking justification by the law, do it either ignorantly or wickedly."—*Ibid.*, June 10, 1852, p. 24.

A few years later Uriah Smith, long-time editor of the *Review and Herald*, expressed his belief in the blessed truth of righteousness by faith when, in commenting on Revelation 7:13, 14, he wrote:

"Though the 144,000 are accused of rejecting Christ and trusting to their own works for salvation, because they refuse to violate the commandments of God, Rev. xiv, 1, 12, in the great day that calumny will be wiped off. It will be seen that they have rested their hope of life on the merits of the shed blood of their divine Redeemer, making Him their source of righteousness. There is peculiar force in saying of these that they have washed their robes

51

and made them white in the blood of the Lamb."—*Thoughts, Critical and Practical, on the Book of Revelation* (1865 ed.), p. 136.*

Just three years later (1868) J. H. Waggoner, one of our veteran editors and the father of E. J. Waggoner, declared his belief in righteousness by faith in this comment on Romans 3:21:

"There are but three senses, as I conceive, in which this phrase, 'the righteousness of God,' may be used. It must refer primarily to his own attributes; secondly, to the revelation of his will, which is the unfolding of his attributes; and thirdly, to the righteousness of his saints, whose characters are made conformable to his will. In this latter sense it is used in 2 Cor. v, 21. 'That we might be made the righteousness of God in him.' And the righteousness of God without the works of the law, manifested through the faith of Christ, can simply have respect to Jesus Christ's removing our sin, and thus placing us before the throne of justice as free, as sinless, as though we had never broken the law. But the law being the measure of holiness, of perfection, the rule of judgment, is of course a witness of the righteousness so effected; for as condemnation is by law, so must justification be according to law, or else justice will be disregarded. So there can be no determination of character, either good or bad, without the law. But this text says the law is a witness of the righteousness of God; and this only confirms the views I have taken, that it is a revelation of the divine perfection. No language could more clearly show it."—*The Atonement: an Examination of a Remedial System in the Light of Nature and Revelation* (1868 ed.), pp. 62, 63.

In the light of these statements, and also of those quoted in the preceding chapters of this book, it must be clear that during the decades of our denominational history preceding the 1888 General Conference session Seventh-day Adventist ministers understood and believed the fundamental principles of the doctrine of righteousness by faith. Furthermore,

---

* The passage quoted here is found also on page 175 of the 1881 edition (which is the "Third Edition, Revised and Enlarged") of the book just named. The last two sentences are likewise found on page 470 of *The Prophecies of Daniel and the Revelation*, which is the 1944 revised edition of Uriah Smith's books on Daniel and the Revelation. This valuable book was highly recommended by Ellen G. White. (See *Colporteur Ministry*, pp. 123, 124.)

Ellen G. White, as we have seen, continually emphasized these truths in her ministry. No, righteousness by faith was not new light when it was preached in Minneapolis! It was neglected light, as Mrs. White indicated late in the year 1888:

"Elder E. J. Waggoner had the privilege [at Minneapolis] granted him of speaking plainly and presenting his views upon justification by faith and the righteousness of Christ in relation to the law. *This was no new light, but it was old light placed where it should be in the third angel's message.* . . .

"*The faith of Jesus has been overlooked and treated in an indifferent, careless manner. It has not occupied the prominent position in which it was revealed to John.* Faith in Christ as the sinner's only hope has been largely left out, not only of the discourses given but of the religious experience of very many who claim to believe the third angel's message. At this meeting I bore testimony that the most precious light had been shining forth from the Scriptures in the presentation of the great subject of the righteousness of Christ connected with the law, which should be constantly kept before the sinner as his only hope of salvation.

"*This was not new light to me,* for it had come to me from higher authority for the last forty-four years, and I had presented it to our people by pen and voice in the testimonies of His Spirit. But very few had responded except by assent to the testimonies borne upon this subject. There was altogether too little spoken and written upon this great question."—"Looking Back at Minneapolis," Manuscript 24, 1888 (written about November or December, 1888. (Italics supplied.)

In a sermon delivered at the camp meeting held at Rome, New York, on June 17, 1889, Ellen G. White remarked:

" 'I have had the question asked, What do you think of this light that these men are presenting? Why, I have been presenting it to you for the last forty-five years—the matchless charms of Christ. This is what [I] have been trying to present before your minds. When Brother Waggoner brought out these ideas in Minneapolis, it was the first clear teaching on this subject from any human lips I had heard, excepting the conversations between myself and my husband.' "—Manuscript 5, 1889, pp. 9, 10.

Two months later in a *Review and Herald* article, she declared:

"The doctrine of justification by faith has been lost sight of by many who have professed to believe the third angel's message. . . .

"God has raised up men to meet the necessity of this time. . . . Their work is not only to proclaim the law, but to preach the truth for this time,—the Lord our righteousness."—August 13, 1889, p. 514; in *Selected Messages,* book 1, pp. 360, 361. (Italics supplied.)

In 1890 she wrote:

"Some of our brethren have expressed fears that we shall dwell too much upon the subject of justification by faith. . . . If there had not been a remissness in the past to properly instruct the people of God, there would not now be a necessity of calling especial attention to it. . . . The exceeding great and precious promises given us in the Holy Scriptures have been lost sight of to a great extent, just as the enemy of all righteousness designed that they should be. He has cast his own dark shadow between us and our God, that we may not see the true character of God."—*Review and Herald,* April 1, 1890, p. 193; in *Selected Messages,* book 1, p. 372.

Four years later she wrote:

"By many who have been engaged in the work for this time, Christ has been made secondary, and theories and arguments have had the first place. . . .

"Laborers in the cause of truth should present the righteousness of Christ, not as new light, but as precious light that has for a time been lost sight of by the people. . . .

"No wonder faith has staggered at the promises of God, when ministers and workers have failed to present Jesus in His relation to the law of God."—*Review and Herald,* March 20, 1894, p. 177; in *Selected Messages,* book 1, pp. 383, 384.

Truth is often hard to take. This is decidedly so if it seems to indicate defects in our cherished beliefs or methods of labor. And, if the revelation comes through younger and less-experienced men, it is still harder for some older men to accept. This evidently was the case at the meetings in Minneapolis and for some time afterward.

II. *Conflict Over the Ten Horns of Daniel Seven*

In the week-long workers' meeting that preceded the General Conference session in Minneapolis, two prominent, strongminded men clashed over the subject of the ten horns of Daniel 7.

On one hand, Uriah Smith, the editor of the *Review and Herald,* and the author of *Thoughts on Daniel and the Revelation,* a book that had been given a wide circulation, maintained that the Huns constituted one of the ten kingdoms represented by the ten horns.

On the other hand, A. T. Jones, one of the editors of the *Signs of the Times,* who also had made an extensive study of Daniel 7, contended for the Alamanni in place of the Huns.

The debate between these two stalwarts waxed hot. Sides were taken, and the camp was divided. The controversy over the Huns and the Alamanni was "a minor matter, indeed, but it rubbed already stubborn fur the wrong way."—SPALDING, *op. cit.,* vol. 2, p. 291. This division of opinion at the workers' meeting set the stage for the division of opinion concerning the message of righteousness by faith presented by E. J. Waggoner and A. T. Jones.

III. *Conflicting Views Over the Law in Galatians*

Before the General Conference session at Minneapolis, the *Review and Herald* had published an article in which the author, O. A. Johnson, in a discussion on "The Two Laws" took the position that the law in Galatians included the ceremonial law.*

---

* *Review and Herald,* April 13, 1886. Said Johnson, "Now while the decalogue is called the law of God, it is never called the law of Moses. Neither is there anything in this law relating to ordinances or sacrifices. See Jer. 7:22, 23.

"Besides this law another law was added 'because of transgression,' and it was given through the mediator Moses. Gal. 3:19. This law was written in a book and kept by the side of the ark. Deut. 31:24, 26."

After this *Review* article appeared, *The Signs of the Times* carried a series of nine articles (July 8-September 2, 1886) in which E. J. Waggoner, one of the editors, took the position that Paul, in the Epistle to the Galatians, was discussing the moral law.

On February 18, 1887, Ellen G. White wrote from Basel, Switzerland, a letter of rebuke to the two editors of *The Signs of the Times* for having published articles which revealed to our people and to the world that our two best-known church papers were at variance on certain teachings. In this letter Mrs. White did not take a position either for or against Elder Waggoner's views on the law in Galatians. She said:

"I have no hesitancy in saying you have made a mistake here. You have departed from the positive directions God has given upon this matter, and only harm will be the result. This is not in God's order. You have now set the example for others to do as you have done, to feel at liberty to put in their various ideas and theories and bring them before the public, because you have done this. This will bring in a state of things that you have not dreamed of. . . .

"It is no small matter for you to come out in the *Signs* as you have done, and God has plainly revealed that such things should not be done. We must keep before the world a united front. Satan will triumph to see differences among Seventh-day Adventists. These questions are not vital points. . . .

"But how do you think I feel to see our two leading papers in contention? I know how these papers came into existence, I know what God has said about them, that they are one, that no variance should be seen in these two instrumentalities of God. They are one and they must remain one, breathing the same spirit, exercised in the same work, to prepare a people to stand in the day of the Lord, one in faith, one in purpose. . . .

"There has been a door thrown open for variance and strife and contention and differences which none of you can see but God. His eye traces the beginning to the end. And the magnitude of mischief God alone knows. The bitterness, the wrath, the resentment, the jealousies, the heart burnings provoked by controversies of both sides of the question cause the loss of many souls."—Letter 37, 1887; in *Counsels to Writers and Editors*, pp. 75-80.

This statement points out the sad fact that the articles mentioned had sown seeds that would produce a grim harvest. The predicted results became very apparent at Minneapolis.

During the ministerial institute that preceded the Minneapolis session E. J. Waggoner gave some studies on the subjects of the atonement and the law, and this led to a spirit of division and debate.

This contention over the law in Galatians was responsible for much of the opposition that developed in Minneapolis against Elders Waggoner and Jones and the message they presented on righteousness by faith. This Mrs. White plainly stated a few years later (in 1896). After quoting Galatians 3:24 ("The law was our schoolmaster to bring us unto Christ, that we might be justified by faith"), she said:

"In this scripture, the Holy Spirit through the apostle is speaking especially of the moral law. The law reveals sin to us, and causes us to feel our need of Christ and to flee unto Him for pardon and peace by exercising repentance toward God and faith toward our Lord Jesus Christ.

"An unwillingness to yield up preconceived opinions, and to accept this truth, lay at the foundation of a large share of the opposition manifested at Minneapolis against the Lord's message through Brethren [E. J.] Waggoner and [A. T.] Jones. By exciting that opposition Satan succeeded in shutting away from our people, in a great measure, the special power of the Holy Spirit that God longed to impart to them. The enemy prevented them from obtaining that efficiency which might have been theirs in carrying the truth to the world, as the apostles proclaimed it after the day of Pentecost. The light that is to lighten the whole earth with its glory was resisted, and by the action of our own brethren has been in a great degree kept away from the world."—Letter 96, 1896; in *Selected Messages*, book 1, pp. 234, 235.*

These are some of the things that led certain ones to oppose the message of righteousness by faith presented at Min-

---

* Note: For the relationship of the ceremonial law and the moral law to Paul's discussion in Galatians, see *Selected Messages*, book 1, pages 233-235.

neapolis. But these prejudices and contentions were not valid reasons for the course pursued there.

During the Minneapolis session Mrs. White in her addresses urged the brethren not to permit themselves to be carried away by their feelings. She appealed to them to search the Scriptures calmly and prayerfully to know the truth as it is in Christ Jesus. Toward the close of the meeting she made a final earnest appeal for unity and brotherly love. Here are some pointed excerpts from that discourse:

"I entreat you to exercise the spirit of Christians. Do not let strong feelings of prejudice arise, for we should be prepared to investigate the Scriptures with unbiased minds, with reverence and candor. It becomes us to pray over matters of difference in views of Scripture. Personal feelings should not be allowed to influence our words or our judgment. It will grieve the Spirit of God if you close your understanding to the light which God sends you.

"Dr. Waggoner has spoken to us in a straightforward manner. There is precious light in what he has said. Some things presented in reference to the law in Galatians, if I fully understand his position, do not harmonize with the understanding I have had of this subject; but truth will lose nothing by investigation, therefore I plead for Christ's sake that you come to the living Oracles, and with prayer and humiliation seek God. Every one should feel that he has the privilege of searching the Scriptures for himself, and he should do this with earnest prayer that God will give him a right understanding of His Word, that he may know from positive evidence that he does know what is truth.

"I would have humility of mind, and be willing to be instructed as a child. The Lord has been pleased to give me great light, yet I know that He leads other minds, and opens to them the mysteries of His Word, and I want to receive every ray of light that God shall send me, though it should come through the humblest of His servants.

"Of one thing I am certain, as Christians you have no right to entertain feelings of enmity, unkindness, and prejudice toward Dr. Waggoner,* who has presented his views in a plain, straightforward manner, as a Christian should. If he is in error, you should,

---

* Note: E. J. Waggoner was both a minister and a physician.

in a calm, rational, Christlike manner, seek to show him from the Word of God where he is out of harmony with its teachings. If you cannot do this you have no right as Christians to pick flaws, to criticize, to work in the dark, to prejudice minds with your objections. This is Satan's way of working.

"Some interpretations of Scripture given by Dr. Waggoner I do not regard as correct. But I believe him to be perfectly honest in his views, and I would respect his feelings and treat him as a Christian gentleman. I have no reason to think that he is not as much esteemed of God as are any of my brethren, and shall regard him as a Christian brother so long as there is no evidence that he is unworthy. The fact that he honestly holds some views of Scripture differing from yours or mine is no reason why we should treat him as an offender or as a dangerous man, and make him the subject of unjust criticism. We should not raise a voice of censure against him or his teachings unless we can present weighty reasons for so doing and show him that he is in error. No one should feel at liberty to give loose rein to the combative spirit. . . .

"I see the beauty of truth in the presentation of the righteousness of Christ in relation to the law as the doctor has placed it before us. You say, many of you, it is light and truth. Yet you have not presented it in this light heretofore. Is it not possible that through earnest, prayerful searching of the Scriptures he has seen still greater light on some points? That which has been presented harmonizes perfectly with the light which God has been pleased to give me during all the years of my experience. If our ministering brethren would accept the doctrine which has been presented so clearly—the righteousness of Christ in connection with the law—and I know they need to accept this, their prejudices would not have a controlling power, and the people would be fed with their portion of meat in due season. Let us take our Bibles, and with humble prayer and a teachable spirit come to the great Teacher of the world; let us pray as did David, 'Open thou mine eyes, that I may behold wondrous things out of thy law' [Ps. 119:18]. . . .

"Said my Guide, 'There is much light yet to shine forth from the law of God and the gospel of righteousness. This message, understood in its true character and proclaimed in the Spirit, will lighten the earth with its glory. The great decisive question is to be brought before all nations, tongues, and peoples. The closing work of the third angel's message will be attended with a power that will send the rays of the Sun of Righteousness into all the highways and byways of life, and decisions will be made for God as supreme Governor; His law will be looked upon as the rule of His government.' . . .

"We must have the power of God to soften and change the rugged traits of our character, that we may be susceptible to the influence of truth. We should look upon the Word of God with reverence, as something sacred. Christ is true, and without Him we know nothing as we ought to know it. We are lacking in the spirituality of true religion."—Manuscript 15, 1888. See Appendix A, pages 303-311, for the full sermon.

It can be seen that some details in Elder Waggoner's studies Mrs. White did not then approve, but she concurred with and endorsed his emphasis on the great theme of righteousness by faith as presented by him at the conference.

How unfortunate that some of the delegates at the Minneapolis session allowed themselves to be beclouded by prejudice and failed to hear and heed the voice of God! How different the story of the 1888 meeting would have been if all in attendance had been sensitive to the divine call to a richer experience in God's love!

CHAPTER SIX

After Minneapolis, the Revival Spreads

WHEN the Minneapolis meeting closed, many returned to their fields with a new song in their hearts. They had caught a new vision of Christ and the cross of Calvary. By faith they had received Him who is the mighty Saviour. They were gripped by a new determination to make Christ the center of all their preaching. Having tasted of His great salvation, they could now make known to others, with overflowing hearts, the secret of His great loving-kindness.

As already noted, some left the session with a big question mark before them. They had not reached a decision for or against the message of righteousness by faith.

In a time of crisis it seems hard for some people to reach a decision, yet it is difficult to understand why there was any hesitation in this case, for the message was founded on the Bible. Furthermore, God's chosen servant, Ellen G. White, was present and bore testimony for Him in favor of the message, leaving no room for doubt, and stating plainly that the message was from the Lord.

Others returned to their fields with hearts filled with feelings of bitterness and stern opposition. They went back to let the miasma of their evil influence poison the hearts and minds of still others. Writing about this last class, a little later, Mrs. White said:

"There are those who see no necessity for a special work at this time. While God is working to arouse the people, they seek to turn aside the message of warning, reproof, and entreaty. Their influence tends to quiet the fears of the people, and to prevent them from awaking to the solemnity of this time. Those who are doing this, are giving the trumpet no certain sound. They ought to be awake to the situation, but they have become ensnared by the enemy."— *Review and Herald,* Aug. 13, 1889, p. 514.

The following year, Sister White wrote:

"You will meet with those who will say, 'You are too much excited over this matter. You are too much in earnest. You should not be reaching for the righteousness of Christ, and making so much of that. You should preach the law.' "—*Ibid.,* March 11, 1890, p. 146.

This opposition naturally had an unfortunate influence in the field. It left many of the believers in a state of perplexity and bewilderment. Others were led to join in the opposition to the message. The lukewarm, indifferent ones were emboldened to continue in their state of morbid drowsiness. Satan was determined to defeat the purpose of God. He sought to divert the minds of God's people from Christ and His righteousness. He labored with great zeal to extinguish the light shining from God's Holy Book on the subject of righteousness by faith.

But, thank God, the lamp of truth was not permitted to go out. In His love and mercy the Lord wrought in behalf of His people. He used various means and methods in His efforts to lead His remnant people to understand and accept righteousness by faith.

There was, first, the quiet but mighty influence of the Holy Spirit, who was constantly at work to enlighten minds and to subdue hearts. Under the benign influence of this heavenly agency, many stony hearts were softened and made submissive. Souls that had been in rebellion repented and cast in their lot with the loyal ones.

And the Holy Spirit used the good influence of the brethren and sisters who returned from the Minneapolis session on fire for God and His truth. Through their faithful witnessing, hesitant souls, and even aggressive opponents, were made to surrender. We can never overestimate the wholesome and far-reaching influence of a godly life. "A kind, courteous Christian," we are told, "is the most powerful argument that can be produced in favor of Christianity."—*Gospel Workers*, p. 122. And there was something about the experience of the warmhearted advocates of righteousness by faith that marked their new conversion as genuinely Christian.

After the session in Minneapolis, and throughout the nineties, there was a steady stream of articles from the pen of Mrs. White running through the columns of the *Review and Herald* and *The Signs of the Times*. In these articles frequent references were made to this vital subject. These heavenly messages helped to turn the tide in favor of a fuller and wider acceptance of the new experience in faith toward which so many were turning. A few excerpts will suffice to show the tenor of these utterances:

"The present message—justification by faith—is a message from God; it bears the divine credentials, for its fruit is unto holiness." —*Review and Herald*, Sept. 3, 1889, p. 545.

"Messages bearing the divine credentials have been sent to God's people; the glory, the majesty, the righteousness of Christ, full of goodness and truth, have been presented; the fullness of the Godhead in Jesus Christ has been set forth among us with beauty and loveliness, to charm all whose hearts were not closed with prejudice. We know that God has wrought among us. We have seen souls turn from sin to righteousness. We have seen faith revived in the hearts of the contrite ones."—*Ibid.*, May 27, 1890, p. 321.

As Mrs. White surveyed the field and saw the large results of preaching the blessed truth her heart overflowed in these happy, sensitive words:

"We thank the Lord with all the heart that we have precious light to present before the people, and we rejoice that we have a message for this time which is present truth. The tidings that Christ is our righteousness has brought relief to many, many souls, and God says to His people, 'Go forward.' The message to the Laodicean church is applicable to our condition. How plainly is pictured the position of those who think they have all the truth, who take pride in their knowledge of the Word of God, while its sanctifying power has not been felt in their lives. The fervor of the love of God is wanting in their hearts, but it is this very fervor of love that makes God's people the light of the world."—*Ibid.*, July 23, 1889, p. 466.

After the Minneapolis session, Mrs. White joined A. T. Jones and E. J. Waggoner in carrying the glorious message to the churches, laboring from coast to coast at camp meetings, workers' meetings, institutes and Bible schools, and other important gatherings. Sometimes they were together at the same gathering, but at other times they separated, in order to reach a larger number of people. Other workers joined them in promulgating the blessed teaching and the message that they preached bore fruit. This is evident from the reports from the pen of Mrs. White published in the columns of the *Review and Herald.* Concerning a meeting held in South Lancaster, Massachusetts, in early 1889 she wrote:

"I have never seen a revival work go forward with such thoroughness, and yet remain so free from all undue excitement. There was no urging or inviting. The people were not called forward, but there was a solemn realization that Christ came not to call the righteous, but sinners, to repentance. The honest in heart were ready to confess their sins, and to bring forth fruit to God by repentance and restoration, as far as it lay in their power. We seemed to breathe in the very atmosphere of heaven. Angels were indeed hovering around. Friday evening the social service began at five, and it was not closed until nine. . . .

"There were many who testified that as the searching truths had been presented, they had been convicted in the light of the law as transgressors. They had been trusting in their own righteousness. Now they saw it as filthy rags, in comparison with the righteousness of Christ, which is alone acceptable to God. While they had not been open transgressors, they saw themselves depraved and degraded in heart. They had substituted other gods in the place of their heavenly Father. They had struggled to refrain from sin, but had trusted in their own strength. We should go to Jesus just as we are, confess our sins, and cast our helpless souls upon our compassionate Redeemer. This subdues the pride of the heart, and is a crucifixion of self."—March 5, 1889, p. 146.

Late in July, Mrs. White reported a steady and heartening acceptance of the message:

"In every meeting since the General Conference [in Minneapolis] souls have eagerly accepted the precious message of the righteousness of Christ. We thank God that there are souls who realize that they are in need of something which they do not possess— gold of faith and love, white raiment of Christ's righteousness, eyesalve of spiritual discernment. If you possess these precious gifts, the temple of the human soul will not be like a desecrated shrine. Brethren and sisters, I call upon you in the name of Jesus Christ of Nazareth to work where God works. Now is the day of gracious opportunity and privilege."—*Ibid.*, July 23, 1889, p. 466.

Writing about the camp meeting at Williamsport, Pennsylvania, Mrs. White reported:

"The churches in Pennsylvania have been passing through discouragements, and some of their members have apostatized. But as the precious message of present truth was spoken to the people by Brethren Jones and Waggoner, the people saw new beauty in the third angel's message, and they were greatly encouraged. They testified to the fact that they had never before attended meetings where they had received so much instruction and such precious light. They were now determined to return to their homes and to their churches to impart to their friends and neighbors the light they had received. They felt that they now understood better how to win souls to Christ.

"The churches are lukewarm. They have listened to doctrinal discourses, but they have not been instructed concerning the simple art of believing. In every meeting which we attend, we find many who do not understand the simplicity of faith. They do not know what constitutes genuine faith, and they miss a rich experience simply because they do not take God at His word. They need to have Christ set forth before them."—*Ibid.*, Aug. 13, 1889.

From the camp meeting in Rome, New York, she sent this joyous expression:

"When the doctrine of justification by faith was presented at the Rome meeting, it came to many as water comes to the thirsty traveler. The thought that the righteousness of Christ is imputed to us, not because of any merit on our part, but as a free gift from God, seemed a precious thought."—*Review and Herald,* Sept. 3, 1889, p. 546; in *Selected Messages,* book 1, p. 360.

At the Ottawa, Kansas, camp meeting in 1889, there was at first considerable resistance to the revival emphasis. Concerning this and the ultimate victory, Mrs. White wrote:

"At the Kansas meeting my prayer to God was, that the power of the enemy might be broken, and that the people who had been in darkness might open their hearts and minds to the message that God should send them, that they might see the truth, new to many minds, as old truth in new framework. The understanding of the people of God has been blinded, for Satan has misrepresented the character of God. . . . Many have been living in an atmosphere of doubt, and it seems almost impossible for them to lay hold on the hope set before them in the gospel of Christ. . . .

"On Sabbath, truths were presented that were new to the majority of the congregation. Things new and old were brought forth from the treasure house of God's Word. Truths were revealed that the people were scarcely able to comprehend and appropriate. Light flashed from the oracles of God in relation to the law and the gospel, in relation to the fact that Christ is our righteousness, which seemed to souls who were hungry for truth, as light too precious to be received.

"But the labors of the Sabbath were not in vain. On Sunday morning there was decided evidence that the Spirit of God was working great changes in the moral and spiritual condition of those assembled. There was a surrendering of the mind and heart to God, and precious testimonies were borne by those who had long been in darkness."—*Review and Herald,* July 23, 1889, pp. 465, 466; in *Selected Messages,* book 1, pp. 355, 356.

In Iowa and other places there was much to do to gain the victory over opposition. But, in every place, God wrought with

His Spirit on human hearts, and great victories were gained. Many were the expressions of joy and gratitude that came from the lips and pens of the brethren who attended these gatherings. As an example, we quote from a brief report by S. H. Lane, one of the leading workers of that day, regarding the Rome, New York, camp meeting:

"The presentation of the subject of justification by faith by Sister White and Elders Jones and Waggoner, did more to encourage all present than the investigation of all other subjects. It brought hope and good cheer to every heart. This was manifested in many ways. The prayers and testimonies were of a stirring nature, and were filled with courage on account of the love of God which caused many to repent and not despair, and to believe without presumption. Nearly all left the meeting praising God."— *Review and Herald*, Sept. 10, 1889, p. 570.

The revival work carried on in the camp meetings across the continent exerted a profound influence in breaking down the opposition, and in gradually leading workers and members to a common view and appreciation of the subject of righteousness by faith. And then came the General Conference session of 1889, to be held in Battle Creek, October 18 to November 5, just one year after the meeting at Minneapolis. What would this meeting bring forth?

Elder O. A. Olsen was now at the helm. Elders Jones and Waggoner were at the conference, and of course Sister White. The spirit of contention that characterized the session in Minneapolis was absent at the 1889 meeting in Battle Creek. A spirit of harmony and brotherly love prevailed throughout the meetings. This is evident from the following lines written by Mrs. White sometime during the session of 1889:

"We are having most excellent meetings. The spirit that was in the meeting at Minneapolis is not here. All moves off in harmony. There is a large attendance of delegates. Our five o'clock morning meeting is well attended, and the meetings good. All the testimonies to which I have listened have been of an elevating character. They say that the past year has been the best of their life; the light shining forth from the Word of God has been clear and distinct—justification by faith, Christ our righteousness. The experiences have been very interesting.

"I have attended all but two morning meetings. At eight o'clock Brother Jones speaks upon the subject of justification by faith, and great interest is manifested. There is a growth in faith and in the knowledge of our Lord and Saviour Jesus Christ. There are quite a number who have not had an opportunity to hear upon this subject before, but they are taking it in, and are being fed with large morsels from the Lord's table. The universal testimony from those who have spoken has been that this message of light and truth which has come to our people is just the truth for this time, and wherever they go among the churches, light, and relief, and the blessing of God is sure to come in."—Manuscript 10, 1889; in *Selected Messages,* book 1, pp. 361, 362.

It is evident, therefore, that during the interval between the General Conference sessions of 1888 and 1889 the message of righteousness by faith yielded "the peaceable fruit of righteousness" (Heb. 12:11). Furthermore, the General Conference session of 1889 "fed with large morsels from the Lord's table" those who were hearing this message for the first time. Thus this session both reaped and sowed the message of righteousness by faith. And it was acclaimed as "just the truth for this time" wherever it was preached.

With the conference over, Ellen White was in the field again, working alone or with Elders Jones and Waggoner. At the Bible School held at Battle Creek, on the morning of February 4, 1890, she spoke of "The Present Message," and reported briefly on her activities:

"I have traveled from place to place, attending meetings where the message of the righteousness of Christ was preached. I considered it a privilege to stand by the side of my brethren, and give my testimony with the message for the time; and I saw that the power of God attended the message wherever it was spoken. You could not make the people believe in South Lancaster that it was not a message of light that came to them. The people confessed

68

their sins and appropriated the righteousness of Christ. God has set His hand to do this work.

"We labored in Chicago; it was a week before there was a break in the meetings. But like a wave of glory, the blessing of God swept over us as we pointed men to the Lamb of God that taketh away the sin of the world. The Lord revealed His glory, and we felt the deep movings of His Spirit. Everywhere the message led to the confession of sin and to the putting away of iniquity."—*Review and Herald*, March 18, 1890, p. 161.

And so it was much of the time during the three years between the Minneapolis meeting and Mrs. White's departure for Australia late in 1891.

And there were numerous articles, too, by a number of well-known denominational writers on the subject of righteousness by faith, appearing from time to time in *The Signs of the Times*, and some in the *Review and Herald*. These carried such names as S. N. Haskell, J. O. Corliss, E. J. Waggoner, A. T. Jones, M. C. Wilcox, F. M. Wilcox, E. W. Whitney, E. Hilliard, H. E. Sawyer, G. C. Tenney, M. E. Kellogg, G. D. Ballou, I. E. Kimball, D. T. Bourdeau, W. W. Prescott, William Covert, Charles Whitford, and others.

Pamphlets and tracts setting forth the doctrine of righteousness by faith were published. Among them was a ninety-six-page brochure by E. J. Waggoner entitled *Christ Our Righteousness*. Furthermore, this theme was presented in Sabbath school lessons and in Week of Prayer readings. But the greatest contribution, in written form, came through the numerous books by Ellen G. White, beginning with 1888 and running throughout the nineties. The list is impressive:

1888   *The Great Controversy.**
1889   *Testimonies for the Church*, volume five.
1890   *Patriarchs and Prophets*.
1892   *Steps to Christ*.

---

* This 1888 edition, printed prior to the Minneapolis meeting, was the forerunner of our present 1911 *Great Controversy*. Two earlier editions, 1858 and 1884, represented Mrs. White's steady and consistent emphasis through the years on salvation through Christ the only Saviour.

1892 *Gospel Workers* (old edition).
1894 *Christian Education* (old edition).
1896 *Thoughts From the Mount of Blessing.*
1898 *The Desire of Ages.*
1900 *Christ's Object Lessons.*

In all these books Ellen G. White sets forth the plan of salvation in all its beauty and importance. The various phases of justification, sanctification, and final victory through faith in Christ's righteousness are presented with clarity. The heart of the reader is warmed and charmed by the moving appeals and the Christ-centered attractions of these books and her efforts to help people grasp the simplicity of faith.

This steady barrage of articles, books, pamphlets, and tracts that flowed from our presses into the field exerted a tremendous influence in enlightening and uniting the hearts and minds of Seventh-day Adventists on the centrality of gospel teaching in the life and work of the church.

CHAPTER SEVEN

The Ministerial Institutes and Their Fruitage

ELDER O. A. OLSEN, who was elected president of the General Conference at the 1888 meeting in Minneapolis, carried a great burden for the spiritual welfare of the church, and very much desired to develop a stronger and more spiritual ministry. He was also dedicated to building a ministry stronger theologically and that would be particularly keen in the knowledge of gospel teaching.

The reader will recall, however, that at the time of his election in October, 1888, he was in Europe and was unable to assume his responsibilities as president until early May, 1889. In the meantime a ministers' and workers' institute provided for at the General Conference session had been held in Battle Creek, the men meeting in the college building. This was especially for those engaged in public labor, and younger ministers were urged to attend. It ran from January 17 to March 28, with about fifty in attendance. The announcement for the institute emphasized that "Elder A. T. Jones will take a leading part in the instruction."—*Review and Herald,* Jan. 1, 1889, p. 16.

Cheered by the good success of this ten-week institute, Elder Olsen and members of the General Conference Committee arranged for two more such schools for ministers to be held between the General Conference sessions of 1889 and 1891. These were conducted as planned and proved among other things to be influential in breaking down much of the opposition that had been aroused at the memorable Minneapolis meeting. It was the plan that Elders Jones and Waggoner were to be among the instructors at these institutes.

These Biblical training sessions were a new venture in denominational experience and history and covered a two-year course of studies. Plans were developed and executed to meet the needs of a large class of ministers already in the field whose circumstances would not permit them to take an extended course in one of our colleges, and who needed the benefit of a limited course adapted to their age and immediate needs. Special emphasis was laid upon the central Bible theme of justification and sanctification through faith in Christ, the all-sufficient Saviour.

As originally planned, the first of these two schools began immediately after the close of the General Conference session of 1889, and lasted twenty weeks, from November 5, 1889, to March 25, 1890. The east vestry of the Tabernacle served as the place of meeting. Fifty students were in regular attendance; also, as circumstances allowed, students attending branch schools in foreign languages (Scandinavian, German, and French). A special class of instruction for laymen was held in conjunction with the school for ministers.

The second, conducted from October 31, 1890, to February 27, 1891, lasted only sixteen weeks instead of twenty as originally planned. This was attended by more than twice as many students as had attended the preceding Bible school for ministers. Foreign-language students studying French and German also attended this Bible school, which closed before the General Conference session of March 5 to 25, 1891.

Both in attendance and in spiritual results achieved, the two Bible schools for ministers were successful. Speaking of this venture when delivering his opening address on March 5 at the General Conference session of 1891, O. A. Olsen said:

"Two ministers' schools have been held since our last general gathering. The first one commenced immediately after the close of the last General Conference, and continued twenty weeks; the second one of sixteen weeks has just closed, and we are glad to say that they have been a success even beyond our expectations. The number in attendance at the first . . . reached a little more than fifty, and in the last one the regular attendance has reached over one hundred and thirty." *—*General Conference Bulletin*, March 6, 1891, p. 4.

Having noted the success of the two institutes, we turn to a more detailed review of accomplishments. Elder Olsen attested to the spiritual enrichment provided the first of the two Bible schools for ministers:

"The efforts of all the instructors in every branch was to make the instruction thoroughly practical and applicable to present needs. Neither was the religious interest neglected; every day had its regular devotional exercise, and many of these were very precious seasons.

"One important feature of the Bible school was the labors of Sister White. For over a month she attended quite regularly our morning devotion, which, during this time, occupied one hour and a half or more. These were seasons of special interest, and will long be remembered by those who were present. Sister White enjoyed great freedom, and on several occasions the power of the Lord was manifest in a large measure. . . .

"To show the reader how the class regarded the school, and its success, we insert here some preambles and resolutions adopted by the school at its closing sessions:

"WHEREAS, Our experience in this school the past few months has shown us marked evidences of the Lord's guidance in leading

---

* In this connection the following chronological table of General Conference sessions and ministerial institutes may be of interest:
    1. 1888 GENERAL CONFERENCE SESSION IN MINNEAPOLIS: Oct. 17, 1888-Nov. 4, 1888.
    2. 10-week ministers' schools: Jan. 17, 1889—about March 28, 1889.
      (See: *Review and Herald*,
        Jan. 1, 1889, p. 16;
        Sept. 17, 1889, p. 592.)
    3. 1889 GENERAL CONFERENCE SESSION: Oct. 18, 1889-Nov. 5, 1889.
    4. 20-week Bible school for ministers: Nov. 5 or 6, 1889-March 24 or 25, 1890.
      (See: *Review and Herald*,
        April 1, 1890, pp. 200, 201; 204, 205.)
    5. 16-week Bible school for ministers: Oct. 31, 1890-Feb. 27, 1891.
      (See: *Review and Herald*,
        Nov. 4, 1890, p. 688;
        March 3, 1891, p. 144.)
    6. 1891 GENERAL CONFERENCE SESSION: March 5, 1891-March 25, 1891.

the General Conference Committee to plan for this special course of instruction; and,

"WHEREAS, We have received great benefit, intellectually and spiritually, from this instruction and association; therefore,

"*Resolved,* That we express our thanks to the General Conference Committee, the educational committee, and the instructors, for their ardent and patient efforts, which, through the blessing of God, have better fitted us to act our part in the closing work of the last message to the world.

"*Resolved,* That we ask the General Conference Committee to lay plans at its earliest convenience, for another ministerial course of instruction, similar to the one just closing, to be held in the winter of 1890-91; and that we hereby pledge to the committee our hearty cooperation and influence to secure as large an attendance as possible.

". . . The school just closed was the first effort of the kind among us, and much connected with it can be improved in many ways; but we feel very thankful for the blessing of God and the success that has attended the present effort. We cannot value too much the importance of this blessing. May God greatly bless this enterprise to the advancement of this important work."—*Review and Herald,* April 1, 1890, p. 201.

The spiritual blessing of this same Bible school for ministers is further asserted by Dan T. Jones, secretary of the General Conference:

"The last few months have marked an important era in our work. . . . During the past five months, an educational work outside of the regular college work has been systematically carried on for the education of workers in all the different lines of our work, and schools have been successfully maintained in four different languages. . . .

"Another matter of especial importance in connection with these schools was the effort made for the spiritual interests of the students. The first hour in the morning was devoted to work of this character. These meetings were of especial interest the last few weeks of the term. Eld. Olsen took charge of them, and Sister White attended many of the meetings, and bore her testimony with much freedom and power. The restraint which had existed on the part of some connected with the school was removed by explanations that were made, and a tender spirit came in. The subjects of faith and the love of God were largely dwelt upon, greatly to the encouragement of all present.

"As the news of the good meetings went out, many came in from the Battle Creek church, the office, the college, and the sanitarium, till the east vestry of the Tabernacle, which will seat about 300, was filled to overflowing each morning. The interest was such that the meetings were often permitted to continue for two hours. All were greatly benefited, and many who had been cold and formal in their work in the past, received such an experience in the things of God as to give them new courage and hope for the future. At the morning meeting on the last day of the school nearly all spoke, and their unanimous testimony was that they had been greatly benefited by the school and by their associations together, and that they could go to their fields of labor with better courage and greater hopes of success than ever before."—*Ibid.*, pp. 204, 205.

It should be noted that as planned both A. T. Jones and E. J. Waggoner were among the instructors (see *Review and Herald,* April 1, 1890, p. 200).

While the foregoing statements by O. A. Olsen and Dan T. Jones do not mention the issue concerning the message of righteousness by faith, Mrs. White clearly alludes to this in statements written on March 10 and 11, 1890, to her son William and his wife. She had just spoken in the Battle Creek Tabernacle to the students at their morning devotions:

Monday, March 10. "I have just come from the meeting. The room was full, the three apartments were in one. The Lord again poured upon me the spirit of supplication. Faith did take hold of the arm of infinite power. We did have the blessing of God. . . .

"Some confessions were made and quite a number who had been in darkness made confessions of their finding Jesus and being free in the Lord. . . .

"The word spoken is fully received by the largest number present. The men who have held things have no power now. There is a strong current setting heavenward, and if we wait on the Lord we shall surely see of His salvation. He will work in our behalf. He will not let this ministerial institute break up in confusion and darkness."—Letter 30, 1890.

March 11: "My heart is filled with thanksgiving and praise to God. The Lord has poured upon us His blessing. The backbone of the rebellion is broken in those who have come in from other places."—*Ibid.*

Thus, the twenty-week ministers' Bible school, which followed the General Conference session of 1889, exerted a telling influence in breaking down the opposition to the message of righteousness by faith. This will be noted more in detail when in a subsequent chapter we shall quote again from Mrs. White's letter to her son and his wife, and note confessions made by several leading men whom she specifically names.

Seven months after the close of this ministers' Bible school, another one opened on Friday, October 31, and like the twenty-week school it was held in Battle Creek in the Tabernacle. A few days later (November 2), encouraged by the large attendance and the school's prospects of good success, O. A. Olsen wrote:

"The prospects for the school this winter are very encouraging indeed. . . .

"Our ministers' Sabbath school and social meeting held yesterday forenoon and afternoon were seasons of much interest. It was remarked by some that it seemed as though we had begun just where we left off last spring. This is the way that it should be, and we hope to make still greater advancement. We expect in the season now before us to make advancement not only in our knowledge of the Bible, and in how to apply ourselves to study, but also in spiritual experience.

"Let our brethren and sisters everywhere remember the ministers' school in their prayers, that God may grant it His signal blessing."—*Review and Herald,* Nov. 4, 1890, p. 688.

While the plans for this second school called for both A. T. Jones and E. J. Waggoner to assist in teaching, only Elder Waggoner could be present (see *Review and Herald,* March 4, 1890, p. 688).

On December 2, in an article announcing the coming

Week of Prayer, December 20-27, 1890, Elder Olsen informed the field concerning progress made in the ministers' Bible school:

"We are also much encouraged by the prospects for the ministers' school that now has been in progress about three weeks. The attendance is large, nearly 100 at present, and there are still more to come. The best of interest is manifested. Teachers and students are enjoying much of the Spirit of God. We have been expecting this, for we felt that the present situation of our work demanded it. Has not the time come for the work to advance all along the line? We long to see our people everywhere drink deeper draughts from the well of salvation, and show forth more of the real spirit of the message. The time has certainly come for an individual consecration to God and His work as never before."—*Ibid.*, Dec. 2, 1890, p. 746.

The school recessed during the Week of Prayer, which proved to be a season particularly rich in spiritual blessings for the Seventh-day Adventist community at Battle Creek. Dan T. Jones reported:

"During the Week of Prayer very interesting and valuable meetings were held in Battle Creek. The ministers' school took a vacation, and all the ministers and other students in attendance devoted their entire time to pastoral work in the Battle Creek church. Meetings were held each morning at 5:30, especially for workers. Elder Olsen attended them, and gave a series of talks on methods of work. These proved to be valuable seasons.

"Another meeting was held for ministers and workers at eleven o'clock. The employees in the office [publishing house] were given the hour from 11:00 to 12:00 A.M., and they assembled in the office chapel for worship and religious instruction. The employees of the sanitarium held a meeting from 12:00 to 1:00 P.M. Meetings for the church were held each day at 2:30 P.M., and all met together in the auditorium of the Tabernacle at 7:00 in the evening, when a sermon was preached or an address delivered on the same subject as the reading for the day.

"On the last day of the Week of Prayer the article from Sister White, published in the *Review and Herald* Extra, was read by Prof. Prescott. Elder Olsen followed with a few remarks, when a call was made for those who wished to get nearer to God and enjoy more of His blessing, to come forward, and almost the entire congregation arose. Such a move on the part of the people has seldom been seen in Battle Creek. The meetings were continued at intervals through another week, with good results. Some have been converted. Donations for foreign missions amounted to $2,125."—*Ibid.*, Jan. 6, 1891, p. 12.

On the last page of the same paper we find O. A. Olsen's report:

"At Battle Creek the program for the meetings, as mentioned in the *Review* Extra, was carefully carried out, and the interest in the meetings increased daily. The church district meetings, and the special meetings at the college, sanitarium, and *Review* office were all excellent. The ministers' meetings were especially interesting, and all felt that it was a most profitable occasion. . . . May the interest that has been manifested during the Week of Prayer continue to deepen till finally God's people are clothed with that glory and power which the Lord has promised shall go with the last message to the world."—*Ibid.*, p. 16.

An editorial note on the same page confirms the foregoing statements:

"We are happy to present in this number quite full references from others to the Week of Prayer, particularly as it was enjoyed in Battle Creek. What they have said is about what we should have had to say, and it does not prevent our repeating it; for it is worthy of being repeated; and we can fully indorse all the statements made. The references to the meeting on the Sabbath, December 27, are not overdrawn. Seldom is a congregation more deeply moved than was the congregation on that occasion. . . . Surely the Lord is to be praised for these tokens of His goodness." —*Ibid.*

The Ellen G. White article entitled "Be Zealous and Repent," * which appeared in the *Review and Herald* Extra of

---

* Note: On Sabbath, December 27, the last Sabbath of the Week of Prayer, Mrs. White was in Washington, D.C. Her article entitled "Be Zealous and Repent," which appeared in the Extra, is found in *Ellen G. White Present Truth and Review and Herald Articles*, vol. 2, pp. 453, 454.

December 23, 1890, and which greatly stirred the large congregation assembled in the Battle Creek Tabernacle on the last Sabbath of the Week of Prayer, was a straightforward and vibrant appeal for God's professed children to repent of their Laodicean state and to confess their sinful unbelief and resistance to God-given light and truth. They were to open their hearts and minds to one prevailing interest—Christ our Righteousness. It is little wonder that in the solemnity of the Week of Prayer this message produced such outstanding results. Neither is it surprising that the meetings were continued, at intervals, through another week.

Speaking of this, a news note in the *Review and Herald* declares:

"The meetings did not stop in Battle Creek with the Week of Prayer, and some good occasions have been seen since that time. Sister White returned to Battle Creek, from Washington, December 31. She spoke in the Tabernacle on the evening commencing the Sabbath, January 2, and also Sabbath forenoon. In the afternoon the large congregation was separated into four divisions, and many testimonies expressive of an earnest purpose to serve God with more faithfulness in time to come, were given. In the evening, it would be safe to say that fully 1,000 persons came together to celebrate the ordinances of the Lord's house, including the instruction of John 13:1-17."—*Ibid.*, p. 16.

As we shall see in a later chapter dealing with the confessions of certain ministers, it was on the last Sabbath of the Week of Prayer in Battle Creek that one of our leading workers confessed that his attitude toward the message of righteousness by faith preached at Minneapolis had been wrong. And, as we shall also see, it was during the first two weeks following the Week of Prayer that, through the influence of Mrs. White's Week of Prayer article and her personal ministry afterward, another of our outstanding ministers of that time was led to confess that he too had maintained wrong positions with respect to the message preached at Minneapolis.

Nine weeks after the close of the Week of Prayer of 1890 the ministers' Bible school closed on Friday, February 27, 1891. The *Review and Herald* of March 3, 1891, reported the concluding service. On the day that the ministers' Bible school closed, Mrs. White made the following entry in her diary:

"I have attended the closing meeting of the ministerial Bible school—a school composed of conference delegates and those who have been attending the ministerial institute. At this meeting several were called upon to say something. Remarks appropriate for the occasion were made by Elders Olsen, Waggoner, Prescott, and Smith; also by Elder Haskell, who has been mercifully preserved during his tour around the world.

"I spoke in regard to matters that were deeply impressing my mind. I referred to the fear that had been expressed by some who were not members of the ministerial institute, and who had not been present at all the Bible classes of the school—a fear that there was danger of carrying the subject of justification by faith altogether too far, and of not dwelling enough on the law.

"Judging from the meetings that I had been privileged to attend, I could see no cause for alarm; and so I felt called upon to say that this fear was cherished by those who had not heard all the precious lessons given, and that therefore they were not warranted in coming to such a conclusion. None of the members of the class who had been studying the Word to learn 'What saith the Scriptures?' entertained any such fear. The Bible, and the Bible alone, has been the subject of investigation in this school. Every lesson has been based, not on the ideas and the opinions of men, but on a plain 'Thus saith the Lord' "—Manuscript 21, 1891, written Feb. 27 in Battle Creek, Michigan.

A few days earlier, in a letter to a friend, Mrs. White had written of the value of the Bible school in these words:

"Our meetings have been highly profitable, and from this meeting the ministers will go all over the world to preach the gospel."
—Letter 28, 1891, written Feb. 21 in Battle Creek, Michigan.

Not only was this school highly profitable, but it was a necessity. On March 3, a few days after its close, Mrs. White wrote more in her diary concerning it:

MINISTERIAL INSTITUTES AND THEIR FRUITAGE

"I attended the ministerial council* and made some important remarks in regard to the necessity of the ministerial school, and the importance of ministers' spending some time in obtaining a drill in Bible study, which would qualify them to do better work. Thus they would place themselves in the most favorable position to obtain a knowledge of God and His Son Jesus Christ, whom to know aright is life eternal, and would obtain a knowledge of how to work. This is necessary because there has been so much counter-working in our midst that the churches have received very confusing theories in regard to the truth for this time. It is essential that our ministers speak the same things in our churches and give the trumpet no uncertain sound. Our ministers need first to be converted to the truth themselves. Then they can go forth everywhere, bearing the message of truth for this time.

"Teachers of Bible truth need not to be ever learning and never coming to the knowledge of the truth in regard to justification by faith and the imputed righteousness of Christ. As soon as the truth is grasped, and the Holy Spirit's power impresses the image of Christ on the soul, tarry not, go forth proclaiming everywhere, as did the apostles, the word of life. Teaching, you will be taught by the Holy Spirit."—Manuscript 19, 1891.

During the General Conference session that began a few days after the close of the Bible school for ministers, Mrs. White expressed in another letter her high appreciation of the school:

"The ministerial institute was a season of close searching of the Scriptures. The doors of hearts were not barred with iron, lest rays of light should penetrate the darkened chambers of the mind and the sanctifying power should cleanse and refine the soul temple. Right in the midst of their study, during the past winter, there have been times when there was not a question with the class but that the Comforter, the Holy Spirit of God, was doing its work. 'Then opened he their understanding, that they might understand the scriptures' (Luke 24:45). And the precious oracles were to them verily the voice of God. Hearts were affected, and they praised God with weeping and rejoicing. Rich and precious testimonies were borne, and they went forth to labor, trusting to be made ef-

---

* This council was held from February 25 till the opening of the General Conference session, March 5, 1891. (See *Review and Herald,* Feb. 17, 1891, pp. 106, 112.)

ficient by the agency of the Holy Spirit."—Letter 3, 1891, written March 20, in Battle Creek, Michigan.

O. A. Olsen spoke enthusiastically of the success of these two Bible schools when he addressed the delegates assembled for the opening meeting of the General Conference session in 1891. He said:

"The amount of good accomplished by these schools it is impossible for us to estimate. The blessing of God has been present in a large measure. The students have not only received a better knowledge of the truth, but the converting power of God has been manifested in a marked degree. We feel assured that the influence of the schools will have an excellent effect upon the work wherever it reaches."—*General Conference Bulletin*, March 6, 1891, p. 4.

It was the "converting power of God," as Elder Olsen says, manifested in connection with these Bible schools for ministers that made them a strong influence in breaking down the opposition aroused at the General Conference session in Minneapolis in 1888. Who can measure the reformation produced by this influence?

The spirit of acceptance and consecration seen at the Bible schools was carried into the sessions of the General Conference held in 1891. This session offered a liberal store of spiritual food to all in attendance. The General Conference Committee arranged to extend, to as large a number as possible, some of the benefits of a school such as the Bible school for ministers which had just closed, by devoting to Bible study one hour a day during the General Conference session. This plan was carried out with the best of results. In a letter written to two friends a few days before the close of the session, Mrs. White said:

"We have had a deeply interesting conference. . . . I attended all the morning meetings except three, and spoke to the ministers with great freedom. The Lord has been in our midst, and we have seen of His salvation. I never attended a General Conference where there was manifested as much of the Spirit of the Lord in the study of His Word as on this occasion. Meeting after meeting was held for three weeks. Each morning there was a meeting at half past five for the ministers, and these were special seasons of refreshing from the presence of the Lord. These ministers' meetings were of a solemn character. There was depth of feeling, thanksgiving, and praise offered to God for His precious blessings bestowed in the searching of His Word."—Letter 3, 1891, written March 20, in Battle Creek, Michigan.

The following report was printed while the meeting was still in progress:

"No General Conference ever held by S. D. Adventists has elicited so great an interest as has been aroused by the one now in session in this place, both as to the feelings of those who are here on the ground, and the number of those abroad who are intently following its proceedings. The list of the daily *Bulletin* has now run up to over 3,500, which is quite an indication as to how the brethren in all parts of the field are looking to this meeting.* A good measure of the Lord's blessing has attended all the exercises thus far, and many are earnestly seeking a larger measure of His grace. We believe many prayers are going up from many devoted friends of the cause for the success of this gathering."—*Review and Herald,* March 24, 1891, p. 192.

There was a spirit of seeking the Lord at this meeting. The following paragraphs from a final report of the session reveal that—

"the business of the conference was well arranged, and passed off like clockwork. The committee worked hard and prayerfully. A large amount of business was transacted, but all the proceedings were most pleasant and harmonious. Evident tokens were given on several occasions during the conference, of the Lord's special interposition to remove difficulties and open the way before His cause. These blessings were sources of encouragement and confidence in the work.

"In addition to all this, many are able to testify that they enjoyed a rich personal religious experience, both before and during

---

* The *Bulletin* covering this session was printed as a *Review and Herald* Extra (*The Review and Herald*, Feb. 17, 1891, p. 112; *Ibid.*, Feb. 24, 1891, p. 128). There were 3,500 subscribers to the *Bulletin*. Seventh-day Adventist world membership then comprised 29,711 members. The *Bulletin* for 1891 contained 262 pages. Price: Twenty-five cents per copy!

the meeting; by which they are enabled to look back upon the occasion as one of important instruction in Bible themes, and of great spiritual profit.

"And so the conference has closed in a manner, so far as we have been able to learn, satisfactory to all; and the brethren have gone forth to their various fields of labor, strong in faith as to the future progress and triumph of this work and firm in the conviction that we now stand on the very verge of the promised outpouring of the Spirit, the latter rain, through which the message will close in power, and be cut short in righteousness. To which all hearts respond, May it be even so."—*Ibid.*, March 31, 1891, p. 200.

In some important respects, however, even this deeply spiritual General Conference session failed to meet in full the plans of God and the hopes and expectations of His servant Ellen G. White. The church moved out slowly to occupy positions opened by Providence. The divine plan for the Advent people envisioned a full and speedy acceptance of the light and a rapid dissemination of the truth of righteousness by faith—the third angel's message in verity—to all the world. Nevertheless, the General Conference session of 1891, like the one preceding in 1889, exerted a strong influence in breaking down the opposition aroused at Minneapolis in 1888 against the message of righteousness by faith.

For a number of years after the memorable meeting in Minneapolis, each General Conference session gave a prominent place in its program to the importance of this doctrine. Mrs. White's messages to those assemblies—whether delivered by herself in person or read by someone else in her absence—dealt in one way or another with this theme. Moreover, either E. J. Waggoner or A. T. Jones was always invited to present a series of studies on this topic. W. W. Prescott also gave several talks on this theme. All this helped to make clear the meaning of the message of righteousness by faith, to draw the brethren closer together in Christian fellowship, and to raise higher and higher the gospel banner.

If, after the Minneapolis Conference, the persons involved in opposing the light had united their efforts with those of more simple faith in spreading the message throughout the whole field, a mighty work would have been accomplished in a short time. This thought is borne out in a message sent by Mrs. White from Melbourne, Australia, on January 9, 1893, to the forthcoming General Conference session, which convened in Battle Creek, Michigan, February 17 to March 6. From that message, read at the morning social meeting of Monday, February 27, we share the following insight:

"The opposition in our own ranks has imposed upon the Lord's messengers a laborious and soul-trying task; for they have had to meet difficulties and obstacles which need not have existed. While this labor had to be performed among our own people, to make them willing that God should work in the day of His power, the light of the glory of God has not been shining in clear concentrated rays to the world. Thousands who are now in the darkness of error might have been added to our numbers. All the time and thought and labor required to counteract the influence of our brethren who oppose the message has been just so much taken from the world of the swift-coming judgments of God. The Spirit of God has been present in power among His people, but it could not be bestowed upon them, because they did not open their hearts to receive it.

"It is not the opposition of the world that we have to fear, but it is the elements that work among ourselves that have hindered the message. The efficiency of the movements for extending the truth depends upon the harmonious action of those who profess to believe it. Love and confidence constitute a moral force that would have united our churches, and ensured harmony of action; but coldness and distrust have brought disunion that has shorn us of our strength.

"The Lord designed that the messages of warning and instruction given through the Spirit to His people should go everywhere. But the influence that grew out of the resistance of light and truth at Minneapolis tended to make of no effect the light God had given to His people through the Testimonies. *Great Controversy*, volume 4, has not had the circulation that it should have had, because some of those who occupy responsible positions were leavened with the spirit that prevailed at Minneapolis, a spirit that clouded the discernment of the people of God.

"The work of opponents to the truth has been steadily advancing while we have been compelled to devote our energies in a great degree to counteracting the work of the enemy through those who were in our ranks. The dullness of some and the opposition of others have confined our strength and means largely among those who know the truth, but do not practice its principles. If every soldier of Christ had done his duty, if every watchman on the wall of Zion had given the trumpet a certain sound, the world might ere this have heard the message of warning. But the work is years behind. What account will be rendered to God for thus retarding the work?"—*General Conference Bulletin,* Feb. 28, 1893, p. 1.

In the years after 1888 there was yielding of hearts to the influence of God's Spirit. A good work was done. But there were those who were slow to grasp the light, and there could have been a larger, fuller work of grace wrought in the world had there not been such dullness and opposition to the light from heaven.

CHAPTER EIGHT

George I. Butler
Moves Into the Light

THE MINNEAPOLIS meeting and the aftermath of that
session of the General Conference are correctly described by
L. H. Christian, who as a young man was present for several days:

"It was a stormy meeting. Some men were urging the importance of
righteousness by faith. Their work and their teaching were the beginning of
a large revival, as every student of Adventist history knows, but there were
some who were not clear on the matter, and it took three or four years
before they came into entire harmony with these views. Mrs. White . . .
urged that they be given time, and before long practically every one of them
did accept the full light."—*The Fruitage of Spiritual Gifts*, p. 43.

The revival that followed the 1888 session was a preparatory
experience for a large witness on the part of the church. But in spite
of this the view is held by some that the leadership of the
Seventh-day Adventist Church at the General Conference in
Minneapolis rejected the truth of righteousness by faith and may
have affirmed this rejection by some sort of formal action, or that
there was at least a general rejection on the part of those attending
the session.* This would naturally raise the question of the propriety

---
*The records would indicate that some forty years after the Minneapolis Conference, and not
until then, a serious charge was made of denominational or General Conference rejection. This is
found in a privately published, undated pamphlet issued in the late 1920s titled, "The Exodus
and the Advent Movement." The author, a well-known pastor, evangelist, and Bible teacher,
while frequently quoting from the *Testimonies* and the *Review and Herald*, offers no documentary
support for his bold assertions of rejection. In 1888 he was but a child and could not have been an
eyewitness. In his pamphlet he declares without equivocation:

"The Advent movement reached its Kadesh-barnea at the Minneapolis General Conference
in the fall of 1888. . . .

"The rejection of God's special message in 1888 . . . marked the beginning of a spiritual retreat
toward the world or Egypt. . . .

"The antitype is true to the type. Since the rejection of the message of righteousness by faith in of a formal confession on the part of the General Conference in session to right matters with God.

The facts are that reception of the matter of righteousness by faith was mixed at the Bible studies at which they were discussed, and no action was taken on the acceptance or rejection of the subject. This has been shown in the foregoing chapters. To make a confession today acknowledging such a repudiation would imply a false charge against the Minneapolis session. It would level a charge against the delegates of committing a sin that they never committed as a delegation, though some erred as individuals. Their hearts were set against the heavenly message, and by throwing their influence against both the message and the messengers they grieved God's Spirit. Yet most of those persons repented of their sin, as we shall make clear, and thus removed their guilt by placing the sin of unbelief and hardness of heart upon the Sin Bearer, Jesus Christ.

We know of no text in the Bible that requires all the people of God to confess the sins committed by some individuals among their predecessors. God does not hold the children responsible for the sins of their fathers. The Bible declares: "The soul that sinneth, it shall die. The son shall not bear the iniquity of the father, neither shall the father bear the iniquity of the son: the righteousness of the righteous shall be upon him, and the wickedness of the wicked shall be upon him" (Eze. 18:20).

The same principle has been stated by Sister White in these words, referring to the guilt of those who crucified Christ: "Those who live in this day are not accountable for

---

1888, we as a people have practically lost sight of . . . the very kernel and life of the gospel."—pp. 12, 20, 32.

Contrast this with Ellen White's declaration in 1907: "We have as Bible Christians ever been on gaining ground" (*Selected Messages*, book 2, pp. 396, 397).

In the 1930s and in more recent years the unsupported assertion of denominational rejection has been repeated and seemingly has gained acceptance. Not one person who attended the Minneapolis Conference, including Ellen G. White, ever at any time bore testimony in support of such assertions of rejection as quoted above. Many who were living when this new interpretation was projected firmly declared orally and in writing that there was no denominational rejection. They were there and knew what took place. See Appendix D, "Delegates at 1888 Session Bear Witness on Conjectures of Conference Rejection," p. 330.

the deeds of those who crucified the Son of God."—*Review and Herald,* April 11, 1893, p. 226.

We have not found any statement in the writings of Mrs. White calling upon the General Conference in session to confess the sins of the brethren who sinned individually in Minneapolis, but we do find in her writings these two statements penned in 1892:

"The sin committed in what took place at Minneapolis remains on the record books of heaven, registered against the names of those who resisted light, and it will remain upon the record until full confession is made, and the transgressors stand in full humility before God."—Letter 19d, 1892, Sept. 1, to O. A. Olsen.

"The words and actions of all who took part in this work [in Minneapolis] will stand registered against them until they make confession of their wrong."—Letter 24, 1892, Sept. 19, to Uriah Smith.

These statements make it clear that the only ones who should confess, or who could obtain forgiveness for the guilty ones, were the transgressors themselves. What was done in Minneapolis is past history. We cannot, by any means or method, change it one iota. The only thing we can do is to confess our own sins, whatever they are; and by the grace of God avoid a repetition of the sin committed by those who opposed the message of God in 1888 and afterward.

A. W. Spalding wrote of the revived message of justification delivered at Minneapolis, and in many places in North America after this meeting, and he said that this message "requires constant renewal in the consciousness of the church and of every individual. For satisfaction with truth inherited is the peculiar danger of the Laodicean church. Let them who think they stand, beware lest they fall."—*Op. cit.,* vol. 2, p. 303.

How many persons were included in the opposition we have no way of knowing. By searching through letter files, manuscript files, and periodical files, we have discovered that at least twenty-three workers were involved in it in one way or another. Most of these men were present in Minneapolis as delegates. There were others less known, out in the field, who participated more or less in the opposition. To suggest that there was wholesale collusion and organized opposition is not correct. Most of the men concerned, within a few months or years confessed their sins, and did a noble work for God thereafter. A few of them persisted in their obstinate objections and ultimately dropped out of the work and left the church.

George I. Butler—president of the General Conference from December 29, 1871, to August 10, 1874, and from October 6, 1880, to October 17, 1888, when the General Conference session was held in Minneapolis—was absent from this session because of illness. Before the session opened he had received letters from the West Coast, where E. J. Waggoner and A. T. Jones were serving as editors of *The Signs of the Times,* warning him concerning the line of studies these two men were planning to present at Minneapolis, and those letters prejudiced his mind against those brethren and their message before they presented the first study.

The author of one of these letters was a young minister named W. M. Healey, an eloquent preacher and an astute debater. Shortly after the Minneapolis meeting Mrs. White wrote him a long letter reproving him for what he had done. From her letter to him we quote the following paragraphs:

"I learned that you were one who wrote letters of warning to Elder Butler. I asked him if I might see the letter, but he said that he had destroyed it. Strange proceedings! My brother, Is the Lord leading you? or is the enemy working upon your mind as upon the minds of others? I have come to the conclusion that this is the case. . . .

"You wrote that plans were all laid, and that A. T. Jones, Dr. Waggoner, and W. C. White had things all prepared to make a drive at the General Conference. And you warned Elder Butler —a poor sick man, broken in body and in mind—to prepare for the emergency; and in that conference Elder Butler felt called upon to send in telegrams and long letters, 'Stand by the old landmarks.' Just as though the Lord was not present at that conference, and would not keep His hand on the work!

"My testimony was ignored, and never in my life experience was I treated as at that conference; and I give you, my brother, with some others of our brethren, the credit of doing what you could to bring this state of affairs about. You may have thought that you were verily doing God service, but it served the cause of the enemy rather than the cause of God."—Letter 7, 1888, Dec. 9.

Because of such prejudicial letters he had received, Elder Butler took it upon himself to send letters and telegrams to warn the delegates against Elders Waggoner and Jones and their message. Though absent, he thus became one of the principal sponsors of the opposition to the message of righteousness by faith. Because he was a leader of great strength and prominence, his attitude naturally had great weight. And in the light of his own teaching on this subject (see chapter 5) his opposition served only to confuse the issue.

Elder Butler's broken health and the prolonged illness of his wife, who had suffered a stroke, compelled him in 1888 to drop out of the denominational work. He was inactive for a number of years. During this period of retirement he had time to reflect, to pray, and study. Under the influence of the Spirit of God, he was changed into a new man. After the death of his wife, he re-entered the work.*

Five years after Minneapolis the following statement from the pen of Elder Butler under the title, "Personal," appeared in the *Review:*

"In view of the many official positions which I have held in the past among our people, and my quiet retirement from active service in the work for the last four or five years, and especially because of many queries raised in the minds of some, and inquiries made to myself and others, and reports that I had lost faith in whole or in part in the message and work of Seventh-day Ad-

---

* In the *Review and Herald* of December 17, 1901, appears a statement by George I. Butler telling of his satisfaction at being elected president of the Florida Conference.

ventists, after some reflection, I have thought it best to write a brief statement for publication for our good *Review,* of my condition, position, feelings, etc. . . .

"Great changes have occurred in the work during the four or five years I have been in retirement; very likely I am not as well prepared to judge of the extent and character of these changes as are those who have been less isolated. I have no feeling of dislike, bitterness, nor unkindness in my heart toward those who have led out in these changes. I can cheerfully say more: I fully believe that God has blessed greatly to the good of His people and the cause the greater agitation of the doctrines of justification by faith, the necessity of appropriating Christ's righteousness by faith in order to our salvation, and the civil and religious liberty principles now so much dwelt upon. To be sure, I thought I believed in all of these before. I never, for a moment since my conversion, supposed I could be saved by my own good works, or be justified in any other way than by faith in Jesus Christ, as my only Saviour, or that I could do anything acceptable to God without the help and grace of our Lord Jesus Christ. I never for a moment supposed that we could keep the law acceptably, or a single precept of it, in our own strength. Yet I am well satisfied that additional light of great importance has been shining upon these subjects, and fully believe that God has greatly blessed it to the good of those who have accepted it.

"I freely admit that for a period I stood in doubt in regard to the agitation of these subjects I have here so freely endorsed. I did not attend the General Conference at Minneapolis, where differences were agitated, being at the time sick in Battle Creek. But for a variety of reasons not necessary here to refer to, my sympathies were not with those leading out in bringing what I now regard as light, before our people. I would not attempt to conceal from the reader the fact that the last few years have been a period of great trial in my Christian experience—the most severe in my life. These have been years of affliction, weakness, sorrow, perplexity, temptation, and trial, but not of apostasy. Many things have seemed mysterious and hard to understand or explain. Such scriptures as 1 Peter 4:12, 13 have had an added force to my mind: 'Beloved, think it not strange concerning the fiery trial which is to try you, as though some strange thing happened unto you.' . . .

"I make no excuses for manifold mistakes and errors which may have been seen in my life. I plead for no sympathy. I desire, I trust, above all things, to close my earthly record with joy. I have prayed many times with David: 'Forsake me not in my old age.' My life has been one of pressure, care, perplexity and anxious thought, labor and trial. God has been very good to me, much better than I deserve. I hope never to despair, never to fall out by the way. Christ seems very precious to me, the best friend by far I ever had. My heart burns within me many times to be able yet to bring souls to the truth. I hope yet to labor again in some humble way in His vineyard."—June 13, 1893, p. 377.

Several months later the *Review* of August 15, 1893, carried an article titled "Steps to Christ" from the pen of George I. Butler. This was written after he had read and re-read the book of that title by Ellen G. White. In his review he referred to the book as "this precious little volume." "I would not wish to see a single thought contained in it changed, or a sentence altered," he wrote. He declared that the book makes plain the way of salvation, and thus revealed his own agreement with Mrs. White on the central truths of the gospel.

The following year—1894—we see Butler and Jones working together at the same Florida camp meeting, laboring for souls—this according to a report from the South by R. M. Kilgore. Said Elder Kilgore:

"All were thankful for the presence of Elder A. T. Jones, and appreciated his efforts in their behalf very highly. There were three discourses given each day. Elder Jones spoke twice, and Elder Geo. I. Butler and myself filled the other hour. A lively interest was manifested on the part of all in the truth presented, and the brethren and sisters drank in the spirit of the message with rejoicing. The spiritual growth in the meetings from the beginning to the close was apparent. This was also true with the people from without. The last night the spacious auditorium was well filled with attentive hearers."—*Ibid.*, Dec. 4, 1894, p. 764.

Elder Butler's changed attitudes and his return to the work of the church in 1901 brought great joy to the heart of Mrs. White. On different occasions she expressed her satisfaction at seeing this veteran minister back in the harness. In a letter written in May, 1902, from St. Helena, California, she spoke thus of Elder Butler:

"[He] is strong in physical and spiritual health. The Lord has proved and tested and tried him, as He did Job and as He did Moses. I see in Elder Butler one who has humbled his soul before God. He has another spirit than the Elder Butler of younger years. He has been learning his lesson at the feet of Jesus. After caring so long for his suffering, afflicted wife, he has come forth from the furnace fire refined and purified. I respect and love my brother as one of God's servants."—Letter 77, 1902.

In a manuscript written in the same year she further declared her approval of Elder Butler's return to the work, observing: "Elder Butler is president of the Southern Union Conference, and I believe that this is right."—Manuscript 124, 1902.

To the delegates assembled in Oakland, California, for the General Conference session of 1903, Mrs. White expressed her approval and joy at seeing Elder Butler active again. She said:

"I rejoice that Brother Butler is with us in this work [in the Southern field]. I have known that the time would come when he would again take his place in the work. I want you to appreciate the trials that he has passed through, and to help him all you can. God desires the gray-haired pioneers, the men who acted a part in the work when the first, second, and third angel's messages were first given, to stand in their place in His work today. They are not to drop out of sight."—*General Conference Bulletin,* April 14, 1903, p. 205.

In the following year she made it clear in one of her letters that Elder Butler was back in the work by divine appointment. She said: "The Lord has appointed Elder Butler and Elder Haskell and his wife to labor in the South."—Letter 121, 1904.

Six years later, in 1910, Sister White, in a letter to Elder Butler, gave him the following comforting and encouraging assurance:

"I have not lost faith in you, Elder Butler. I greatly desire that the old soldiers, grown gray in the Master's service, shall continue to bear their testimony right to the point, that those younger in the faith may understand that the messages which the Lord gave us in the past are very important at this stage of the earth's history."—Letter 130, 1910.

From my personal observation I can testify that though Brother Butler struggled for a while against the counsel given by the Lord through Mrs. White on the question of righteousness by faith, he was a staunch supporter of the Spirit of Prophecy.

In the Autumn Council of the General Conference held at Loma Linda, California, in 1915, one of the most perplexing problems that confronted the denomination was the serious financial condition of our medical college. A subcommittee appointed to study the problem brought in a report, the substance of which may be summed up as follows:

This institution can no longer operate without receiving heavy annual subsidies. The only source from which these subsidies can come is the General Conference. The only way the General Conference could provide these subsidies would be to call home a large number of our foreign missionaries, and give the foreign missions offerings thus saved to the medical college. This is unthinkable! Therefore, we recommend that the school be closed.

We sat almost paralyzed in our seats. How could we close our beloved medical school? And yet, how could we continue to operate it without the necessary funds?

After a time of painful silence, an old, gray-haired, trembling brother arose in the front row of seats and began to speak, in a quavering voice, somewhat as follows:

"Brethren, I am bewildered. I can hardly believe my eyes and my ears. What is this I hear you say? We must close this school? I am old now, and I do not know much. You are young and strong, and you must know what has to be done. Soon the vote will be taken, but before it is taken, let me say this:

95

"You know who I am, George I. Butler. I used to be president of the General Conference, and I think I received more testimonies from the servant of the Lord than any of you, and most of them rebuked me. We were at times urged to do what seemed impossible, but when we went forward by faith, the way opened. Brethren, I believe in God and in His prophets!"

Then, waving before us a pamphlet containing the messages that had come to us from the servant of the Lord to establish and operate a medical college in California, he made an earnest appeal for faith and confidence in the divine counsels. Before sitting down, he added this:

"Now, Brother Daniells [president of the General Conference] will soon call for a vote. When he does, there is one old hand that will not go up.

"This hand," he said, as he stretched out his quivering arm, "has not learned how to vote to close what God says should be open."

Slowly he lowered his trembling hand and sat down.

I thrust my right hand into my pocket and said to myself: "I know another hand that will not go up!"

Not one hand went up! The school was permitted to live. Not one missionary was called home in order to give the foreign missions offerings to the school. Since that crisis hour our medical school has grown from a small, insignificant institution to become one of the large medical schools in the United States.

This experience is related here to testify that G. I. Butler came out of the crisis of 1888 a firm believer in the messages and counsels sent us by God through the Spirit of Prophecy, and a man with a heart changed and made new by the grace of God.

And the experience of Elder Butler in the years following the Minneapolis meeting were duplicated in one way or another in the lives of other prominent men who, like him, moved out into the light of truth and accepted it.

CHAPTER NINE

Uriah Smith
Falls on the "Rock"

URIAH SMITH, editor of the *Review and Herald,* long-time secretary of the General Conference, and Bible teacher at Battle Creek College, was one of the men who opposed the message of righteousness by faith at Minneapolis. He became one of the most influential men in the opposition group, but his position changed in later years, as we shall see.

Elder Smith was a refined, dignified gentleman with considerable influence as a pioneer of the church. Never did he stoop to engage in rough and bitter attacks on his opponents. But he knew how to exert his influence in favor of what he believed. This was all to the good when he was on the right side of a question, but unfortunate if he happened to be on the wrong side. To his credit, it must be said that in the columns of the paper which he edited he did not say much against the messages delivered by A. T. Jones and E. J. Waggoner at Minneapolis; however, he did say enough to make it clear that he did not support these views. So his influence was negative.

Uriah Smith's opposition to the message of righteousness by faith was a source of great concern to Ellen G. White. She prayed and labored much for him. Happily, as we shall see, her interest in him was not in vain.

Shortly before the end of December, 1890, Mrs. White returned from one of her frequent field trips to her home in Battle Creek, Michigan, where the second of the Bible schools for ministers was in progress. Here, as noted in chapter seven, "The Ministerial Institutes," the Seventh-day Adventist community had just passed through a most helpful Week of Prayer. On Sabbath, December 27, which was the last Sabbath before her return to Battle Creek, Mrs. White's appeal for repentance, published in the *Review and Herald* Extra of December 23, 1890, had been read by Prof. W. W. Prescott to a full house in the large Battle Creek Tabernacle. This reading had moved the great assembly as it had rarely been moved before, and helped prepare the ground for additional services during the following week—meetings in which Mrs. White took an active part. Elder Smith came under the influence of these exercises and began to see the light. Mrs. White addressed two most earnest appeals to him, one of thirteen pages written December 31, 1890, and the other of four pages, January 6, 1891, which had a favorable influence.

Mrs. White had spent the Week of Prayer period in Washington, D.C., and God's increasing blessing had rested upon her daily ministry there throughout that week. She left Washington on Sunday, December 28, to speak in a small but well-packed hall in the country near Baltimore. She had intended to go on to Philadelphia and other places. But unexpectedly a severe illness came upon her. It appeared that her heart was involved. Consequently, it was thought best that she return to her home in Battle Creek. After a night of suffering she left Washington by train on Monday morning, December 29, and reached Battle Creek on Tuesday afternoon, the thirtieth. What happened immediately after her return to her home she describes in a letter to Elder and Sister J. S. Washburn, of Washington, D.C., written Thursday, January 8, 1891, in Battle Creek. She stayed with the Washburns while in Washington.

"We had a favorable journey from Washington to this place. I suffered considerably with heat and somewhat with heart disturb-

98

ance, but much less than I anticipated. . . . We arrived at Battle Creek about three o'clock [Tuesday afternoon, Dec. 30, 1890], and found the folks all well and glad to see us.

"We learned that Sabbath [Dec. 27] there had been a wonderful meeting similar to those we had in Brooklyn, Danvers, and in Washington. Nearly the whole congregation presented themselves for prayers, and among them Brethren Prescott and Smith. The Extra in the *Review and Herald* [of Dec. 23, 1890] was read, and the testimony of all was that the power of God attended the reading of the article. They said that this made a deep impression.

"Brother Olsen made some remarks inquiring why the power of God attended the presenting before them of the testimony to the churches in that article when the person who wrote it was not present. He asked them to carefully consider that matter. Was it not the Spirit of God speaking to them in unmistakable voice in vindication of the testimonies, and the work He had laid upon Sister White?

"Professor Prescott made a confession dating back to Minneapolis, and this made a deep impression. He wept much. Elder Smith said that testimony meant him; said that he felt that it was addressed to him, but he stopped there and went no further. But both placed themselves as there repentant, seeking the Lord.

"Well, they said they had never had such a meeting in Battle Creek, and yet the work must be carried on, for it was just begun. . . . The Lord sent me here, I fully believe, and that threatened difficulty of the heart did not trouble me at all after we reached Battle Creek.

"Tuesday night [Dec. 30, 1890] I was in agony of soul all night so that I could not sleep. Elder Smith's case was weighing heavily upon me. I was working with him, pleading with God, and I could not cease my crying unto God.*

"Friday night [Jan. 2, 1891] I was asked to speak; the house was full, and I gave some account of the workings of the Spirit of

---

* Referring, in her diary entry, begun on Tuesday, December 30, 1890, to this trying night, Mrs. White shows that its agony was brightened with hope, for she says:

"Tuesday night a great burden came upon me. I could not sleep. Elder Smith was before me and my supplications went up to heaven in his behalf all night. I was in a spirit of agony of wrestling with God, and great hope took possession of my soul for him. He is one of our old hands, one of our reliable men, and the Lord will give him His keeping power."—Manuscript 54, 1890.

The next morning she wrote a 13-page message of appeal to Elder Smith, opening up to him the peril of his course and the influence it had upon others. She reminded him that there were wrongs that reached back to 1882. which developed around a situation at the college and involved Elder Smith and Professor Bell. This had laid the foundation for his Minneapolis experience.

God with me in the meetings which I had attended. I related as well as I could the success of these meetings. We had a special meeting of deep interest after I had spoken, and many excellent testimonies were borne, especially from those who were earnestly seeking the Lord. It was a good meeting.

"On Sabbath [Jan. 3, 1891] I spoke from Matthew 11:16-27. I made a decided application of this lesson to those who had great light, precious opportunities, and wonderful privileges, and yet their spiritual growth and advancement was not in accordance with the blessings of the light and knowledge given of God. There was a solemn impression made upon the congregation, and fully two thousand persons were present. I had great freedom in speaking. In the afternoon the meetings were divided, and I hear there were excellent meetings in these divisions.*

"Monday [Jan. 5, 1891] Elder Smith came to me and we had an earnest, faithful talk. I could see that he had a very different spirit from that he had months ago. He was not hard and unimpressible; he felt the words I spoke to him, laying before him faith-

---

* In a diary entry dated January 3, 1891, Mrs. White unburdens her heart as follows regarding this January 3 Sabbath meeting and regarding God's people. She says:

"Sabbath, January 3, 1891. I spoke in the Tabernacle to a crowded house. I had not an idea of saying as plain and pointed things as I did say, but the Lord spoke through the human agent. I felt pressed, and could not withhold the message given. I pray the Lord that the words spoken may find access to hearts.

"The Tabernacle was crowded to its utmost capacity. Oh, how I yearned in spirit for the men who, by resistance of light which God has given, have for the past two years hedged up the way that the Spirit of God shall not find access to their hearts. I heard a voice say to them, 'You still are unbelieving. *Stand aside* or close up the ranks by coming into line and uniting in the work wholeheartedly.'

"Must this burden always rest upon me here in Battle Creek? Must I always carry this heavy load? Must my testimony be of that character to reprove, rebuke? May the Lord have mercy upon me and help me, that I shall be found true and faithful to do God's will, to keep the way of the Lord, to do justice and judgment!

"A good work has been begun here, but it is not complete. There are men who do not know or understand. Will it stop short at some of the cruel stumblingblocks, and the church, because they do not make thorough work, wade through another year of darkness? God forbid! Oh, that there may be found righteous ones to plead in behalf of His people, and that their prayers will prevail!

"I should rejoice greatly to see the spirit of confession followed up throughout the church. Many are now obtaining a glimpse of their true condition and of their real necessities. If they persevere, make thorough work, and continue to draw nigh to God, He will draw nigh to them and will lift up for them a standard against the enemy. There will certainly be an outpouring of the Spirit of God. The church cannot overrate their sinful neglect of duty, their unfaithfulness, and their neglect to receive light and practice the truth. Not improving their opportunity has brought defective eyesight, and has weakened their faith and corresponding zeal in earnest effort to walk in the light. Through their unbelief—because of the attitude and position of the church—sinners in our borders have become hardened and have been fearfully established in unbelief.

"When Jesus is within the sanctuary above, when we have an Advocate in the courts of heaven, how earnestly should the corresponding work of intercession be going on upon the earth! While we may see and should sense the guilt of sin, we are to appreciate the mercy of God through the atonement. The Lord has promised that because of the propitiatory sacrifice He will, if we repent, certainly forgive our iniquities. Now, while Christ is pleading in our behalf, while the Father accepts the merits of the atoning Sacrifice, let us ask and we shall receive. Let all confess their sins and let them go beforehand to judgment that they may be forgiven for Christ's sake, and that pardon may be written against their names."—Manuscript 40, 1891.

fully the course he had taken, and the harm he had done through this position. He said he wanted to come into harmony with the testimonies of the Spirit of God.* I had written to him thirteen pages [Dec. 31, 1890] and sent them to him—very plain words. Tuesday [Jan. 6, 1891] he called again to see me and asked if I would meet with a select few, that he had something to say. I told him I would.†

"Yesterday, Wednesday [Jan. 7, 1891], the meeting was held in my room in the office, and Elder Smith read the letter I had sent him, read it to them all, and said he accepted it as from the Lord. He went back to the Minneapolis meeting and made a confession of the spirit he had occupied, casting on me very heavy burdens. Brother Rupert confessed also, and we had a very profitable, excellent meeting.

"Brother Smith has fallen on the Rock, and is broken, and the Lord Jesus will now work with him. He took my hand as he left the room, and said, 'If the Lord will forgive me for the sorrow and burdens I have brought upon you, I tell you this will be the last. I will stay up your hands. The testimonies of God shall hold this place in my experience.' It is seldom that Elder Smith sheds a tear, but he did weep, and his voice was choked with the tears in it.

"Now you see I have reason to be glad and rejoice and praise the Lord. Professor Bell was present. Elder Smith confessed to him the wrong that he had done him in the school trial in 1882. Oh, how glad I was to see and hear and know that these things that had barred the Spirit of God from coming into our meetings were removed."—Letter 32, 1891.* (Ed. note: See page 102 for footnote.)

---

* This visit of Uriah Smith to Mrs. White on Monday, January 5, 1891, is, apparently, the visit to which she refers when, immediately under her diary date line reading "Battle Creek, Tuesday, January 6, 1891," she says:
"I had [a] conversation with Elder Smith, more favorable than any previous talk. He seems to be desirous to come to the light. He sees that his course has not been right in some things, and this I knew he must see before he could be closely connected with God. Since the Minneapolis meeting he has been counteracting my work by his position. The light that God has given me for the church has not been fully received because of his position. His attitude has said more than words. But after conversing with him freely, and showing him what harm he was doing to those who did not want to believe the message or receive the messenger and the counsel from God, he seemed to see more clearly the position he had occupied. He was determined to make straight paths for his feet, and to take up the stumblingblocks, that the lame may not be turned aside out of the way, but rather be healed of their weakness and inefficiency.
"The Lord is at work, and I will not take the work out of His hands into my own hands. This is my prayer for Brother Uriah Smith, that he shall triumph with the third angel's message, and that the trumpet shall give a certain sound, that a people may be prepared for the great day of God. We have no time to lose."—*Ibid.*
† In a diary entry dated January 6, 1891, Mrs. White gives information concerning Uriah Smith's purpose in wanting to speak to "a select few." She says:
"Elder Smith came in and made a request to have a select number present to whom he wished to speak and as far as possible confess where he had been wrong."—*Ibid.*

Mrs. White's joy over Uriah Smith's confession, his request for forgiveness, and his pledge of loyal support, is expressed again and again in a manuscript that she wrote on Friday, January 9, 1891—the day after she wrote to the Washburns. After speaking of her trip to Washington, D.C., and return to Battle Creek, et cetera, she recounts Uriah Smith's confession, reiterates her expression of gratitude and affirms her conviction that God Himself had ordered her illness and return. Again she recounted how Brother Smith "had fallen on the *Rock* and was *broken*," and she told of her joy, which she found hard to describe.

The humble and heartfelt confession on the part of Elder Smith brought great relief to Mrs. White and many others who were earnestly praying and laboring for a spirit of harmony to replace the spirit of discord and jealousy that had been so noticeable since the Minneapolis session of 1888. The example of this prominent leader's repentance, confession, and change of attitude no doubt influenced others to repent and confess their wrong course, and to change their attitude.

Not satisfied with the confession he made on Wednesday, January 7, 1891, in the presence of Mrs. White and a select few, Elder Smith made another one on the following Sabbath, January 10. Mrs. White was not present, for she spent that Sabbath at Pine Creek, Michigan. But on the following Monday (Jan. 12, 1891), when she was back in Battle Creek, she speaks of his confession in the following words:

"I learn that on Sabbath Elder Smith made quite full confessions and Brother Rupert also confessed. They went back in their

---

* In her diary also, in an entry dated January 7, 1891, Sister White tells about Uriah Smith's confession. She says:

"At three o'clock P.M. the little company assembled in my room. Elder Smith said a few words, then read the letter I had written him after the exercise of my mind Tuesday night. Then Brother Smith, with tears, made a full and free confession of the wrong course he had pursued. He pledged himself, as he took my hand, that he would stand by me and would never cause me grief of soul again. This was a season pleasant for the Lord to look upon and for us all to contemplate. We hoped Frank Belden would follow Brother Smith, but he [did not].

"We long to see all who have not discerned the light to discern truth and righteousness and keep gathering and cherishing every divine ray of light."—Manuscript 40, 1891.

confessions to the meeting at Minneapolis, and confessed their mistakes, in their blindness, and that their spirit and actions on that occasion were wrong. The Lord had precious truth to unfold to His people which they, being filled with unbelief and prejudice, could not appreciate, and they worked counter to the Spirit of God."—Manuscript 40, 1891.

Even this confession made on Sabbath, January 10, 1891, did not satisfy Elder Smith, but the next Sabbath he made still another one. Mrs. White was not present this time, for on Friday, January 16, she had left Battle Creek to speak at a general meeting held at Bushnell, Michigan, January 15-22. But on her return home on Monday, January 19, she heard the news of Elder Smith's confession on the previous Sabbath. She wrote of it in her diary, as follows:

"We learn that the good work has been going on in the church. The last Sabbath, in the afternoon, Elder Smith attended the ministerial institute meeting, in the chapel connected with the office. He spoke again of his mistakes, and went back to Minneapolis and confessed his wrong there and since that time. There was a good spirit in the meeting and advance was made. I felt grateful to God for these tokens of the working of the Spirit of God.

"This work of confession going forward will clear the King's highway. May the good work go on, and may new hope, new strength and courage come to the people of God. These men who have lifted the cross have a stubborn nature, and the miracle-working power of God had taken hold of them and we were rejoiced. We respect Brother Smith. Our confidence in him is restored. We feel more closely united with him in Jesus Christ."—*Ibid.,* diary entry dated Battle Creek, Jan. 20, 1891.

On the following Sabbath (Jan. 24, 1891), Mrs. White *was* in Battle Creek and spoke at a meeting held for the workers attending the ministerial institute. What she heard and saw at that meeting gave her great joy and indicated that her wish that the good work of clearing the King's highway might go forward was being fulfilled. In her diary for that day she says:

"I attended the meeting in the chapel and spoke in the meeting for the ministerial students. We had an excellent meeting. There was a very tender spirit. Many are drawing nigh to God and coming to the light, and the Lord is helping them to clear away the rubbish from the door of their hearts and let Jesus come in. There is now a change in the expression of their countenances. Light from the Lord has been reflected upon their hearts and shines forth in their countenances."—*Ibid.*, diary entry dated Battle Creek, Sabbath, Jan. 24, 1891.

The spiritual enrichment that the ministers experienced at the Bible Institute went out to the ends of the earth wherever there were Adventist people. The King's highway was indeed being cleared, precious neglected light was being accepted, and this light shone with increasing brightness every day. Thus the Lord worked to bring Seventh-day Adventists out of their legalistic bent into the freedom and light of Christ.

How much of this increasing brightness was in a measure attributable to the repentance and confession of Uriah Smith, we do not know. But it was considerable. His new experience in Christ said more than words could portray in correcting wrong influences and in conveying a renewed faith in the testimonies of God's Spirit.

In the years following his repentance and confession Elder Smith enjoyed a good religious experience, but he was not always quick to apprehend the truth in its fullness and to comprehend the works of Providence. He found it difficult at times to join his brethren wholeheartedly in promoting the message of righteousness by faith. He seemed to feel that the matter was being overdone. He, together with others, apparently was of the opinion that Seventh-day Adventists had always believed in righteousness by faith, and that by placing so great emphasis on the subject at that time, they would leave the impression that they had never believed in it, and that it was new light. He failed to recognize fully what Mrs. White had stressed again and again: that it was not new light, but neglected light.*

In His abundant goodness and mercy God moved upon Mrs. White while she was in Australia to send Elder Smith a letter calling his attention to the dangers confronting him, and appealing to him to rethink his position and correct his attitudes. From this letter, dated September 19, 1892, we quote a few excerpts:

"Be careful what steps you take in expressing your differences with your brethren. You cannot tell how it pains me to see some of our brethren taking a course that I know is not pleasing to God. They are full of jealousy, and evil surmising, and are ever ready to show in just what way they differ with Elder Jones or Waggoner. The same spirit that was manifested in the past manifests itself at every opportunity; but this is not from the impulse of the Spirit of God. . . .

"As one long experienced in the truth, it was your place to be among those who should first catch the message from the God of heaven, and voice it to the people; but the enemy presented every matter that seemed objectionable to you in a magnified light, and your imagination has not pictured facts to you. The enemy had prepared a long chain of circumstances, like links in a chain, that you might be prevented from standing where you should have stood. You have lost a rich and powerful experience, and that loss, resulting from refusing the precious treasures of truth presented to you, is still your loss. You are not where God would have had you, and you have missed the providential links one after another in the chain, so that now it is hard for you to see the mysterious connections in the endless chain of providence in His special work.

"I write these words, not to afflict your soul, but to warn you, that you may guard against repeating the same experience, thinking it was one ordered of the Lord. God was seeking to lead you in the past, and it is necessary you understand this, that you may not place stumbling blocks before your own feet, over which you will stumble. I know not whether or not you will receive this as from God; but I beseech you for your own soul's sake, take these words written to you in love, and divest yourself of unbelieving, hard

---

* See *Selected Messages*, book 1, pp. 155, 360, 384.

thoughts. Put off thy shoes from off thy feet, for the place whereon thou standest is holy ground. Lay aside fleshly reasonings. Let every soul now stand before God in his own nothingness, and draw nigh to God.

"The many and confused ideas in regard to Christ's righteousness and justification by faith are the result of the position you have taken toward the men and the message sent of God. But oh, Jesus longs to bestow upon you the richest blessings, and to make you a mouthpiece for Himself, that you should declare to others concerning the grace that dwelleth in you. Jesus has looked upon you with sorrow, because you have not answered His expectations. 'Watchman, what of the night?' This is the question that has been asked, and will continue to be asked and answered, and what will you answer, my brother?

"The Laodicean message has been sounding. Take this message in all its phases and sound it forth to the people wherever Providence opens the way. Justification by faith and the righteousness of Christ are the themes to be presented to a perishing world. O that you may open your heart to Jesus! The voice of Jesus, the great vendor of heavenly treasures, is calling to you, 'I counsel thee to buy of me gold tried in the fire, that thou mayest be rich; and white raiment, that thou mayest be clothed.' But I will write no more. My heart is drawn out in love toward you, and my desire is that you shall triumph with the third angel's message."—Letter 24, 1892.

From the foregoing it is clear that Elder Smith did not discern fully the urgency of preaching the message that he had come finally to receive. He staggered at the spectacle of the new emphasis on revival and was overcautious, halting as he moved forward. He made mistakes after making his confession—but where is the Christian who can say that he has made no mistake after confessing his sins to God? That Elder Smith rendered valuable service to the cause of God after this experience is evident from a letter that Mrs. White wrote ten years later later (Feb. 5, 1902), a year before Elder Smith's death. In that letter she said:

"Elder [Uriah] Smith was connected with us at the beginning

of the publishing work. He labored in connection with my husband. We hope always to see his name in the *Review and Herald* at the head of the list of editors;* for thus it should be. Those who began the work, who fought bravely when the battle went so hard, must not lose their hold now. They are to be honored by those who entered the work after the hardest privation had been borne.

"I feel very tender toward Elder Smith. My life interest in the publishing work is bound up with his. He came to us as a young man, possessing talents that qualified him to stand in his lot and place as an editor. How I rejoice as I read his articles in the *Review* —so excellent, so full of spiritual truth. I thank God for them. I feel a strong sympathy for Elder Smith, and I believe that his name should always appear in the *Review* as the name of the leading editor. Thus God would have it. When, some years ago, his name was placed second, I felt hurt. When it was again placed first, I wept, and said, 'Thank God.' May it always be there, as God designs it shall be, while Elder Smith's right hand can hold a pen. And when the power of his hand fails, let his sons write at his dictation."—*Selected Messages,* book 2, p. 225.

It is regrettable that this talented pioneer, who was such a tower of strength in the young and growing Advent Movement, permitted himself to assume the attitude that brought so much sorrow and loss to the cause of God during a trying period in the history of the movement. But it is a cause of joy and rejoicing to know that, like Peter of old, he acknowledged his mistake, repented of his wrong, and went forward in fruitful service for his Master until the day of his death in 1903, at the age of 71.

For almost fifty years Uriah Smith was connected with the editorial work of the *Review and Herald,* much of that time

---

* NOTE: Elder Smith was not always the choice of the church leaders to be the leading editor of the church paper, though he served in that capacity longer than anyone else.

The *Review* of October 5, 1897, carried the announcement that Elder A. T. Jones had been added to the editorial staff, and that the relationship of the two men as associate editors was revealed by the masthead, which places first the name of Alonzo T. Jones.

Elder Smith was humble enough to stay by as associate editor while the younger man, and a man with whom he had not always agreed, took over the helm of the paper. This reveals a large measure of the grace of God in Smith's life.

In the May 14, 1901, issue of the *Review,* Uriah Smith's name appears once again as "editor"—sole editor.

as editor in chief. He was the author of a number of pamphlets and books, chief of which is his work on the books of Daniel and Revelation, a treatise that has had a very wide circulation and is still in demand. Thousands of men and women have been brought into the fold of Christ and into a saving relationship with Him through reading the messages of truth that have come from his lucid pen.

CHAPTER TEN

Still More Confessions

ABOUT ten months before the revival meetings in Battle Creek during which Uriah Smith made his confession, and approximately two weeks before the close of the first of the two Bible schools for ministers held between the 1889 and 1891 General Conference sessions, at least five of the men who had opposed the message of righteousness by faith yielded to God their stubborn wills, and either confessed their guilt or gave evidence of a changed attitude. These five men were: C. W. Olds, D. T. Fero, J. W. Watt, R. C. Porter, and Matthew Larson. And there were other men, even better known in the movement, whose hearts were changed by the grace of God.

These confessions and changes of attitude were a matter of more than ordinary interest to Ellen White, who attended many of the morning devotional meetings of the ministerial institute, and who, through her ministry, enriched these meetings. In a letter that she wrote to her son Willie and his wife on March 10 and 11, 1890, while the good work of repentance and confession was in progress, Mrs. White makes particular mention of the work of God's grace in changing the hearts of certain men:

"I have just come from the meeting. The room was full, [the east vestry of the Tabernacle] the three apartments were in one. The Lord again poured upon me the spirit of supplication. Faith did take hold of the arm of infinite power. We did have the blessing of God. . . . I spoke about thirty minutes. The Lord gave me power to speak before those present.

"Some confessions were made and quite a number who had been in darkness made confessions of their finding Jesus and being free in the Lord. . . .

"There is more and more freedom coming to the meeting. The darkness is no longer a controlling element. We are expecting more of God's Spirit, and longing and hoping and believing that the Lord will give special blessings. How I long to see these ministers free in the Lord and joyful in their God. . . .

"I am so thankful that the current is changing, and that the Lord is at work for His ministers. Many of them will return to the field of their labor with much light, a deeper experience, and with more courage in the Lord. . . . I feared I should leave this place in depression and discouragement, but the Lord is giving us tokens for good, and He will bring His people where they can praise His holy name. . . .

"Many seem to be getting the blessing of faith and pardon. I called Brother Olds' name and gave him a pointed testimony. He confessed Sabbath afternoon. This morning he talked in a very humble and broken way. Brother Binghouse said he was never so blessed in his life as he has been in the last few days. Brother Warren reveals the blessing of God in his face, for it looks as if the Sun of Righteousness was beaming upon him. He bore a testimony that he never felt the blessing of God to so great a degree in his heart before. Brother Fero has humbled his heart, and he says he is free in the Lord and is wonderfully blessed. Brother Watt talked again this morning and he says he is gaining a deep and rich experience in the knowledge of our Lord and Saviour Jesus Christ. He seems to be altogether a different man, and many whose names I do not know, are coming into the light. Oh, I hope and pray that this work may move forward in great power. We must have the blessing of God deep and rich and full. Brother Olsen stands well, firm and free, and boldly on the right side. . . .

"I no more carry a load because of the fact that I cannot express myself. I am free and I talk as the Spirit of God giveth me utterance, and the word spoken is fully received by the largest number present. The men that have held things have no power now. There is a strong current setting heavenward, and if we wait on the Lord, we shall surely see of His salvation. He will work in our behalf. He will not let this ministerial institute break up in confusion and darkness."—Letter 30, 1890.

On March 11 Ellen White continued her epistle of rejoicing:

"Dear Children, my heart is filled with thanksgiving and praise to God. The Lord has poured upon us His blessing. The backbone of the rebellion is broken in those who have come in from other places. This morning the room was full. We first had prayer, then Brother Olsen spoke; I followed in the same line in which I have been laboring since one week ago last Sabbath. The Lord put words into my mouth to speak, and Elder Bourdeau spoke well. Elder Waggoner spoke very humbly. Brother Steward spoke with much feeling and humility. Brother Fero spoke well. Brother Larson then spoke and confessed that his feelings had not been right. I responded and he took his position on the testimonies.

"Brother Porter was on his feet, all broken up so that he could say nothing for a few moments; then he said that when I had spoken to him personally, before those assembled in the office chapel, he rose up against it, but he felt now that it was just what he needed, and he thanked the Lord for the reproof. He confessed the wrong that he had done me and Elder Waggoner, and humbly asked us to forgive him. . . .

"The whole room was sobbing and praising God, for there was a revealing of His power. He drew graciously near. . . .

"Brother Prescott talked well and plainly; told them that were assembled that God had spoken to us through Sister White this morning. 'Let us,' he said, 'take heed to these words.' He wept like a baby when Brother Larson and [Brother] Porter were making their confessions. Brother Olsen is so glad and feels so relieved, he scarcely knows what to do with himself. Brother Waggoner feels so thankful."—*Ibid.*

W. W. Prescott was deeply stirred at this spring meeting, but it was not until Sabbath, December 27, 1890, as we have already stated, that he surrendered fully to God's invitation to repentance and confessed his guilt in opposing the message of righteousness by faith preached at the 1888 General Conference session. It was while he was reading the Week of Prayer reading by Ellen White that Elder Prescott was so profoundly affected and wept. "He then confessed," wrote Mrs. White, "that at the Minneapolis meeting, and since that time, he had not had altogether right feelings. He asked the forgiveness of all, and especially of Brethren Waggoner and Jones."—Manuscript 3, written Jan. 9 in Battle Creek, Michigan.

Uriah Smith's failure to follow Brother Prescott's act of confession on Sabbath, December 27, 1890, must have reminded Brother Prescott of his own failure, ten months earlier, to follow the example of R. C. Porter and Matthew Larson, who humbly acknowledged their wrong course.

The story of the confession of Uriah Smith, as told by Mrs. White, reveals also the confession of G. G. Rupert—another of the men who in 1888 opposed the message of righteousness by faith preached at Minneapolis.

The reader will recall that when, on Thursday, January 8, 1891, Sister White wrote to Brother and Sister J. S. Washburn, giving them the good news of the confession of Uriah Smith, she added: "Brother Rupert confessed also, and we had a very profitable, excellent meeting."—Letter 32, 1891.

Brother Rupert's readiness to follow and join Uriah Smith in making things right is understood in the light of the following lines, written by Ellen White from Brooklyn, New York, on November 25, 1890, to Uriah Smith, in a letter urgently calling him to repentance and confession:

"Bro. Rupert has a work of confession. I told him two years ago when at Potterville, and he has heard the same again and again from my lips, but Brother Smith has been his stumbling block and the stumbling block of many others."—Letter 73, 1890.

Uriah Smith removed the stumbling block by his confession.

In the spring of 1893, a little more than two years after W. W. Prescott, Uriah Smith, and G. G. Rupert had entered into a new life in Christ, similar confessions were made by I. D. Van Horn and LeRoy Nicola regarding their own opposition to God's message.

In a touching letter to Mrs. White, Elder Van Horn responded to a testimony that she had written him from Melbourne, Australia, on January 20, 1893, pointing out his sad condition since the time of the Minneapolis meeting. This popular minister—so successful in youth work—told of his heartfelt repentance and confession as follows:

"Your letter, written the 20th day of January, 1893, was received by me Tuesday evening, February 21. Now that the ministers' institute* and General Conference, in which was manifested the Spirit and power of God as I have never witnessed before, are in the past, I will take the earliest opportunity to return an answer to you. . . .

"This communication by your hand to me I heartily accept as a testimony from the Lord. It reveals to me the sad condition I have been in since the Minneapolis meeting, and this reproof from the Lord is just and true. Since it came I see more than ever before the great sin it is to reject light. And this is made doubly sinful by my own stubborn will holding out so long against the light that has shown so brightly upon me. I did not realize how great was the darkness that enveloped me, and how strongly I was held under Satan's power, till I received this token of God's love to me which has opened my eyes.

"I am now heartily ashamed of the part I took in the 'merriment,' the 'satire,' 'sarcasm,' and 'wit' that was so much indulged in by myself and others in the same room at that Minneapolis meeting. It was very wrong—all wrong—and must have been very displeasing to the Lord, who witnessed it all. I wish it all could be blotted from my memory.

"A few days before this testimony came I began to see myself far out of the way, as I saw so much of the power of God resting on Brethren Jones, Prescott, and Haskell as they unfolded before me the light and glory of the message as it now should go to the world. Knowing that repentance and confession was the only way

---

* This institute was held from January 27 to February 17, 1893. (See the *Review and Herald* of Feb. 7, 1893.)

out of sin and darkness, I took occasion, in a meeting on the Sabbath day, to confess my great wrong at Minneapolis, and the wrong all the way from that time till now.

"This brought me some light, blessing, and comfort from the Lord. I now believe that He used this means to prepare me to receive this reproof that was soon to come into my hands. I thank the Lord that he showed me so great kindness. Surely His tender mercy to me is greater than I am worthy to receive.

"Three days after this I received the testimony, and late in the evening I went to my room where all alone I read it three times over with much weeping, accepting it sentence by sentence as I read.

"I bowed before the Lord in prayer and confessed it all to Him. He heard my earnest plea, and for bitterness of soul He gave me peace and joy. I could but thank Him for sending me this message, for it is a token of His love. 'For whom the Lord loveth he chasteneth, and scourgeth every son whom he receiveth.'

"The next morning I went into the ministers' meeting and made a more earnest and extended confession of my wrong before my brethren who knew of my course, and it brought great light and blessing into my soul. I am now a free man again, thank the Lord, having found pardon and peace.

"But I begin to see how much I have lost in these four years of darkness and unbelief. I will now make haste and 'buy the gold' the 'white raiment' and the 'eyesalve,' that I may stand before my fellow men, not in my own strength with a few set discourses, but with the righteousness of Christ, and the rich provisions of His grace to give them the 'meat in due season.' I will arise, and in the fear of the Lord, go forward with the advancing light of the message. I will walk softly before the Lord, and will cherish His presence in my heart, that I may have power from Him, who has all power, to resist Satan, shun his snares, and gain the victory at last. . . .

"I shall need counsel and instruction. If you have anything further that would give me more light, showing me more clearly my true condition, I shall be very glad to receive it."—March 9, 1893, Battle Creek, Michigan.*

About two weeks after Elder Van Horn wrote the afore-

---

* At the 1897 General Conference session, held at Lincoln, Nebraska, I. D. Van Horn preached a sermon entitled "Righteousness by Faith." In this sermon, delivered on Sunday

quoted letter of confession to Sister White, LeRoy Nicola wrote her a similar letter, from which we quote the following lines:

"I have been thinking of writing you for a number of months. I want to tell you that my views of some matters in connection with that Minneapolis meeting have radically changed since I last talked with you. The Lord has mercifully shown me some of the mistakes which I made at that time. I know He has forgiven me. I rejoice in the mercy and great love which He has shown me. . . .

"It looks to me very plain that you have unflinchingly and most decidedly stood for four or more years in favor of special principles of inestimable value to our work. How the truth would have been dishonored had some of the counsels at Minneapolis prevailed. This seems very clear to me. I rejoice in the light that has been shining since that meeting. I want to stand in the full light of God's favor, and not in any of the sparks of my own kindling. Every particle of trial in the matter has left me, and I do feel to accept with all my heart the testimony that God has given you. I shall do everything that it is possible for me to do to restore what I have torn down. And I feel that the work of retracing some of my steps would be very incomplete did I not beg your forgiveness for my indifferent course toward you."—March 24, 1893.

After receiving this letter from Brother Nicola, Sister White wrote from Wellington, New Zealand, in her diary of April 23:

"I received two important letters from Elder Olsen and LeRoy Nicola, with a most thorough confession of the part he [Nicola] acted in Minneapolis. It is thorough, and I praise the Lord for the victory he has gained over the enemy who has held him four years from coming into the light. Oh, how hard it is to cure rebellion! How strong the deceiving power of Satan!"—Manuscript 80, 1893.

---

evening, February 28, Elder Van Horn stressed the importance of being clothed with the white raiment of Christ's righteousness. In the course of this discourse he made the following remark:

"Do you know that since the meeting at Minneapolis, the sending forth of the message to put on the righteousness of Christ has been going on? Do you know that like a wave of light it has gone to our people everywhere? Well, have you bought it yet? Has eight years of time gone by, and yet you have not made the purchase?"—*General Conference Bulletin*, March 8, 1897, p. 306.

Commenting further on this the next day, Mrs. White declared: "I knew if he walked in the light that this must come." —Letter 79, 1893.

The letter from Elder Olsen reporting on the 1893 General Conference session brought word about two others in whom Ellen White had felt deep concern. Of this she wrote in her diary of April 24, 1893:

"I have passed many sleepless hours during the night. The good news from America kept me awake. Oh, how my heart rejoices in the fact that the Lord is working in behalf of His people, in the information in the long letter from Elder Olsen, that the Lord by His Holy Spirit was working upon the hearts of those who have been in a large measure convinced of their true condition before God, yet have not humbled their hearts before to confess! The Spirit of the Lord moved them to the point at this conference.

"Elder Morrison, who has been so long president of the Iowa Conference, made a full confession. Madison Miller, who has been under the same deceiving power of the enemy, made his confession, and thus the Lord is indeed showing Himself merciful and of tender compassion to His children who have not received the light He has given them, but have been walking and working in darkness."— Manuscript 80, 1893.

Relative to Elder Morrison, we have the added testimony of A. T. Jones in a letter he wrote May 12, 1921, to C. E. Holmes:

"In justice to Brother J. H. Morrison [it must be said that he] ... cleared himself of all connection with that opposition, and put himself body, soul, and spirit into the truth and blessing of righteousness by faith, by one of the finest and noblest confessions that I ever heard."

The obituary of Madison Miller, written by C. L. Taylor, bears witness to the good fruits of his full repentance.

"Brother [Madison Miller] was a man of deep piety. My personal interviews with him during the last year of his life deeply impressed me, for they revealed to me a heart greatly enriched by grace, and ripened off in the love of truth. His one thought was to be right—right for right's sake. The unconscious influence of his life was such as to make others hungry for better things, and undoubtedly he will reap an abundant harvest in the kingdom of God."—*Review and Herald,* Feb. 8, 1917, pp. 22, 23.

From the facts produced in this chapter, it must be evident to the reader that within a few months or a few years of the Minneapolis meeting, the majority of the persons concerned in the opposition to the light of righteousness by faith repented of their wrong course and took their stand for truth and right. There is evidence, either direct or indirect, that R. A. Underwood, D. T. Jones, R. M. Kilgore, and others also came into harmony with the light. No attempt will be made to go further in relating their individual experiences. Throughout the field, workers and members moved into line and thus strengthened the hands of the large number who had hailed the truth preached by A. T. Jones and Dr. Waggoner from 1888 and on into the years succeeding.

Here we shall permit C. McReynolds, a loyal worker who was present at the Minneapolis session, and who lived until a few years ago, to add his testimony, written about 1931:

"Early in the spring, 1889, word began to come of some of those who had stood with the opposition at the conference beginning to see light, and soon earnest confessions followed. Within two or three years most of the leading men who had refused the light at the conference had come out with clear confessions."—"Experiences while at the General Conference in Minneapolis, Minnesota, in 1888," Ellen G. White Publications Document File, No. 189.

On February 6, 1896, Sister White sent, from Australia, a message addressed "To My Brethren in America," advising the discontinuance of the three-to-five-month-long ministerial institutes, because they were no longer necessary. Here are her own words, as now recorded in *Testimonies to Ministers,* page 401:

"Men are called from the fields, where they should have con-

117

tinued working in the love and fear of God, seeking to save the lost, to spend weeks in attending a ministerial institute. There was a time when this work was made necessary, because our own people opposed the work of God by refusing the light of truth on the righteousness of Christ by faith."

In the above statement Sister White recognized that in the seven years that had elapsed since Minneapolis, the situation had so changed that it was no longer necessary to call the workers together for long-drawn-out institutes to instruct them on the subject of righteousness by faith. This was a cause for rejoicing.

The battle had been long and hard. The victory was not won in a day or a month. No, not even in a year! Several years of toil and tears were required to bring it about. The enemy of souls made a desperate effort to wreck the Advent Movement, but, thank God, he failed. Through the mighty workings of the Spirit of God upon human hearts, the enemy was defeated.*

This must not be interpreted to mean that every opposer was converted. Some who had been prominent in the cause of God withdrew from the work and left the church. And, sad to say, the very men—A. T. Jones and E. J. Waggoner—who were opposed at Minneapolis and who wrought so mightily for God and for the true gospel, lost their way and drifted out of the church.

This did not happen in a year or in a decade, but slowly and surely in the crisis years that followed 1888, the natural weaknesses inherent in Jones and Waggoner took shape in

* By the beginning of the year 1899, most of the opponents among the workers had undergone such a change in their attitude that Elder A. T. Jones felt it incumbent upon him to sound a note of warning lest our ministers swing from one extreme to another. During the General Conference session held in South Lancaster, Massachusetts, from February 15 to March 9, 1899, he gave a study in which he cautioned the brethren against the danger of emphasizing faith to the exclusion of the importance of keeping the commandments of God. Here are his words:

"The Lord sent a message, and sent His word by that message, saying that the faith of Jesus, righteousness by faith, must be preached. He says that He sent the message of righteousness by faith because the people had lost sight of Christ, in the righteousness of Christ as He is. *I am afraid that there has been a tendency to go over to the other end now, and preach the faith of Jesus without the commandments. We must guard ourselves against such a thing as that.*"—*Review and Herald*, June 20, 1899. (Italics supplied.)

their lives and in their ministry. They eventually lost their hold on God and the truth and their ministry became ineffectual. E. J. Waggoner became indifferent. A. T. Jones became antagonistic.*

In 1892, Ellen White penned lines that expressed her fears for the spiritual survival of these two champions of truth. She also made clear that in the event that either man apostatized, the basic truths they had taught at Minneapolis would stand, for they were founded upon the everlasting gospel. She wrote:

"It is quite possible that Elder Jones or Waggoner may be overthrown by the temptations of the enemy; but if they should be, this would not prove that they had had no message from God, or that the work that they had done was all a mistake. But should this happen, how many would take this position, and enter into a fatal delusion because they are not under the control of the Spirit of God. They walk in the sparks of their own kindling, and cannot distinguish between the fire they have kindled, and the light which God has given, and they walk in blindness as did the Jews.

"I know that this is the very position many would take if either of these men were to fall, and I pray that these men upon whom God has laid the burden of a solemn work, may be able to give the trumpet a certain sound, and honor God at every step, and that their path at every step may grow brighter and brighter until the close of time."—Letter 24, 1892.

---

* See Appendix B.

119

CHAPTER ELEVEN

Attitudes in Battle Creek

WHEN Elder O. A. Olsen was elected president of the General Conference at the Minneapolis session in 1888 he was in Europe, where he was in charge of a young, growing work. The records of the time reveal that not all the men chosen to work with him had accepted the message of righteousness by faith as it was presented at Minneapolis. This led to problems that extended through most of his administration. D. T. Jones, the newly elected secretary, did not at once accept the message, nor did R. A. Underwood, who was not a resident of Battle Creek. Harmon Lindsay, elected treasurer, never did.

Furthermore, a number of men filling leading positions in our institutions in Battle Creek were not in sympathy with the message or the men who had presented it. Among these were Captain Eldridge, Frank Belden, and A. R. Henry, the former treasurer of the General Conference and for several years one of the leading spirits in the Review and Herald publishing house.

The conflict that broke out in Minneapolis raged in the headquarters city of Battle Creek for a number of years. Feelings ran high. A. T. Jones and E. J. Waggoner for a time were *persona non grata* with certain of the influential men in that important Adventist center. Someone had the temerity to suggest that the pulpit of the Tabernacle should be closed against A. T. Jones. Even Sister White was discredited by some because her messages gave support to the two men who brought the message of righteousness by faith to the Minneapolis session. In fact, the reader may have noted the implication that as well as the issues over the message of righteousness by faith, there were, deep in the hearts of some who opposed, questionings over the visions and disbelief in God's leadings through the Spirit of prophecy. Of her experience in Battle Creek after her return from Minneapolis, Mrs. White wrote:

"When I came to Battle Creek, I repeated the same testimony in the presence of Elder Butler, but there was not one who had the courage to stand by my side and help Elder Butler to see that he, as well as others, had taken wrong positions, and had misapprehended my words, and had false ideas in reference to my position and work."—Letter 3, 1889, written Jan. 25 to R. A. Underwood.

Consequently, it was not an enviable situation that Elder Olsen stepped into when six months later he arrived in Battle Creek to assume his new duties and responsibilities as president of the General Conference.

Elder Olsen was a God-fearing man, and his soul was troubled over what he saw and heard in Battle Creek. With the help of God, he labored to bring about peace and harmony. He gladly supported Sister White in her noble and persistent efforts to improve the situation, and he rejoiced with her, as we have noted in a previous chapter, when men began to surrender and to confess their wrongs.

R. A. Underwood shortly changed his course and ceased his opposition. D. T. Jones also before long came into harmony with the will of God. He died September 24, 1901, at the age of forty-six, after having "closed up all his business, reviewed his life, acknowledged his mistakes, and with a firm faith and bright hope, as a weary soldier laid off the armor, saying, 'My work is done, and I am ready to go.' "—*Review and Herald*, Oct. 29, 1901, p. 710.

Because of their far-reaching influence, we shall present

the experiences of four other men who were prominent in the opposition group: Frank Belden, Captain Eldridge, A. R. Henry, and Harmon Lindsay. All occupied leading positions in the management of the Review and Herald publishing house, and Harmon Lindsay served, in addition, as treasurer of the General Conference from 1874 to 1875 and from 1888 to 1893.

Frank Belden, a nephew of Ellen G. White, the son of her older sister Sarah, was a poet, a song writer, and a composer of music of no mean ability. Several Seventh-day Adventist song-books and hymnals down through the history of the church have been enriched by his songs. Some of these songs have been translated into various languages and are sung around the world.

As long as Frank Belden remained humble, he was a great blessing to the cause of God. But as his responsibilities grew and his influence extended, he came to depend less and less upon God, the Source of all wisdom and power. This resulted in the promotion of plans and policies detrimental to his own experience and to the best interests of the publishing house.

In various ways Ellen White tried to help her nephew to see the errors of his way. From faraway Australia she wrote long letters to him filled with divine counsel, reproof, and tender appeals. From one of these written November 5, 1892, we quote as follows:

"I should feel sad to see you separated from the cause and work of God. But I would not have you occupy your present position of large responsibility unless you shall come to understand better your relation to God and His claims upon you, and your relation to your fellow men. . . .

"Instead of learning of Christ's meekness and lowliness of heart, you have advanced in self-esteem and self-importance. Selfishness has entwined itself in all your efforts. It has tainted your work, and will ruin your soul unless you change this order of things decidedly and firmly. . . .

"Have you not in a large degree sacrificed spiritual and eternal interests for mere worldly, temporal things? How near has the work and cause of God been to your soul? Has not your self-sacrifice for Jesus been very small? You have another life to sustain than that which is nourished by temporal bread. You have a soul to look to carefully, lest it shall be lost forever. . . .

"Across the waters of the broad Pacific I cry to you, Look and live. Look steadily, constantly, earnestly, to the Lamb of God, that taketh away the sin of the world. The sanctification of the soul is accomplished through steadfastly beholding Him by faith as the only-begotten Son of God, full of grace and truth. . . .

"Frank, my dear nephew, the power of the principles you profess has too often been neutralized by your practice. . . . The Lord can bless you only as you come to Him with humble heart, confessing your errors and sins.

"When you are enlightened by the Holy Spirit, you will see all that wickedness at Minneapolis as it is, as God looks upon it. If I never see you again in this world, be assured that I forgive you the sorrow and distress and burden of soul you have brought upon me without any cause. But for your soul's sake, for the sake of Him who died for you, I want you to see and confess your errors. You did unite with those who resisted the Spirit of God. You had all the evidence that you needed that the Lord was working through Brethren Jones and Waggoner; but you did not receive ·the light; and after the feelings indulged, the words spoken against the truth, you did not feel ready to confess that you had done wrong, that these men had a message from God, and you had made light of both message and messengers. . . .

"Captain Eldridge's influence over you has not been right in some things. Your influence with him might have been much more to his good and the glory of God than it has been. But the past, with its burden of record, has gone into eternity; now in repentance and confession and conversion to God, in childlike submission and obedience to His will, is your only hope of salvation. I am deeply in earnest; I could not abate one jot or tittle of truth to please you or to make you my best friend. No; it is life or death with you. There is no time for us to trifle with eternal realities. We must be saved in God's way, just as He has presented it in His Word, else we can never be saved at all. . . . Thank God, oh, thank Him with heart and voice, that He is still our compassionate Redeemer, ready to forgive sin, and by His own blood to cleanse us from every stain that sin has made."—Letter B-2a, 1892.

But the words fell on unbelieving ears. He would not listen. At about this time he withdrew from the Review office. Concerning this, Ellen White commented:

"In severing his connection with the work of God in the office, Frank [Belden] has done just what I had feared he would do. Had he denied self, standing at his post in obedience to the will of God, and because this is the work of God, putting his whole heart into the work and bearing its responsibilities and burdens as others have borne them before him, even though he should not gain as much financially as in business for himself—had he done this, he would have made it manifest that he was not a timeserver. But how great was his interest for the office, if he could step out when he pleased, when it appeared to be for his interest to do so? Ought the soldiers in Christ's ranks to act in this way? Should soldiers in the army of the nation do this, they would be treated as deserters, and how does the heavenly universe look upon such soldiers in Christ's army? No one who engages in the work of God with an appreciation of its sacredness, could turn from the work to secure any worldly advantages whatsoever."—Letter 20a, 1893; in *Selected Messages,* book 2, pp. 213, 214.

But she still carried a heavy burden of heart for this man. In 1895 she wrote:

"I appeal to you, Frank, by all that is dear and precious and holy, to make thorough work and stand in your Saviour a free man. O that all who stepped in false paths at that notable meeting at Minneapolis, and have felt the same spirit enfolding them about, would let heaven's light into their souls, which would give them a true sense of their course of action, and their manner of spirit since that time! O that they would, before it is too late for wrongs to be righted, make confession in secret to God who seeth in secret the plans and imperfections and the sins of those things which have made Jesus ashamed to call them brethren! Hating Jesus Christ in the form of His saints! O how will God reveal this whole business in a place where they have never looked upon it!"— Letter 13, 1895, written November 13.

Frank Belden continued in his own willful way, until he lost his hold upon God and severed his connection with the cause that he had spent so much time and talent to build up.

Captain Eldridge, manager of the Review and Herald publishing house, shared the sentiments of Frank Belden, who exerted a baneful influence upon him. He severed his connection with the Review in 1893. Mrs. White wrote several long letters to this capable man, laying bare before him the condition of his heart. She made clear that unless he changed his course he would lose his soul. Like a mother she pleaded with him. Two paragraphs taken from a long letter she sent to him from Australia, April 14, 1894, are illuminating:

"Your case is urged upon my mind—your spiritual condition as it was after you accepted the truth, and as it is at the present time. Your principles are not now what they should be or what they might have been if you had appreciated the light of the Sun of Righteousness, and had walked in its rays as they shone upon your path. The Lord brought you, Brother Eldridge, in connection with His established institutions because He had blessed you with talents, which, if sanctified, would be a blessing to His cause and work. But without the Holy Spirit of God to bless and encourage your advancement as a learner, you would not obtain the experience essential for you as a wise manager in a line of work demanding faithfulness in every particular. Unless you should submit yourself to be educated and taught of God, you could not fill successfully the position to which you were called. There must be no confederating together on the part of any of the workers to carry out their own purposes; for one would surely mislead another.

"The union between yourself and Frank Belden did not aid either of you in gaining the experience essential for you individually. You were both entrusted with sacred responsibilities. You were both on trial, under the proving of God. This responsible position called for daily and hourly experience in spirituality, in devotion to God. There was no lack on the part of God; every provision had been made whereby you might individually receive the power essential for the perfection of Christian character."—Letter 20, 1894.

Commenting on his experience, Ellen White, two years later, wrote:

"However skillful Captain Eldridge may have been in guiding vessels upon the high seas, he was incapable of managing the responsibilities at the heart of the work."—Letter 124, 1896.

Hostility toward A. T. Jones and E. J. Waggoner and their message was not the only issue involving Captain Eldridge in a wrong course. There were other problems as well. One that was causing unrest and dissatisfaction in the Review and Herald publishing house was the question of the high wages Brother Eldridge and a few of the principal officers were drawing.

In order that he and his family might live on a scale comparable to some of their wealthy neighbors, the manager of the Review had influenced the board, on the basis of giving full recognition to executive ability, to fix a salary of thirty dollars a week for himself and twenty-five dollars a week for each of the other leading officers in the institution. This was at a time when ordained ministers were receiving twelve dollars each a week, and the employees in the publishing house even less. This, naturally, created an unwholesome atmosphere in the institution.

But apparently the extra income did not help him, for early in November, 1892, Captain Eldridge wrote Sister White that he had decided to leave the work because he and his family could not live on the salary he was receiving. His account with the publishing house at that time was overdrawn to the extent of $1,244, and he owed a similar amount to another institution. In reply Mrs. White wrote him a long letter, from which we quote in part as follows:

"My brother, in your letter you speak of leaving the Review office. I am sorry that you can be willing to separate from the work for the reasons you mention. They reveal that you have a much deeper experience to gain than you now have. Your faith is very weak. Other families, much larger than yours, sustain themselves without one word of complaint, on half the wages you have. We have been over the ground, and I know what I am talking about. It is evident that whether you remain in the Review office or separate from it you have lessons to learn that will be of the highest interest to you. I do not feel at liberty to urge you to remain; for unless you drink deeper of the Fountain of living waters, your service will not be acceptable to God. . . .

"Whatever position a man may fill in connection with the office of publication, he is not to be paid an exorbitant sum, for God does not work in this way. You lacked spiritual eyesight, and you needed the heavenly anointing, that you might see that the work of God was founded in a sacrifice, and only by a sacrifice can it be carried forward. . . .

"My brother, if you have no more heart interest in the work than is indicated by the fact that you can drop it so easily, I have nothing to say, no plea to make for you to remain in the office, or for Brother Belden to return to it. You both reveal that you are not men that can be depended upon. And an example that would be given in offering you additional inducements to remain would not be pleasing to God."—Letter 20a, 1893, written January 9 in Australia; in *Selected Messages,* book 2, pp. 210-214.

Soon after receiving this letter, Brother Eldridge severed his connection with the publishing house. And in a letter written May 1, 1895, to the president of the General Conference, Ellen White remarked that "Captain Eldridge and Frank Belden acted a prominent part; but in mercy to them they disconnected themselves from the office."—Letter 57, 1895, written from Tasmania.

Our records do not reveal what became of Captain Eldridge, but he dropped out of the picture of institutional leadership and in time disappeared from the records of the denomination he had served.

Harmon Lindsay, who was treasurer of the General Conference, and who occupied other positions of trust, resisted the promptings of the Spirit of God at the Minneapolis meeting and through a number of years following. His real attitude is well delineated in a twelve-page letter written to him May 1,

1895, by Ellen White, then in Tasmania. To show the attitude of Brother Lindsay and the issues involved in his disaffection, I quote at length from Mrs. White's letter as follows:

"Since the meeting at Minneapolis you have followed in the tread of the scribes and Pharisees. Never will you have greater evidence of the working of the Holy Spirit than you had at that meeting. Again and again the Spirit of the Lord came into the meeting with convincing power, notwithstanding the unbelief manifested by some present; but you were deceived and prejudiced, and manifested the spirit of those who refused to acknowledge Christ. You have followed in their tread, and have refused to acknowledge the mistakes and errors in resisting the message the Lord in mercy sent you.

"Afterward, at the conference meetings held in Battle Creek, though evidence after evidence was given you, you refused to accept the message sent you by God. You would not humble your pride and repent; your wrong attitude remained unchanged.

"At times . . . you were almost ready to fall on the Rock and be broken, but you strengthened yourself to resist. With others you walked in the same path as did the rebellious Jews; the same spirit that inspired them inspired you, and the results have been similar. You need a teachable spirit. You will never find rest until you yield up your set, stubborn will, and cease to resist the pleadings of the Spirit of God. . . .

"God has given you great light, and you will be held accountable for all the privileges you have had to become acquainted with God and His truth. . . .

"You have not cherished the love of the truth in your heart, though you maintain in some respects the form of godliness. You have sought to manage things according to Harmon Lindsay's will and way, but all this outward work is vain unless God works within. The position you have accepted demands consecrated ability and a pure, sanctified heart. But I have heard you give wrong counsel in regard to the disposition of means given by those who have been moved by the Holy Spirit to sell what they have and help God's work.

"Since the Minneapolis meeting your influence and that of Brother A. R. Henry have been like a malarious atmosphere upon the hearts of God's people. . . .

"Why do you cherish such bitterness against Elder A. T. Jones and Elder Waggoner? It is for the same reason Cain hated Abel. Cain refused to heed the instruction of God, and because Abel sought God, and followed His will, Cain killed him. God has given Brother Jones and Brother Waggoner a message for the people. You do not believe that God has upheld them, but He has given them precious light, and their message has fed the people of God. When you reject the message borne by these men, you reject Christ, the Giver of the message. Why will you encourage the attributes of Satan? Why will you and Brother Henry despise God's delegated ministers, and seek to justify yourselves? Your work stands revealed in the sight of God. 'Turn ye, turn ye . . . ; for why will ye die?' "—Letter 51a, 1895.

Harmon Lindsay served the General Conference in financial lines until the session held in February, 1897, which he attended as a delegate at large. Ellen G. White documents indicate that he was fast drifting from the church. Before long he was in opposition to the cause he once served, and he died a Christian Scientist.

But back again to Battle Creek and attitudes there. A. R. Henry, already mentioned in several Ellen G. White communications, was the son of a Methodist minister, and president of a bank in Indianola, Iowa, when, in 1881, he was called to be manager of the Review and Herald publishing house. From 1883 to 1888 he served as treasurer of the General Conference. For a number of years after 1888 he occupied different positions in the publishing house. He also found time to operate a lumber and building business in Battle Creek. He was a shrewd businessman, and a born leader of men.

What a tragedy that a man who had been blessed by Heaven with such talent, and who enjoyed the love and confidence of his brethren, should have permitted himself to pursue a course that brought sorrow and harm to the cause of God!

Through Ellen White, the Lord sent many messages of warning and tender appeal to Brother Henry. From one of these I quote the following paragraphs:

"I have a warning for you from the Lord. 'All the paths of the Lord are mercy and truth unto such as keep his covenant and his testimonies.' 'The meek will he guide in judgment; and the meek will he teach his way.' I feel very sad in regard to your case, for you are pursuing a course that is deciding your eternal destiny. You are in great trouble of mind, and you have given that mind to be worked by the powers of darkness. Satan is striving to destroy you, body and soul. When in Minneapolis you took a turn that has influenced all your movements since then in the wrong direction. You must know that you are pursuing a course similar to that of Judas, who betrayed his Lord.

"Your supposed wisdom in financial matters has led your brethren to cling to you, and to regard your judgment as superior. They have made a mistake. Notwithstanding all the light God has given His people in regard to the righteousness of Christ, they have not had spiritual eyesight to discern that all wisdom is from God. They have not discerned the truth. Linked up with Harmon Lindsay, you have betrayed sacred trusts, and you have both greatly hurt the cause of God.

"You must answer for your course of action before God. Would it not be well for you to consider what the end of all this will be? You have already gone as far under the inspiration of Satan as it is in any way safe for you to go. It is your privilege now to make a decided change. In the name of the Lord I warn you not to take one step further in the path you have entered upon. This is a life-and-death question. Call a halt, I beseech of you. Call a halt before it is everlastingly too late. . . .

"Will you consider that it was you yourself who acted a part in the work that has brought the displeasure of God upon His instrumentality in Battle Creek. Not you alone, but those also who were connected with you, had warning after warning. God desires that the principles upon which His institution was first established shall be maintained at any cost. There must be a close searching of the Scriptures, to know the way of the Lord. . . .

"You and Harmon Lindsay have rejected the light sent you from heaven, which, if received, would have made you wise men. Your natural traits of character would have been brought into subjection to the Spirit of God, and your great desire would not have been to make provision for yourselves in a way that is not honorable or righteous. These plans to follow the imagination of your unsanctified hearts have brought upon you blindness of mind and increased stubbornness of heart, until you could not feel the necessity of saving your souls unto eternal life. . . .

"I entreat of you, A. R. Henry, to break the power of Satan. No longer be fastened a slave to his chariot wheels. God's power alone can break this chain, break the fetters of Satan. Heaven is worth everything to you. Then break with Satan. Flee to Christ before it is everlastingly too late. A few more steps in the path you are pursuing will place you where light and truth will have no power over you.

"I send you this, for my soul has been wrestling in agony in regard to your case. I want you to be saved. I want you to have life, that life that measures with the life of God. I want to see you a victor. I want to see you an overcomer. Will you be this? Pursue the course you have entered upon, and you will divorce your soul from God; and then what?"—Letter 15, 1898, written April 20 from Sydney, Australia.

Because of the positions occupied by Harmon Lindsay and A. R. Henry when O. A. Olsen arrived in Battle Creek in the late spring of 1889, to take over his duties as president of the General Conference, and because of their natural and acquired abilities, he leaned heavily on them for counsel and assistance in the promotion of the work of God. He often took them with him to attend important institutional boards and conference committee meetings both far and near. At times, he sent one or both of them to such gatherings when he himself could not go.

From the servant of the Lord messages came to the president of the General Conference, warning him of the dangers involved in permitting men like Lindsay and Henry to continue to be associated so intimately with him in the direction of the Lord's work. On May 1, 1895, Sister White wrote to him:

"You have connected with you men who have no living connection with God. You fear to exercise your judgment, lest there shall be an explosion. This is why I feel so sad. I have written out matters that I dared not send to you unless there were persons of a firm, decided character who would stand by your side as true yoke-fellows, to sustain you. The two men who have been especially associated with you, should, in their present spiritual condition, have no part in planning and carrying forward the work of God in any of its various lines. If they were to see themselves as God sees them, and fall upon the Rock and be broken, a decided change would appear in them. Confessions would be made to free their souls from every corrupting influence."—Letter 57, 1895.

Four months later from Australia, Sister White wrote Elder Olsen the following lines:

"For years I have carried a consuming burden for the cause of God in Battle Creek. I am now deeply troubled over the shape which matters are taking there, and the influence which is being exerted on the work everywhere. I ask you, my brother, how can you entrust A. R. Henry and Harmon Lindsay with so much responsibility in the work, and send them hither and thither to all parts of the field? They are not by precept and example giving the third angel's message. The atmosphere which surrounds their souls, and which is revealed in spirit and influence, shows that they have lost the Spirit of God out of their hearts and their experience. They are made responsible for many, many things, while they do not feel their accountability to God."—Letter 53, 1895, Sept. 10.

A few days later Ellen White sent President Olsen this message calling for action:

"Elder Olsen, the present state of things has continued long enough. Your eyesight has become imperfect. You link up with men whom God is not leading. You accept as sound the propositions of men who in some things start you on a wrong track; for you sanction these propositions, and give them authority and power. I am not sorry that these things, which have been so long brewing in unsanctified minds, have become more pronounced, that you may the better discern their true character before some other agent shall come in to preside over the conference in your place. I now beg of you to arise in the name of the Lord, and He will help you to retrieve the errors of the past, that are leading to serious results."—Letter 55, 1895, written Sept. 19 from Australia.

At first it was difficult for Elder Olsen to sense fully the perils of the situation. But not long after he received this letter from Sister White, changes came. A. R. Henry retired to his business in Battle Creek. Ellen G. White continued to carry a heavy burden for him. In her closing remarks on the last day of the 1901 General Conference in Battle Creek, she asked:

"Where is Brother Henry today? Who during this meeting has labored for him? . . . I wish to ask, 'Is it not best for us to do all in our power to heal souls that are wounded nigh unto death?' "
—*General Conference Bulletin,* April 25, 1901, p. 463.

The records show that A. R. Henry remained a member of the church until the day of his death, June 26, 1909, at the age of seventy years.

Now turning to Brethren Jones and Waggoner. Notwithstanding the unfriendly attitude of some of the brethren at the Battle Creek headquarters toward them, they were given a prominent part in the work of the church. Until Ellen White sailed for Australia, late in 1891, frequently they were associated with her, attending camp meetings, workers' meetings, and other gatherings. Both were invited to take a prominent place in the large ministerial institutes conducted in Battle Creek in 1889, 1890, 1891. At all the General Conference sessions for a number of years after 1888 they were the principal speakers, leading out in Bible teaching. At the morning meetings during the 1889 General Conference session A. T. Jones presented the Bible studies and spoke on the subject of righteousness by faith.* In 1891, E. J. Waggoner offered sixteen Bible studies, and A. T. Jones gave a talk on religious liberty. He also preached a Sabbath afternoon sermon.

At the 1893 session Elder Jones delivered twenty-four Bible studies, and in 1895 twenty-six (in addition to a religious liberty talk on Sabbath afternoon, March 2). In 1897, A. T. Jones

---

* The practice of stenographically recording the Bible studies given during a General Conference session was first adopted at the 1891 session. Consequently, the *General Conference Bulletin* of 1889 does not contain the studies presented by Elder Jones. Ellen G. White, however, refers to these. The bulletins of the following sessions contain the studies presented at these important sessions of the church.

presented eleven more, and E. J. Waggoner nineteen. In 1899, A. T. Jones had eight such studies, and E. J. Waggoner four. In 1901, A. T. Jones had three, and Waggoner five. The frequent appearance of these men at the General Conference sessions indicates that for many years they were considered the leading Bible exponents in Seventh-day Adventist ranks and were held in high esteem by most of the responsible leaders of the General Conference.

Furthermore, in the late 1890's Elder A. T. Jones was made the editor of the *Review and Herald*. The masthead for the issue of October 5, 1897, read

Alonzo T. Jones)
) Editors
Uriah Smith)

But the full significance of this is seen in the announcement signed by the Directors, which accompanied the move, appearing in the same issue:

"IMPORTANT ANNOUNCEMENT

"The Board of Directors of the Review and Herald Publishing Company are glad to announce to the many friends of the cause, that Elder A. T. Jones has been added to the regular editorial staff of the *Review and Herald*. Brother Jones will devote his time to editorial work on the *Review;* and now, instead of speaking to comparatively few of our people in annual gatherings, he will address *all* of them *every week.*

"This will give to our churches and scattered brethren everywhere the privilege of receiving, each week, the words of faith, hope, courage, and good cheer that have been the means of so much blessing to many all over both America and Europe.

"Elder Smith will continue as associate editor; and as he has recovered from the serious illness which was incurred in Syria, and which has troubled him more or less since his return in 1895, we hope to have much more from his pen filled with the oldtime fire of the message. Elder Smith's long experience in the cause enables him to write as but few others can. He is one of the only two or three of the old pioneers of forty years' labor in this work who are left to us."—*Review and Herald*, Oct. 5, 1897.

Four years later, that Elder Jones might be freed for evangelistic work in the field, he was released from the responsibilities of editorship. The change is noted by Elder A. G. Daniells, a strong exponent of righteousness by faith, in the May 14, 1901, issue of the *Review*. Once again Elder Smith's name appears as "Editor"—sole editor.

"EDITORIAL CHANGE

"Among the changes effected since the session of the General Conference, the readers of the *Review* will observe that which relates to the editorship of our denominational paper. Elder A. T. Jones is this week succeeded as editor in chief by Elder Uriah Smith, who for forty-seven years has been connected with the editorial department of the *Review and Herald*.

"By this change Elder Jones is again free to engage in evangelistic work in the field. Our people, who have hitherto been so richly blessed in listening to his stirring messages, will be pleased to learn that similar privileges await them. Moreover, the large family of *Review* readers will be assured that the paper will continue to exert an increasing influence for good under the efficient management of Elder Smith, who has so long and so helpfully ministered to our people in every land, through the columns of the *Review*. . . .

"A. G. DANIELLS, *Chairman*
General Conference Committee"

One thing is clear: For many years the leaders of the church took steps to keep Elders Jones and Waggoner prominently in the lead as Bible teachers in the ranks of the church.

So in old Battle Creek there was defeat and victory, victory and defeat. What is more, there was discernible in the historical developments of the time a fulfilling of God's plans and purposes for the remnant church; and of these glorious developments we shall see numerous evidences in the closing chapters of this narrative.

CHAPTER TWELVE

The Minneapolis Spirit
at the 1891 Session

THE first General Conference biennial session * was held March 5-25, 1891, in the commodious Tabernacle in Battle Creek, Michigan. This important gathering was the last General Conference session attended by Ellen G. White before her departure for Australia, where she spent almost nine years.†

Sister White addressed the delegates a number of times during the 1891 session, but unfortunately only two of her addresses were recorded in the *General Conference Bulletin*. In her last message to the assembly delivered on Tuesday evening, March 24, and titled "Our Present Dangers," she spoke out against a spirit that was manifest at this 1891 meeting that was displeasing to God and that needed to be corrected. "You possess in a large degree," she declared to the delegates, "the same spirit that was revealed in the conference at Minneapolis."—*General Conference Bulletin*, 1891, p. 257.

This spirit *did not take shape in a conflict over righteousness by faith*. This needs to be emphasized. We should seek to know, therefore, what took place in the 1891 meeting that reflected the meaning of Mrs. White's words.

---

* From 1863 till 1889, there were twenty-eight regular sessions: one per year, except in 1872, when instead of holding the session early in 1872 it convened December 29, 1871. A second session was held in 1873, and special sessions added in 1876, 1878, 1879, and 1880, making two for each of those years; and 1876, when there were three. From 1891 till 1905, the sessions were biennial. From 1909 till 1962 they were quadrennial, save for the 1918, 1941, and 1946 sessions, each of which followed a five-year period, and 1936, which followed a six-year period. From 1863 till 1962 there were forty-nine sessions, of which thirty-two were held in Battle Creek, Michigan—the 1901 session being the last one held there. (See *1964 Yearbook of the Seventh-day Adventist Denomination*, Annual Statistical Report, p. 2.)

† Mrs. White arrived in Australia on December 8, 1891 (see *Life Sketches of Ellen G. White*, p. 332), and left Australia on August 29, 1900, returning to the United States (*The Bible Echo*, Sept. 17, 1900, p. 616).

THE MINNEAPOLIS SPIRIT AT THE 1891 SESSION

In Minneapolis in 1888 the spirit that caused so much sorrow and harm was a spirit of criticism and jealousy, and also of opposition to divine counsel, while the sensitive point of conflict was the message of righteousness by faith. In Battle Creek, in 1891, there was likewise revealed by some a spirit of disobedience and opposition to the counsels of God, but on issues other than those prominent in 1888. Neither in the minutes of the 1891 session nor in references to this gathering can we find that there was any repetition of the basic issue of the Minneapolis conflict. E. J. Waggoner was present and presented sixteen studies on the book of Romans, stressing especially the subject of righteousness by faith, without meeting any open resistance.

While there was no open opposition to the doctrine of righteousness by faith at the 1891 session, this must not be regarded as evidence that all the opposers to this central gospel truth had been converted. A few men as late as 1897, who filled important positions in Battle Creek, had not yet taken their stand. These men were in attendance at the 1891 session but they did not openly oppose the message of righteousness by faith.

Ellen White felt much concern for these men, and she expressed this concern at the session. This is revealed in a manuscript entitled "Article read in the auditorium of the Battle Creek Tabernacle to a large assembly, at the General Conference of 1891," from which we quote as follows:

"The Lord has been calling His people. In a most marked manner He has revealed His divine presence. But the message and the messengers have not been received but despised. I longed that those who have greatly needed the message of divine love would hear Christ's knock at the door of the heart, and let the heavenly Guest enter. But at the hearts of some Jesus has knocked in vain. In rejecting the message given at Minneapolis, men committed sin. They have committed far greater sin by retaining for years the same hatred against God's messengers, by rejecting the truth that the Holy Spirit has been urging home. By making light of the message given, they are making light of the Word of God. Every appeal rejected, every entreaty unheeded, furthers the work of heart hardening, and places them in the seat of the scornful.

"These rejectors of light cease to recognize light. Their souls are surrounded by a malarious atmosphere, and though some may not show open hostility, those who have spiritual discernment will realize the icy coldness which surrounds their souls."—Manuscript 30, 1890.

That the presence of these unconsecrated men had a chilling influence on the delegates at this session cannot be denied. But the fault of the 1891 session was its failure to heed oft-repeated counsels sent by the Lord regarding a variety of important matters. This Ellen White made clear in her last recorded address to the delegates. On Tuesday evening, March 24, she said:

"You who have been educating yourselves and others in a spirit of criticism and accusing, remember that you are imitating the example of Satan. When it suits your purpose, you treat the Testimonies as if you believed them, quoting from them to strengthen any statement you wish to have prevail. But how is it when light is given to correct your errors? Do you then accept the light? When the Testimonies speak contrary to your ideas, you treat them very lightly.

"It does not become any one to drop a word of doubt here and there that shall work like poison in other minds, shaking their confidence in the messages which God has given, which have aided in laying the foundation of this work, and have attended it to the present day, in reproofs, warnings, corrections, and encouragements. To all who have stood in the way of the Testimonies, I would say, God has given a message to His people, and His voice will be heard, whether you hear or forbear. Your opposition has not injured me; but you must give an account to the God of heaven, who has sent these warnings and instructions to keep His people in the right way. You will have to answer to Him for your blindness, for being a stumbling block in the way of sinners."—*General Conference Bulletin,* April 13, 1891, p. 257.

As the session was drawing to a close Mrs. White was keenly

disappointed over the fact that the delegates had failed to heed the counsels that God had been sending His people through her. There had been a failure to obey the Lord in a number of important areas of responsibility. What were these points of issue at the 1891 General Conference session?

1. Congestion resulting from large numbers of Adventists moving to Battle Creek.

For some time Mrs. White had urged that something be done to encourage decentralization as the remedy to the congestion in Battle Creek. In her first recorded.address to the session she devoted the whole hour to a portrayal of the situation that existed as a result of the large influx of Seventh-day Adventists into this denominational center. She read from a published testimony of 1868 (*Testimonies,* vol. 2, pp. 113-116), and as she read, added the sentences here enclosed in brackets:

"With many of our brethren and sisters there is a strong inclination to live in Battle Creek. [Many think they are getting the next door to heaven, if they get into Battle Creek. Thus they have expressed it to me again and again.] Families have been coming from all directions to reside here, and many more have their faces set that way. [We can well testify of that by the inflowing since the last Testimony was given.] Some who have come to Battle Creek held offices in the little churches from which they moved, and their help and strength were needed there. When such arrive at Battle Creek, and meet with the numerous Sabbathkeepers there, they frequently feel that their testimonies are not needed, and their talent is therefore buried.

"Some choose Battle Creek because of the religious privileges it affords, yet wonder that their spirituality decreases after their sojourn there a few months. Is there not a cause? The object of many has been to advantage themselves pecuniarily—to engage in business that will yield them greater profits. Their expectations in this particular may be realized, while they have dearth of soul, and become dwarfed in spiritual things. They take no special burden upon themselves, because they think they would be out of place. They do not know where to take hold to labor in so large a church, and therefore become idlers in their Master's vineyard.

[Now mark!] All who pursue this course only increase the labor of those who have the burden of the work in the church. They are as so many dead weights. There are many in Battle Creek who are fast becoming withered branches. . . .

"Brethren who wish to change their location, who have the glory of God in view, and feel that individual responsibility rests upon them to do others good, to benefit and save souls for whom Christ withheld not His precious life, should move into towns and villages where there is little or no light, and where they can be of real service, and bless others with their labor and experience. Missionaries are wanted to go into towns and villages and raise the standard of truth, that God may have His witnesses scattered all over the land, that the light of truth may penetrate where it has not yet reached, and the standard of truth be raised where it is not yet known. The brethren should not flock together because it is more agreeable to them, but should seek to fulfill their high calling to do others good, to be instrumental in the salvation of at least one soul. But more may be saved than one."—*General Conference Bulletin,* 1891, p. 181. (In a talk given on March 17, 1891.)

Notwithstanding the gravity of the situation and the earnestness of the appeal for something to be done to decentralize, there was no response. No action was taken. The message fell on deaf ears. There was no move to obey the directions of the Lord in this matter.

2. Consolidation of institutions under one general management.

During the 1889 session, on Tuesday, November 5, a set of resolutions was presented recommending the consolidation of Seventh-day Adventist publishing houses under one management to be centered in Battle Creek. These resolutions were framed by an appointed committee, which made the following recommendations:

"Your committee appointed to take into consideration the publishing interests of the denomination, have carefully considered this subject; and in order to meet the increasing demand of our work, and to avoid all sectional feeling and personal interests which are now liable to arise from the present plan of conducting our business by having separate organizations, and also to unify the work and secure the more hearty cooperation of all, would respectfully recommend—

"1. That steps be taken at once to form a corporation for the purpose of taking entire control of all our publishing interests, thus bringing the work under one general management.

"2. That the officers of this association be a board of twenty-one trustees, to be elected by the General Conference, with power to organize themselves by electing a president, vice-president, secretary, assistant secretary, a corresponding secretary, and a treasurer.

"3. That at least twelve persons on this board be representative men not connected with any local publishing house, taken from different parts of North America, according to the numerical strength of the denomination.

"4. That when this association is organized, one third of the trustees be elected for one year, one third for two years, and one third for three years.

"5. That the stockholders of the Review and Herald Publishing House and the Pacific Press Publishing Company take into consideration the advisability of turning over all their interests to this new organization, and if thought advisable to do so, that steps be taken as soon as possible to bring about this result.

"The objects of this new organization shall be:

"1. To hold the title of all our denominational publishing houses and the equipments thereof.

"2. To own, publish, and control the sale of all denominational books, tracts, and periodicals.

"3. To secure, as far as possible, by purchase or otherwise, the plates and copyrights of all denominational books now published by our different publishing houses, or that may be written in the future.

"4. To encourage the preparation of books, pamphlets, and tracts upon the different points of our faith.

"5. To appoint editors and managers, to take a general supervision of the work of the various offices.

"In view of the fact that it may take some time to bring about, in full, this much-to-be-desired result, and in order to move in that direction as far and as fast as possible, we recommend that at first, this association assume control of all denominational publications and periodicals now published in the foreign languages and of such works as belong to the General Conference of Seventh-day Adventists, but that the incorporation be made with a view to assuming entire control of all our publishing interests.

"In order that no time may be lost, your committee would further recommend that a standing committee of twenty-one be elected by the General Conference at its present session to take this whole question into consideration, with power to act. We would also suggest that the very best legal advice be consulted in bringing this new organization into existence.

"Your committee would further recommend that a similar organization be effected for the purpose of controlling all our educational interests, and owning the property—thus bringing them under one general management. Also, another to control our health institutions."—*General Conference Bulletin*, Nov. 6, 1889, p. 149.

After a general approval of these recommendations, the 1889 General Conference session appointed a large standing committee to give careful study to the implementation of this plan, with the understanding that they would report to the 1891 session.[*] Accordingly, the committee appointed met, drew up their detailed resolutions, and on Sunday, March 15, presented their report to the 1891 session. Because of the importance attached to this document and to enable the reader to follow the reasoning that prompted it, the entire resolution is quoted here:

"Your committee, appointed at the last session of this conference to take into consideration the consolidation of the publishing work under one general management, with power to act, if in their judgment they thought best to do so, would report that we have given the matter referred to us much thought. It being a matter of great importance, requiring careful attention at every step, we have thought it prudent to move cautiously, even though the work might move slowly.

"Your committee has taken steps to examine into the plans upon which the publishing work of other denominations is managed. We have carefully investigated the plans adopted by the

---

[*] See *General Conference Bulletin,* Nov. 22, 1889, p. 158.

Baptists, Presbyterians, Lutherans, Reformed Church, Methodists, and others. We find that in all these, the general points which you wish to gain by consolidation are practically carried out; namely, that the entire publishing work of each denomination is under one general management, and that such portions of the surplus profits accruing from it as are not needed in carrying on the publishing work, are applied to the carrying forward of the general work of the denomination.

"The publishing houses have been built up by the denomination. Many persons who own no stock in these institutions have done much by donations and otherwise to sustain them, and to extend their influence—as much perhaps as many have done who are stockholders. Therefore it is evident that these institutions should be controlled by the denomination.

"Competent attorneys have been consulted on the question of forming a legal corporation to carry out the objects had in view by this conference, relative to the consolidation of your entire publishing work.

"For many reasons, we are not in favor of multiplying corporations. We think the objects so much desired can be brought about without this.

"After carefully considering the matter, and discussing different plans, your committee have reached the conclusion that an organization already in existence would, with some slight changes in its constitution and bylaws, be as efficient in carrying out your desires and purposes as any new corporation that could be formed. We refer to the General Conference Association. The object of this association, as stated in Article III of its constitution, is as follows:

" 'The *object* of this corporation is to diffuse moral and religious knowledge and instruction, by means of publishing houses for such purpose, publications therefrom, and the further means of missionaries, missionary agencies, and all other instrumentalities and methods appropriate and available for and tending to the advancement of the ends and aims above specified.'

"It will be observed at once that the objects of this association, as set forth in its constitution, are the same as the objects which the General Conference had in view at its last session in appointing the committee of twenty-one on consolidation of its publishing interests.

"By referring to Article VI of the Constitution of the General

Conference Association, we see that the association is controlled by a board of only five trustees. We believe this board to be too small for the carrying out of the objects which you have in view; as a board, to control the entire publishing work, should represent the entire field.

"Your committee would therefore suggest:

"1. That the constitution of the General Conference Association be so changed or amended as to provide for a board of twenty-one trustees.

"2. That the board of trustees be made up of men representing all parts of the field.

"3. That the bylaws also be changed to conform to this increase in the number of trustees.

"4. We would further suggest that this board meet semiannually to counsel together, and lay plans for the carrying forward of the publishing work. The local boards of the different publishing houses, and managers in charge of the publishing work in the different institutions, will then be expected, in harmony with the plans that have been laid, to render an outline report of its working to this board at its semiannual meetings, and a complete tabulated report and balance sheet once each year.

"The General Conference Association so organized and equipped for managing a publishing work, can hold stock bequeathed or assigned to it, and otherwise discharge the duties of such a corporation as you have had in mind, fully as well as any new corporation that might be organized for this special purpose, and the objectionable feature of multiplying organizations will thereby be avoided.

"In this report your committee has simply outlined the general plan. If it meets your approval, we would suggest that the following resolution be adopted by the conference:

"*Whereas*, all of our institutions are designed to be parts of one harmonious whole, working to one grand end; and,

"*Whereas*, It is the sense of this body that the best and most enduring interests of our cause require that the management of our various institutions shall be as widely representative as is consistent with good business principles; and,

"*Whereas*, The scope of the law under which the General Conference Association of the Seventh-day Adventists is incorporated, permits said association to become the recipient of trusts, loans, gifts, and advances, to promote the purposes of our cause, and authorize the creation and perpetuation of a board of trustees of sufficient number to meet our ideas of a representative management; therefore,

"*Resolved,* That said corporation is hereby earnestly requested to at once amend its articles of association so as to permit the carrying out in a practical way the general principle set forth in the foregoing preambles.

"If this resolution should be adopted promptly, and the work of amending the constitution begun at once, it can probably all be completed before the close of this conference, and the board suggested in the resolution elected before the conference adjourns." —*General Conference Bulletin,* March 16, 1891, pp. 123, 124.

In the meeting following the one in which this report of the committee on consolidation of publishing interests was presented, this matter was taken up, and the committee's "preambles and resolutions" were adopted. (*Ibid.,* March 17, 1891, p. 135.) Before the session closed, the constitution and bylaws of the General Conference Association were amended as proposed, and a board of twenty-one members was elected. (*Ibid.,* March 19, 1891, p. 163; March 24, 1891, pp. 217, 218; March 26, 1891, p. 248.)

But this whole plan, however sincerely the brethren may have created and adopted it, was contrary to both the spirit and the letter of counsel against consolidation that had been given to the General Conference leaders at different times by the servant of the Lord. Much earlier, in the autumn of 1885, in a letter to George I. Butler and S. N. Haskell, Mrs. White had written expressing disapproval of consolidation on the grounds that too much responsibility was being placed in the hands of too few men:

"In another letter I have spoken in reference to your accumulating so many responsibilities in Battle Creek when there is so little managing talent that is consecrated to the work of God to take care of these interests. I have spoken in disapproval of the enlargement of the sanitarium, on the ground that so large a share of its responsibilities are resting upon one man."—Letter 12, 1885, begun Oct. 28, 1885, in Orebro, Sweden, and finished later in Prussia.

The following spring in a letter to George I. Butler, the president of the General Conference, Ellen White had written showing that it was easy for circumstances to arise that might influence the whole church adversely because of the possible weakness of a few.

"The evils of centering so many responsibilities in Battle Creek have not been small. The dangers are great. There are unconsecrated elements that only wait for circumstances to put all their influence on the side of wrong."—Letter 34, 1886, written March 1, in Basel, Switzerland.

And during the conference itself, one such warning was sounded: Ellen G. White called conference presidents and managers of institutions together in the committee room at the Tabernacle and read a testimony that was based on Isaiah 8: 12-14, which was a decided reproof to the leaders regarding confederacy. At this time two matters were before the men: one the question of union with non-Adventists in the religious liberty work, and the other the question of consolidating the publishing and other interests of the denomination. The majority applied the testimony to the religious liberty question, and proceeded with the work of consolidation. (See W. C. White sermon at College View, Nebraska, Nov. 25, 1905, in White Estate Document File, No. 105b.)

Notwithstanding the counsel that God had given repeatedly against concentrating too much power and too many interests in Battle Creek, the brethren in the 1891 General Conference session planned to gather together and center there the management of all the publishing interests of the church.

In 1894, in a letter from Australia to "the General Conference Committee and the publishing boards of the Review and Herald and Pacific Press," Mrs. White wrote:

"The present is a time of special peril. In 1890 and 1891 there was presented to me a view of dangers that would threaten the work because of a confederacy in the office of publication in Battle Creek. Propositions which to their authors appeared very wise would be introduced, looking to the formation of a confederacy that would make Battle Creek, like Rome, the great head of the work, and enable the office of publication there to swallow up everything in the publishing line among us. This is not God's wisdom, but human wisdom.

"These matters have been coming up again and again in different aspects, but this policy of consolidation would, if adopted, result in marring the work. God would have His work move firmly and solidly, but no one branch is to interfere with or absorb other branches of the same great work. From time to time, for years in the past, God has been pleased to give me special light on these points."—Letter 71, 1894, written April 8.

The plan to consolidate our institutions under one management clearly represented a flagrant violation of the principle quite clearly set forth in the Spirit of Prophecy writings before and very clearly after the 1891 session. Note the following, published in 1902:

"At times it has been urged that the interests of the cause would be furthered by a consolidation of our publishing houses, bringing them virtually under one management. But this, the Lord has shown, should not be. It is not His plan to centralize power in the hands of a few persons* or to bring one institution under the control of another. . . .

"Never should our publishing houses be so related to one another that one shall have power to dictate as to the management of another."—*Testimonies,* vol. 7, pp. 171-173.

But this was not the only issue of the 1891 conference.

---

* See "The Spirit of Independence," in *Testimonies,* vol. 9, pp. 257-261.

CHAPTER THIRTEEN

The Issues of Selfishness and Worldly Policy

AT DIFFERENT times prior to the 1891 General Conference session the Lord through His servant spoke out against unequal wages paid to a few leading officers in the publishing house. Mrs. White urged that adjustments be made. On November 25, 1890, just a few months before the conference convened, she wrote this to the publishing house leaders:

"I was instructed that the Lord's will was not fulfilled when the leaders in the office were willing to take such large wages; but how quickly was the bribe taken, how quickly selfishness was manifested. This is greatly at variance with the principles upon which the publishing house was established; and it is not in harmony with the spirit and work of God."—Manuscript 6, 1890.

Then immediately before the session Ellen White called attention to this question again as follows:

"There are those who do not discern the sacredness of the work, who will surely bring in principles that are not correct. They will work to secure wages, and then think their duty is done. They will bring in a selfish, grasping spirit, which will result in robbery of God. Strange fire will be mingled with the sacred fire. Others will catch this spirit; for the plague spot of selfishness is as contagious as the leprosy. 1 Peter 4, chap. 5:1-11.

"Just as long as you conduct the business connected with the cause and work of God according to the Word of God, according to the specific directions given by Him to give to all Israel, the Lord will be your shield, your guide, your buckler, and your exceeding great reward. But blindness in part has happened unto Israel. A heavy cloud is now hanging over the publishing institution and the General Conference Association."—Manuscript 19, 1891, dated March 3.

In view of the plain, pointed counsel given by the Lord regarding this matter, one would naturally expect some action to have been taken by the delegates to counsel the publishing leaders concerned to remedy the situation. But the session closed without any such action recorded.

Referring to this three years later, in a communication sent from Australia to "the General Conference Committee and the publishing boards of the Review and Herald and the Pacific Press, Mrs. White wrote:

"How slow were some to yield up their selfishness in the matter of wages, even after clear and definite light had been given on this subject. Never before had there been such a delay to correct their wrong course of action. Unholy ambition took possession of their thoughts and minds, and, not having experience—as it is evident they did not have—in the workings and methods of God, they would not receive the light given them by God. Since the light was given, a long period of time has passed, time sufficient for them to make decided changes; but instead of doing this, they were continually seeking occasion to justify themselves in retaining the money they had received. They showed themselves to be untrustworthy, and they could not be left to put their mold upon the cause of God. All their excuses and subterfuges could not avail with God. The Lord has given light which they chose not to heed. 'He, that being often reproved hardeneth his neck, shall suddenly be destroyed, and that without remedy.' "—Letter 71, 1894, written April 8.

From time to time the servant of the Lord had counseled the leaders in our institutions to adhere strictly to Christian principles in all their business transactions. During the 1891 session she brought this matter again to the attention of the delegates. Her remarks regarding this important question are not recorded in the *General Conference Bulletin,* but they are referred to in the *Bulletin* as follows:

"At 2:30 P.M. [Sabbath, March 7, 1891] Sister White spoke with freedom and power about the dangers, duties, and privileges of our time. She dwelt especially upon the danger of leaving our first love, and of the importance of all, expecially those connected with our leading institutions, having a vital connection with Christ, the True Vine. Patterning after the world, and adopting a worldly policy by withholding or suppressing the plain and important truths for our time for fear of arousing prejudice, are dangers which must be guarded against. Men in responsible positions should go to God in earnest supplication for divine help as often as did Daniel. All the people should pray for those upon whom great responsibilities rest that God may guide them by His unerring counsel. A deep solemnity rested upon the congregation as the Spirit of God sent these things home to the heart."—*General Conference Bulletin,* March 8, 1891, p. 34.

The very day Mrs. White gave the talk summarized in the above quotation she wrote in her diary the following lines:

"I spoke with much freedom to the congregation assembled in the Tabernacle. I could not forbear speaking the words the Lord had given me in regard to our different institutions, and the necessity of men who fear God being connected with these institutions. I presented before those present the sacred responsibilities connected with the office of publication, telling them that those who accept these responsibilities should be men of faith, men of piety and deep experience. Jesting and joking should not be sanctioned in the office, neither should harshness nor sourness be shown to those employed or those seeking counsel. . . .

"There can be no sinless swerving from the way of the Lord. Perplexities will arise. Religion will be erased from the souls of some of the workers. Selfish plans will be laid, and engagements entered into, that will blot out the principles which God has specified should rule in every department of this institution. Voices will be heard making resolutions and propositions which are not wise, which come from unsanctified, unholy human minds. These will be accepted. In many hearts the truth of God will cease to be a living, all-pervading, sanctifying principle. High-toned integrity will be supplanted by selfishness and a desire to lord it over others."—*Manuscript* 19, 1891.

The following day, Sunday, March 8, and early in the session, Ellen White made another entry in her diary. After describing her attendance and participation in the Sunday morning ministers' meeting, she wrote this:

"My soul is exceedingly troubled. The publishing institutions are receiving a mold that is not after the similitude of God. I am listening to words from the lips of my Guide. Every business transaction is receiving the inspection of God. Every movement now made should be charged with the highest sense of sacred responsibility. High-toned integrity should be practiced between man and man. All business transactions may be of the purest equity; for God has made every provision that they should be. But they are not.

"Let God be kept ever before you. Let Him be recognized in every transaction that takes place between man and his fellow man. Keep the way of the Lord, to do justice and judgment. If you are ready to hear and to do the words of Christ, if you are much upon your knees in humble prayer, saying from the heart, 'Thou, God, seest me,' great evils will be averted. I beg of you for Christ's sake to take heed to these words. Then the soul will be fortified with heavenly principles."—*Ibid.*

Perhaps closely akin to the problems of "worldly policy" was the growth of "commercial work" done at both the Review and Herald and the Pacific Press and of its influence on both management and employees. This will be discussed in a later chapter.

Ten years after the conference of 1891, and shortly after her return from Australia, Mrs. White attended the 1901 General Conference session, which was held in Battle Creek, April 2-23. Immediately following the president's opening remarks the first morning, she delivered an address that resulted in tremendous and far-reaching changes in the conduct of our worldwide work. The principal burden of her speech concerned reorganization. In the opening paragraphs of her address she referred back to the 1891 session, and spoke of the work that should have been accomplished there:

"I feel a special interest in the movements and decisions that shall be made at this conference regarding *the things that should have been done* years ago, and especially ten years ago, when we were assembled in conference, and the Spirit and power of God came into our meeting, testifying that God was ready to work for this people if they would come into working order. The brethren assented to the light God had given, but there were those connected with our institutions, especially with *the Review and Herald Office and the conference,* who brought in elements of unbelief, so that the light that was given was not acted upon. It was assented to, but no special change was made to bring about such a condition of things that the power of God could be revealed among His people.

"The light then given me was that *this people should stand higher than any other people on the face of the whole earth,* that they should be a loyal people, a people who would rightly represent truth. The sanctifying power of the truth, revealed in their lives, was to distinguish them from the world. They were to stand in moral dignity, having such a close connection with heaven that the Lord God of Israel could give them a place in the earth.

"Year after year the same acknowledgment was made, but *the principles which exalt a people were not woven into the work.* God gave them clear light as to what they should do, and what they should not do, but they departed from that light, and it is a marvel to me that we stand in as much prosperity as we do today. It is because of the great mercy of our God; not because of our righteousness, but that His name should not be dishonored in the world. . . .

"It is not for men in any part of the world, in any line of His work, to depart from God's principles in any business transaction. God wants the world to see that business can be carried on in accordance with the principles that mark the character of God in Christ. What are God's commandments?—They are the wall which is built round His people. There is to be no departure from His principles, no bringing in of worldly policy principles. No worldly customs or practices are to be brought in for this people who are to be representatives of Christ to follow. When we keep the commandments of God, we are in touch with God, and He is connected with us."—*General Conference Bulletin,* 1901, p. 23. (Emphasis supplied.)

It is clear that one of the things Ellen White had hoped to see changed during the 1891 session was the worldly policy that had crept into our institutions. In closing this chapter, we repeat again, that as far as the records go, there is no evidence that there was any open conflict at the 1891 session over the doctrine of righteousness by faith. Except for the chilling influence of the unconverted, there was no apparent opposition on this point. There was, however, a failure to heed the earnest counsel that had come to the church, both before and during the session, through the Spirit of prophecy. God-sent light was neglected. This "do-nothing" attitude prevented essential reforms and hindered the progress of the work of God. This was, in part, why Ellen White in her last warning to the assembly said, "You possess in a large degree the same spirit that was revealed in the conference at Minneapolis."—*Ibid.*, 1891, p. 257.

CHAPTER FOURTEEN

Church Organization a Boon

DURING the last decade of the nineteenth century and the earliest years of this century a number of important messages freighted with counsels and warnings came to church leaders in Battle Creek from the pen of God's messenger. In order to understand and appreciate the import of these it is necessary to be familiar, to some extent at least, with conditions and situations that existed at that time. Without this historical background we might misunderstand or misapply the meaning and purpose of these messages. This at times has been done by well-meaning persons.

During the early 1890's some messages of reproof were directed to certain leaders who opposed the message of righteousness by faith. However, as has been shown, the opposition in this area gradually disappeared and ceased to be a primary reason for the Heaven-sent messages of reproof.

There were other reasons for the repeated counsels that came to the leaders. Conditions at church headquarters in Battle Creek called loudly for a change. The Lord called not only for a revival of practical, spiritual faith but for a reformation as well. Two unhappy situations obtained, even beyond the matters discussed in the two preceding chapters, that called particularly for change. The first concerned church organization, which at that time sadly needed revision and repair. Second, the handling of commercial business by our publishing houses was bringing the frown of God upon the church. In these situations there were unsavory elements of human planning that required correction, and God in His providence and in His time brought about the necessary changes.

During the first decade and a half of its existence, the Advent Movement had neither organized church nor organized conference. No legal entity of any kind existed for holding church property. In fact, it did not own any property. And to add to its embarrassment it did not even have a name.

The little publishing office in Rochester, New York, with its hand press was held in the name of James White. But there was no conference Bible house or agency for distributing literature. There was nothing to bind the believers together for service. There was no recognized church government to control, guide, and protect the young movement in the accomplishment of its task of giving the threefold message to the world. A. W. Spalding wrote of those days as follows:

"The decade following the disappointment was a time of chaos in Adventist circles. Not only did the failure of their hopes cut deep and result in a large falling away, but those who remained were in confusion. Miller and his associates never intended to create a new church; and when they were cast out of their mother churches, they were held together, not by any organic arrangement, but solely by the bonds of a common faith. The experience prejudiced them against church organization. After the disappointment their faith was torn by diverse teachings and irreconcilable leaders. At the same time their bias against organization continued and prevented such union as a definite polity and headship might afford. George Storrs wrote before the disappointment, and his words were echoed afterward: 'Take care that you do not seek to manufacture another church. No church can be organized by man's invention but what it becomes Babylon *the moment it is organized.'"—Origin and History*, vol. 1, p. 291.

Many years later this situation was cited by Ellen G. White as a reason why church organization was essential. In a letter she wrote from Australia on December 19, 1892 to the delegates assembled for the 1893 General Conference session she reviewed the past and explained:

155

"As our numbers increased, it was evident that without some form of organization there would be great confusion, and the work would not be carried forward successfully. To provide for the support of the ministry, for carrying the work in new fields, for protecting both the churches and the ministry from unworthy members, for holding church property, for the publication of the truth through the press, and for many other objects, organization was indispensable."—*General Conference Bulletin*, 1893, p. 22; in *Testimonies to Ministers*, p. 26.

Although the need for organization must have been apparent, there was strong opposition to it on the part of the majority of conscientious believers. Some argued, still following the opinion of George Storrs, that they would be retracing the steps of Babylon if they organized, and that such a course would be inconsistent on the part of a people proclaiming a message to "come out" of "Babylon." The opposition from both the workers and the members was strong, and the cause of God for some years suffered loss because of it.

But as early as December 24, 1850, the matter was forcefully presented to Ellen White in vision. We quote:

"I saw how great and holy God was. Said the angel, 'Walk carefully before Him, for He is high and lifted up, and the train of His glory fills the temple.' I saw that everything in heaven was in perfect order. Said the angel, 'Look ye, Christ is the head, move in order, move in order. Have a meaning to everything.' Said the angel, 'Behold ye and know how perfect, how beautiful, the order in heaven; follow it.' "—Manuscript 11, 1850, Dec. 25.

In the fall of 1853, when the Lord's advancing work was passing through a real crisis in a number of places because of the absence of a sound, solid organization, young Ellen White wrote out faithfully the famous vision regarding church and gospel order. She said in part:

"The Lord has shown that gospel order has been too much feared and neglected. Formality should be shunned; but, in so doing, order should not be neglected. There is order in heaven. There was order in the church when Christ was upon the earth, and after His departure order was strictly observed among His apostles. And now in these last days, while God is bringing His children into the unity of the faith, there is more real need of order than ever before; for, as God unites His children, Satan and his evil angels are very busy to prevent this unity and to destroy it."—First published in the "Supplement" to the *Christian Experiences and Views of Ellen G. White;* now found in *Early Writings,* p. 97.

James White, like his gifted wife, recognized the need of a well-defined organization and saw clearly that if the infant movement was to grow and prosper, there must be a structure of church order and discipline. Through the 1850's we find him advocating a simple organization. The columns of the *Review and Herald,* of which he was the first editor, carried articles in which he kept urging our people to move forward in this matter, and in the month of September, 1860, he called a group of representative men from the various States in which we had believers, to meet in Battle Creek for the purpose of carefully studying the whole problem, and especially as it related to the publishing interests. After due deliberation, a committee consisting of J. N. Andrews, J. H. Waggoner, and T. J. Butler, was appointed to bring in recommendations for consideration by the whole body. The report rendered by this small group of men read as follows:

"1. We recommend to the conference the organization of a publishing association that may legally hold the Review office.

"2. That the association shall consist of seven members selected by this conference, who shall apply to the legislature for an act empowering them to hold the office property, and carry on the business of publication.

"3. That members may be admitted to this association on the payment of one dollar annually, and they may become life members on the payment of twenty-five dollars.*

---

* Membership in the association, as finally provided for by Article IV, Section I, of the bylaws of the association, was on the following basis: "Any person keeping the commandments of God and the faith of Jesus Christ may become a shareholder in this Association on the payment of ten dollars into its treasury, and each person may hold as many shares as they shall thus purchase, and for each and every share held by them, they shall be entitled to one

"4. That the officers of the association shall consist of a business agent, a committee on publication, a treasurer who shall also act as secretary, and an auditor, to be elected annually.

"5. The business agent shall be the presiding officer of the association.

"6. This association shall be called the Advent Review Publishing Association [changed at time of organization to Seventh-day Adventist Publishing Association].

"7. It shall be located at Battle Creek, Michigan.

"8. The whole amount obtained by donations, subscriptions, sales of publications, or otherwise, shall be expended in the publication of periodicals, books, and tracts, and for charitable and benevolent purposes."—*Review and Herald*, Oct. 16, 1860, p. 171.

This report was unanimously adopted. By action of the body, James White, J. H. Waggoner, J. N. Loughborough, G. W. Amadon, Uriah Smith, George T. Lay, and D. R. Palmer were appointed to implement the organization and to make application to the legislature for incorporation under the laws of the State of Michigan.

The next item for consideration was the adoption of a denominational name, for it was seen that without it the movement could not well handle its business affairs, nor could it hope to succeed in its God-appointed work. After lengthy deliberation, on Monday, October 1, 1860, the name "Seventh-day Adventist" was adopted.* This was simple but comprehensive and appropriate, and after its adoption the messenger of the Lord wrote shortly concerning it:

"The name Seventh-day Adventist carries the true features of our faith in front, and will convict the inquiring mind. Like an arrow from the Lord's quiver, it will wound the transgressors of God's law, and will lead to repentance toward God and faith in our Lord Jesus Christ."—"Testimony for the Church," No. 6, published in 1861; now found in *Testimonies*, vol. 1, p. 224.

The incorporation of the Publishing Association and the

---

vote in all the business meetings of the Association."—*"Acts of Incorporation and By-laws of the Seventh-day Adventist Publishing Association,"* p. 8, Art. IV, Sec. I (published in 1861).
* See *Review and Herald*, Oct. 23, 1860, p. 179.

adoption of a denominational name were steps in the right direction. But they were only a beginning. The 1860 meeting adjourned without any action having been taken to recommend the organization of local churches and conferences. More work had to be done to bring the hesitant ones into line with the Lord's plan. Consequently, articles on gospel order were published in the *Review and Herald,* and meetings were held for the purpose of clarifying the issue. In one of her articles Sister White devoted a section to "Organization." * This stirring appeal was later included in volume 1 of *Testimonies for the Church,* and reads in part as follows:

"August 3, 1861, [at Roosevelt, New York] I was shown that some have feared that our churches would become Babylon if they should organize; but those in Central New York have been perfect Babylon, confusion. And now unless the churches are so organized that they can carry out and enforce order, they have nothing to hope for in the future; they must scatter into fragments. Previous teachings have nourished the elements of disunion. A spirit has been cherished to watch and accuse, rather than to build up. If ministers of God would unitedly take their position, and maintain it with decision, there would be a uniting influence among the flock of God. Separating bars would be broken to fragments. Hearts would flow together and unite like drops of water. Then there would be a power and strength in the ranks of Sabbathkeepers far exceeding anything we have yet witnessed."—*Testimonies,* vol. 1, pp. 270, 271.

A general meeting was held in Battle Creek, October 4-6, 1861, at which special study was given to the principles underlying the organization of believers into churches. Before the meeting adjourned, two important actions relating to the question were taken. These read as follows:

1. *"Resolved,* That this conference recommend the following church covenant: We, the undersigned, hereby associate ourselves together, as a church, taking the name, Seventh-day Adventists,

---

* See *Review and Herald,* Aug. 27, 1861, pp. 101, 102.

covenanting to keep the commandments of God, and the faith of Jesus Christ."

2. *"Resolved,* That we refer this subject [of the proper manner of organizing churches] to the ministers present, instructing them to hold a Bible class on it, and write an address to the brethren to be published in the *Review."—Review and Herald,* Oct. 8, 1861, p. 148.

The proposed address appeared in the *Review and Herald* a week later. It dealt with (1) the manner of organizing a church, (2) officers and their duties, (3) the reception of members, and (4) letters of transfer.

As a result of these definite recommendations, various groups of believers were soon organized into churches.

James White and the other leading brethren who had been promoting the organization of local churches had also, by voice and by pen, been emphasizing the urgent necessity of organizing the churches, when formed, into local conferences. Convinced of the wisdom of such a move, the representatives from Michigan in attendance at the aforementioned gathering in Battle Creek, October 4-6, 1861, proceeded to organize the believers in their State into a conference. Joseph Bates became the first president. Resolutions were adopted as follows:

"Resolved, That we recommend to the churches in the State of Michigan to unite in one conference, with the name of The Michigan Conference of Seventh-day Adventists. . . .

"Resolved, That the conference [in session] be composed of ministers and delegates from the churches. . . .

"Resolved, That the officers of this conference consist of a chairman, clerk, and a standing committee of three. . . .

"Resolved, That our ministers' papers consist of a certificate of ordination, also credentials to be signed by the chairman and clerk of the conference, which credentials shall be renewed annually."— *Ibid.*

In October, 1862, final steps in organizing the Michigan Conference were taken. During that year six conferences were organized: Southern Iowa (March 16), Northern Iowa (May

10), Vermont (June 15), Illinois and Wisconsin (September 28), Minnesota (October 4), New York (October 25). On January 25, 1863, the two Iowa conferences were united into a single organization known as the Iowa Conference. On May 31, 1863, the churches in Ohio were formed into a conference. Then, as the work spread across the continent, local conferences were organized in other States and in the provinces of Canada. (See "Historical Summary" in *SDA Year Book*, 1913, p. 246, and C. C. Crisler, *Organization*, pp. 101, 102.)

These good steps in church organization brought the believers living in a given community together in a local church, and bound the local churches in a geographical area into a conference for united action in the service of God. However, there was then no general organization to bind the local conferences together for counsel and cooperative evangelism. Each conference was a law to itself. There was need of a central organization through which the general interests of the church might be fostered. In order to meet this need all the local conferences were invited to send delegates to a general session to be held in Battle Creek May 20-23, 1863. At this session the General Conference of Seventh-day Adventists was duly organized. Officers were elected, and an executive committee of three was named. The nominating committee's report was brief:

President, James White; Secretary, Uriah Smith; Treasurer, E. S. Walker.

This report was unanimously accepted, but Elder White declined to serve, feeling that it was wiser to have someone fill the position who had been less active than he in the movement for church organization. The session then turned to John Byington, of New York, a former Methodist minister, and he was elected president. The executive committee of three consisted of John Byington, J. N. Andrews, and G. W. Amadon.

In an editorial describing this 1863 session Uriah Smith reported with a sense of jubilation:

"Perhaps no previous meeting that we have ever enjoyed, was characterized by such unity of feeling and harmony of sentiment. In all the important steps taken at this conference, in the organization of a General Conference, and the further perfecting of State conferences, defining the authority of each, and the important duties belonging to their various officers, there was not a dissenting voice, and we may reasonably doubt if there was even a dissenting thought. Such union, on such points, affords the strongest grounds of hope for the immediate advancement of the cause, and its future glorious prosperity and triumph."—*Review and Herald,* May 26, 1863, p. 204.

The organization of the General Conference linked together in one body all the existing churches and local conferences. It made provision for all new churches and conferences that would be organized, as the Advent Movement would spread around the world, to become a part of this one body.

These various steps in organization brought order and stability and strength to a movement that had been torn by divisive forces within itself. It also brought courage and confidence into the hearts of the believers. The Advent Movement was now a well-organized body, united in purpose and discipline and faith, ready for action and more widespread evangelistic witness. The value of organization was soon clear to all as new life and vigor were pumped into the very lifeblood of the movement everywhere. The work grew and prospered as never before.

From State to State the evangelists went, holding evangelistic meetings, baptizing new members, organizing churches that were soon to bind themselves together in State conferences. Institutions came into being, adding medical and educational interests to the publishing. The message leaped the expanse of ocean and soon a work was begun in Europe, to be followed soon by Australia, the islands, Africa, and other continents. For twenty-five years the organizational structure of the 1860's was adequate and functioned well, but there came a time when it was outgrown.

Problems Attending Worldwide Growth

THE enemy of souls was not slow in recognizing the advantages of the simple, effective organization, adopted under God's leadership by Seventh-day Adventists. From the very first he set about to frustrate the plan of organization where he might find opportunity. In one area at least, he had success. Little by little churches, conferences, individuals, and institutions came to look to Battle Creek for guidance in nearly everything. The expenditure of even insignificant sums of money for church work required the approval of the leaders at general headquarters. In time, Battle Creek became a center of concentrated authority. Too much power was placed in the hands of a few men.

When the work of the movement was small and confined to narrow limits, the general leaders did not find it difficult to keep in close touch with all parts of the field, but as the church spread across the American continent and to opening lands beyond the seas, they found it a real problem to maintain this close touch. Opportunities for advance in mission lands were often lost because of long delays in receiving approval for certain projects from headquarters. In those days of slow transportation, before the arrival of fast steamers, automobiles, and airplanes, months of patient waiting were required for many overseas fields to receive answers to their requests from Battle Creek. This constituted a real hindrance in the expansion of the mission program.

Instead of recognizing the inefficiency of this awkward con-

163

centration of power in the hands of a few, efforts were made to draw the lines tighter. As we have seen, the idea was conceived that all institutional interests should be controlled from Battle Creek, and recommendations to this end were adopted by the 1889 General Conference session. The Review and Herald publishing house sought to control the Pacific Press. The Battle Creek Sanitarium obtained title to a sanitarium in Mexico, and as a result, when Dr. J. H. Kellogg, the general medical superintendent, left the denomination, both institutions were lost to the cause. An example of educational monopoly occurred in Lincoln, Nebraska, when Union College was established in 1891. The title to the institution was held in Battle Creek, and the school board was appointed by the General Conference. Several appointees actually were residents of Battle Creek.

This centralization of power in the hands of a few boards under the control of a small group of men at denominational headquarters not only hindered progress because of the endless red tape involved but prevented the development of an increasingly larger corps of capable leaders throughout the world field. Men came to look to headquarters instead of to God for wisdom and guidance; good men blessed with intelligence, with power to think and to act, were permitting others to think for them. This was wrong. It tended to make church workers weak and helpless in God's sacred service. A change had to come.

In line with this tendency to concentrate power and facilities in Battle Creek, the institutions there were constantly being enlarged. As a result, more and more members were being drawn into the city. To correct this growing evil of overcentralization of power in Battle Creek, the Lord sent to church leaders one message after another from the pen of Ellen White pointing out the dangers involved, and counseling them to change their plans and policies and reach out by sharing the burdens of leadership with other representative men. During her two-year sojourn in Europe, Ellen White dispatched several documents bearing on this question. From Orebro, Sweden, on October 28, 1885, she wrote to Elders Butler and Haskell as follows:

"Too many have marked out a prescribed line which they wish others to follow in the work. Workers have tried to do this with blind faith, without exercising their own judgment upon the matter which they had in hand. If those who were placed as directors were not present, they have followed their implicit directions just the same. But in the name of Christ, I would entreat you to stop this work. Give men a chance to exercise their individual judgment. Men who follow the leading of another, and are willing that another should think for them, are unfit to be entrusted with responsibility. . . .

"Our leading brethren have made a great mistake in marking out all the directions that the workers should follow, and this has resulted in deficiency, in a lack of a caretaking spirit in the workers, because they have relied upon others to do all their planning, and have themselves taken no responsibility. Should the men who have taken this responsibility upon themselves step out of our ranks, or die, what a state of things would be found in our institutions!

"Leading men should place responsibilities upon others, and allow them to plan and devise and execute, so that they may obtain an experience. Give them a word of counsel when necessary, but do not take away the work because you think the brethren are making mistakes. . . .

"I think I have laid out this matter many times before you, but I see no change in your actions. The Lord would have every responsible man to drop responsibilities upon others. Set others at work that will require them to plan and to use judgment. . . .

"Do not think that these men who do follow out your ideas are the only ones that can be trusted. You have sometimes thought that because they do your will to the letter, they were the only ones in whom you could place dependence. If anyone exercised his own judgment, and differed with you, you have disconnected from him as one that could not be trusted.

"Take your hands off the work, and do not hold it fast in your grasp. You are not the only man whom God will use. Give the

Lord room to use the talents He has entrusted to men, in order that the cause may grow. Give the Lord a chance to use men's minds. We are losing much by our narrow ideas and plans. Do not stand in the way of the advancement of the work, but let the Lord work by whom He will. Educate, encourage young men to think and act, to devise and plan, in order that we may have a multitude of wise counselors."—Letter 12, 1885; in *Testimonies to Ministers,* pp. 301-303.

A few days later, from Christiana, Norway, in the fall of 1885, Mrs. White wrote to Elder G. I. Butler, the president of the General Conference, saying:

"God does not require you to take such a course that the workers in ——— or anywhere else shall not feel at liberty to make advance movements unless they can consult you, and ask what your judgment of the matter is, before they advance. I cannot sanction the idea that you must have a personal oversight of all the details of the work. If I did, the result would be that no worker would dare to exercise his own judgment in anything. The workers would have to rely upon one man's brain and one man's judgment, and the result would be that men would be left in inefficiency because of their inactivity. There are altogether too many of this class now, and they amount to next to nothing. I write this because I feel deeply on this point."—Letter 5, 1885; in *Testimonies to Ministers,* pp. 298, 299.

In an article from her pen that appeared in the *Review and Herald* a few months later, Mrs. White said:

"The Lord does not apportion to any one man some special territory in which he alone is to labor. This is contrary to His plans. He designs that in every place where the truth is introduced, different minds, different gifts, shall be brought in to exert an influence upon the work. . . . Because a person has ability in one direction, it is no sign that his judgment on all other subjects is perfect, and that the wisdom of some other mind does not need to be united with his. . . .

"The Lord does not want any of His children to be shadows of others; but He would have each one be his own simple self, refined, sanctified, ennobled by imitating the life and character of the great Pattern. The narrow, shut-in, exclusive spirit which keeps

166

everything within the compass of one's self, has been a curse to the cause of God, and always will be wherever allowed to exist."— April 13, 1886, p. 225.

In a manuscript written in 1886 in Basel, Switzerland, the servant of the Lord said:

"God says to every man to whom He entrusts responsibilities, 'Put not your trust in man, neither make flesh your arm.' Look to God. Trust in His infallible wisdom. Regard as a sin the practice so common, even among Seventh-day Adventists, of becoming the echo of any man, however lofty his position. Listen to the voice of the great Shepherd, and you will never be led astray. Search the Scriptures for yourself, and be braced for duty and for trial by the truth of God's Word.

"Let no friendship, no influence, no entreaty, let not the smiles, the confidence, or the rewards of any man induce you to swerve from the path in which the Lord would lead you. Let Christlike integrity and consistency control the actions of your life. The man who sits most at the feet of Jesus, and is taught by the Saviour's spirit, will be ready to cry out, 'I am weak and unworthy, but Christ is my strength and my righteousness.' "—Manuscript 15, 1886.

As the years passed by, the situation did not improve. Nine years after writing the foregoing message, Ellen White sent the following rebuke and earnest entreaty to certain men in responsible positions:

"Men, fallible men, are not to think it is their prerogative to control, to mark out, or to prescribe the labors of their fellow men. When God works upon the human instrumentality, let men be very careful how they intermeddle. . . . The work of God has often been hindered by men considering that they had power to say, 'Go here' or, 'Go there,' 'Do this' or, 'Do that' without consulting the individual himself or respecting his convictions as a laborer to-gether with God.

"God has promised His presence to every believer; and let those who are in positions of authority, presidents of conferences and board councils, and everyone who has to do with the human mind respect the individuality of mind and conscience. These workers

167

are in copartnership with Jesus Christ, and you may interpose yourself so as to interfere with God's plans; for the human agent is under His special authority and dictation.

"When men composing boards and councils are themselves walking at a distance from God, of what value is their discernment and wisdom to decide in reference to the work of God's delegated servants? The human mind is open to jealousies, evil surmisings, and selfish considerations, and God's plans are often turned aside by the caprice and by the plans of unconsecrated men. If the door is not closed to the enemy, he will enter and will figure largely in human inventions. The Lord requires the men who have a directing influence in His work, to be wholly consecrated to Him. He wants them to have hearts of flesh and not of steel. . . .

"Christ is our example, and every soul placed in a position of trust needs the subduing influence of the Spirit of God upon his heart day by day. Christ wept with those that wept. In all their afflictions, He was afflicted, and was touched with the feelings of their infirmities. He is a tender and faithful High Priest. He considers the cases of the tempted and tried ones as verily His own, and He ministers unto them. These weak ones of the flock are to be carefully nourished with the manna Christ has supplied. They are to be educated not to look to men and trust in men, whatever may be their calling.

"God would have all such confederacies broken to atoms and remodeled upon Christlike principles. The foundation stone must be mercy. Human minds are not to be trammeled and harnessed up and driven by human hands. The Lord Jesus must hold the reins in His own hands, pierced to bring peace and comfort and hope to every soul who will believe on Him. He gives to the purchase of His blood the guardianship of His grace; they shall move in His light, clad in the robes of His righteousness. To every man is given his work, and while souls are brought into church capacity, work is assigned them of God. They are to move as minds that are under the controlling influence of God."—Manuscript 43, 1895, March 17.

In this same forceful statement Mrs. White called for courtesy and marked respect among all workers, particularly leaders.

"Men are educated to look to men, to be dependent on men. One man, by virtue of his position, exercises authority over them as if they were to be led by lines, this way and that as dumb animals. God has not directed in this way. God is our chief, God is our instructor, and to Him we must look. We must ask the Holy Spirit's guidance, and expect to be led and controlled by it. The church organization is to be respected, but it is not to be made in any way a galling yoke. Men are not to assume the prerogative of God, and think to rule and coerce and oppress the souls of God's purchased possession. All heaven is indignant at what men, with complacency, will do to their fellow men, claiming at the same time to be representatives of Jesus Christ. They too often represent the spirit and character of Satan.

"Christ has found His pearl of great price in lost, perishing souls. He sold all that He had to come into possession of that pearl; He even engaged to do the work Himself, and to run the risk of losing His own life in the conflict. How then should men regard their fellow men? Christ has demonstrated the way. He says, 'A new commandment I give unto you, That ye love one another; as I have loved you, that ye also love one another.' When these words are heeded and obeyed in the spirit and in the letter, we will be doers of the word, and not hearers only. When these words are practiced by those who claim to have wisdom to guide the sheep of the Lord's pasture, they have far less selfishness, far less boasting, far less putting forth the finger and speaking vanity.

"Jesus is to superintend all events in the present and future of His church. John was instructed to write the things which he had seen, 'and the things which are and the things which shall be hereafter; the mystery of the seven stars which thou sawest in my right hand, and the seven golden candlesticks. The seven stars are the angels of the seven churches; and the seven candlesticks which thou sawest are the seven churches.'

"Oh, that men would revere the great head of the church, and would manufacture less human methods, bringing down spirituality to the very dust with human inventions. God has been left out, and the church is not prepared to advance to the conflict under the banner of Jesus Christ. It is not doing the work for suffering souls, which Christ owns as if done to Himself. But the church, defective as it is, and enfeebled with so much chaff, is the only object on earth upon which He bestows His highest regard. In His estimation, the church in heaven and the church on earth are identical. He has promised to come personally into the midst of

169

His church. He says to everyone holding a position of trust, 'Learn of me; for I am meek and lowly in heart: and ye shall find rest unto your souls. For my yoke is easy, and my burden is light.' "—*Ibid.*

Mrs. White declared moreover that—

"men in official position must realize that their position gives them no license to be unkind or discourteous, no license to be oppressive, and to let their tongues, which should be sanctified, speak words which will open a door of temptation, and help the great adversary in his work of discouraging souls. God has given us a work to do in saving souls from the companionship of Satan."—*Ibid.*

But the warnings and counsels fell on dull ears. It was not easy for men overloaded with the snowballing problems of a worldwide work to sense fully the significance of the counsels given to spare them from the perils they saw but dimly and knew not how to remedy.

CHAPTER SIXTEEN

Frustrating Attempts at Reorganization

T HE first halting step to relieve congestion at headquarters and to improve the efficiency of administration was taken by the General Conference Committee, November 18, 1888, when it was voted, as a temporary measure, to divide the North American field into four districts with a member of the General Conference Committee in charge of each district. But no arrangement was made to provide for an executive committee to plan for the development of the church in each territory. No provision was made for a treasurer to receive and disburse funds. The only office was that of the superintendent, appointed and directed by the General Conference. He was the General Conference representative for the district assigned to him.

At the 1889 session of the General Conference, O. A. Olsen, who had recently taken over his duties as president of the General Conference, called attention—

"to the propriety of districting the territory covered by the General Conference in this country, and placing a district under the special charge of a member of the General Conference Committee; such member to have the special oversight of his district in the conducting of institutes, general meetings, camp-meetings, and other work."—*The Seventh-day Adventist Year Book* for 1890, p. 148.

This plan was approved during the session, and the territory in Canada and the United States was promptly divided into six districts, to be known as District No. 1, District No. 2, et cetera. The responsibility for defining the duties and prerogatives of the heads of these districts was left with the General Conference Committee. In a meeting of this committee held December 28, 1889, the following report was adopted:

"1. That the member of the General Conference Committee having charge of a General Conference district, be called a general superintendent.

"2. That it be the duty of each general superintendent to attend the annual State conferences held in his district.

"3. That the general superintendent have the oversight of all ministerial institutes and annual conventions held in his district; that he attend these, as far as possible, and provide for the attendance of competent teachers, leaders, and counselors at all these meetings.

"4. That it be the duty of the general superintendent to become acquainted with the officers of the State conferences, tract societies, and Sabbath school and health and temperance associations in his district, and ascertain the efficiency of their methods of labor; and to counsel, caution, and instruct them, as the state of their work may demand. Also to report to the corresponding secretary of the General Conference any irregularity or inefficiency that endangers the prosperity of the societies of which he has the oversight.

"5. That it be the duty of the general superintendent to have a special care for weak conferences and mission fields in his district, and for such portions of the territory as are being neglected; and to bring to the attention of the General Conference Committee the condition and wants of such fields."—*Ibid.*, for 1891, p. 56.

In his opening address to the delegates assembled in General Conference session at Battle Creek, Michigan, February 17 to March 6, 1893, Elder Olsen referred to the district plan as follows:

"The division of the General Conference territory in this country into districts, and placing a superintendent over each, is proving of much advantage. The most serious difficulty met, has been that several of the superintendents of districts, being presidents of local conferences, have been laden with the responsibilities of local work. The district superintendent should be free to give his whole attention to the work in his district. This point should be borne in mind in the General Conference and State conference appointments."—*General Conference Bulletin,* 1893, p. 278.

Then, looking into the future, he added that "it will be important at this conference to consider the question of further organization. This is made necessary in order to meet the demands of our enlarging work."

Elder Olsen tried to be realistic in facing the real need. He said:

"We would recommend that this conference provide for district conferences, formed of local conferences, composing the General Conference districts in this country, and that the sessions of the said district conferences be held in the alternate years between the sessions of the General Conference. This same plan should also be extended to the work in other lands. Conferences in such fields could be grouped into districts, and granted their necessary prerogatives under the General Conference. These conferences might hold meetings alternately with the General Conference, as before stated, and there should be full delegations composing the districts, with representatives from the General Conference. Each district conference would be expected to consider and plan for the work in its own district, at its sessions, and also to provide, by the election of delegates, for representation at the General Conference."—*Ibid.,* p. 285.

Referring to the property-holding capacities of the General Conference Association, he observed that this had reached the saturation point:

"Another consideration which makes the organization of district conferences necessary is the requirements of our financial work. Proper provision must be made for the legal holding of property set apart for the use of the cause of God, and the legal transaction of such business as may be connected with the cause in its various departments. The General Conference Association, which has met the requirements in this direction for a few years, will be unable to do so in the future. It has already nearly reached its limits as to the holding of real estate, and should not be made to carry more responsibilities in that and other directions. Organizations designed to serve the purpose of the General Conference Association should be organized in the districts. These organizations would be amenable to the district conferences, and on account of the direct connection which these conferences sustain to the General Conference, the work of said legal organizations would be connected with the work as a whole."—*Ibid.*

In response to these recommendations by the president, the session adopted the following resolution:

"In view of the growth and extension of the work in Europe and other parts of the world,

"52. *We recommend,* That the arrangement of General Conference districts be extended also to those fields, and that the Australian and New Zealand conferences be known as District No. 7, and Europe as District No. 8.

"53. *We recommend,* That the presidents of the conferences and the General Conference districts in connection with the General Conference Committee arrange for council meetings to be held the alternate year with the General Conference, and to be known as district conferences, at which time ministerial institutes can be held, and plans for the work in the districts, and such other questions considered and arranged as pertain to the development and advancement of the work within the limits of the district."— *Ibid.,* p. 478.

After the close of the conference the General Conference executive committee gave further study to this matter and passed this further action:

"That district conferences be held in each General Conference district, as far as practicable, in the years alternating with the biennial sessions of the General Conference; that the representation of such conferences consist of State conference committees, the presidents and secretaries of State tract societies, and Sabbath school associations, and the State canvassing agent of each State or territory, in the district; that the district superintendent be the presiding officer of the district conference, a secretary being selected at the first meeting of each session."—*Yearbook,* 1894, p. 85.

In stating the objectives of the district conferences they moved in tight formation with the General Conference:

FRUSTRATING ATTEMPTS AT REORGANIZATION

"The object of the district conferences [shall] be to counsel concerning the interests of the cause in the territory of the conference, and for planning for the extension of the work in all the various lines, no action being taken on matters which have not been considered in principle, at least, by the General Conference; and that devotional exercises and meetings for Bible instruction be held each day of the session."—*Ibid.*

O. A. Olsen's opening address at the 1893 General Conference session, while calling for district conferences empowered to direct and foster the work in their respective territories, failed to make provision for district conference executive committees to function between the district conference biennial sessions. This failure was soon recognized, and in his opening address to the 1895 General Conference session Elder Olsen spoke out plainly on this point, as follows:

"At the last session of this body, the holding of district conferences was considered and recommended. Such conferences have been held in all the districts except Europe. This subject should be further considered, and the question of the authority of these conferences and the business to be transacted in them further defined, especially for the benefit of those more remote from the center of the work.

"Many responsibilities are placed on these district superintendents, and their position and work should meet with proper recognition. It seems to us that arrangements could be made for the presidents of the local conferences to form a committee with the superintendent of the district as chairman. This committee could be called together for counsel and action by the superintendent, whenever there were important questions involving the interests of the work in the district. On such occasions many questions could be considered which would otherwise have to go before the general body."—*General Conference Bulletin,* 1895, pp. 151, 152.

But there was to be a close tie-in with the Battle Creek leadership. Said Elder Olsen:

"To avoid confusion, it would be well for the president of the General Conference to attend these meetings as far as possible. In cases where this is not consistent, the decisions of these district committees ought to be presented to him for consideration. In this way a larger number would engage in consultation, the unity of the work would be preserved, and every interest of the cause properly guarded."—*Ibid.*

For some reason the brethren in the American homeland failed to carry out O. A. Olsen's recommendations, approved by the 1893 General Conference session, to organize district conferences (later known as union conferences) with district committees. But in Australia it was different. There, when Elder Olsen attended the Australian camp meeting, January 15 to 25, 1894, and met with the representatives from Australia and New Zealand to consider this recommendation, appropriate action was taken. Ellen White was present in this gathering, and as the proposal was in line with what she had advocated, she naturally lent her influence in its favor. Her son, W. C. White, who had been serving as superintendent of the Australasian district, was also present, and was elected president of the newly formed Australasian Union Conference. Another promising worker in attendance at this camp meeting was A. G. Daniells, president of the local conference, and who later served as president of this important union for several years, before becoming president of the General Conference.

In the report W. C. White prepared for insertion in the 1894 *Yearbook* regarding the formation of this the first Seventh-day Adventist union conference, the objects and aims of the organization were outlined as follows:

"The object of this conference is to unify and extend the work of the third angel's message, under the general direction of the General Conference, in the Australasian field. As the work extends in that field other conferences will be organized. In the organization of the union conference these local conferences will be brought together for counsel and instruction in the work, and for mutual encouragement and development of the important interests carried forward by the denomination in that field.

"The officers of the conference are: A president, a vice-president, a secretary, a treasurer, and an executive committee. The president of the conference will always be the superintendent of the district appointed by the General Conference."—Page 61.

The reader should note, however, that the above took place in Australia, not in North America.

Four years later, during the General Conference session held at Lincoln, Nebraska, February 19 to March 8, 1897, an effort was made to improve the efficiency of church operations, to share responsibility, and thus to heed the oft-repeated counsels from the Lord. Observe carefully this set of resolutions:

"1. That the presidency of the General Conference Association, the presidency of the mission board, and the presidency of the General Conference work in North America be placed on three different men.

"2. That the General Conference territory be divided into three grand divisions; viz., (a) the United States and British North America, (b) Europe, (c) Australasia; the remaining territory to be under the watchcare of the mission board.

"3. That a mission board of nine members, with headquarters and incorporation in some Atlantic State, be elected to take charge of all mission funds, and all mission fields not included in the three grand divisions mentioned in section 2.

"4. That union conferences be organized in Europe and America as soon as deemed advisable, and that these union conferences hold biennial sessions, alternating with the General Conference.

"5. That the executive committee chosen by the General Conference shall consist of thirteen members, composed of the presidents of the General Conference, the union conferences, the superintendents of the six General Conference districts in the United States, the president of the mission board, and three other persons, the president of the General Conference being the chairman of this committee.

"6. That, in recognition of the example of the apostles as recorded in the sixth chapter of the Acts, businessmen be chosen to attend to the business interests of the work, leaving the ministers more free to engage in the ministry of the Word."—*General Conference Bulletin*, 1897, p. 215.

The *General Conference Bulletin* for the 1899 session reports the implementation of some of these resolutions. After referring to the second, third, and fourth resolutions, George A. Irwin, president of the General Conference, said in his opening address:

"In harmony with these recommendations, the headquarters of the mission board was removed from Battle Creek, Michigan, to Philadelphia, Pennsylvania, and an incorporation formed under the laws of the State of New York.

"July 8-14, in response to a previous call, a general meeting for Europe was held at Hamburg, Germany, at which time the European Union Conference was formally organized, with Elder O. A. Olsen as its president. Elders H. P. Holser, W. W. Prescott, Lewis Johnson, and L. R. Conradi were associated with him as an executive committee, and have local charge of the four principal subdivisions of the countries that go to make up the conference; namely, Central Europe, comprising Switzerland, France, Italy, Sicily, Sardinia, Corsica, and Turkey in Europe; Great Britain, comprising England, Ireland, Scotland, and Wales; Scandinavia, comprising Norway, Sweden, and Denmark, with the oversight of Finland; Germany, comprising Germany, Bulgaria, Rumania, Servia, Austria-Hungary, and Holland, with the watchcare of the Russian Mission Field.

"During the close of 1897 and the beginning of 1898, general district meetings were held in each of the six districts in the United States; *but no formal organizations were effected.*"—*Ibid.,* 1899, p. 6. (Italics supplied.)

The establishment of a mission board on the Atlantic coast brought confusion and weakness, for thus the world field was left without a central authority. On the other hand, the over-concentration of power in Battle Creek continued, as far as the North American continent was concerned, through the failure under the presidency of George A. Irwin, Elder Olsen's successor, to organize the North American districts into union conferences as directed by the 1897 General Conference session.

To compound the difficulty, at that time the General Conference had none of the departments it now has for fostering various lines of activity such as Sabbath school, publishing, medical, and educational work. Instead, these various interests were organized into separate and independent associations with their own constitutions and bylaws, and with their own constituencies, with power to elect their own officers and to plan and promote their own lines of work. With the passing of the years these associations had assumed more and more power; indeed, arbitrary, kingly powers were being exercised from the general headquarters in Battle Creek. Arthur Spalding wrote of these associations and their relationships one to the other as follows:

"All these agencies were independent or semi-independent, and worked together or at cross purposes according to the degree of divine grace in the hearts of their members and officers. Nominally the General Conference was the parent of them all; but the reciprocative organizations creaked in operation, sometimes got out of hand, and were disciplined to a degree, like the obstreperous adolescent children of an ill-managed family, by the increasing arbitrariness and severity of the parent.

"Thus there came to be what Mrs. White denounced as the exercise of 'kingly power.' The fortunes and fates of several of these organizations were controlled by interlocking directorates, wherein a few men in Battle Creek (and in lesser degree in Oakland, on the Pacific Coast) who were influential members of nearly all the boards could put their veto or their approval upon the work. Distrusting this state of things, the people restricted their liberality, and scarcity of funds exasperated the situation.

"Certain of the organizations, however, being more vigorous and assertive, appeared to suspicious eyes ready to grasp all power and authority, and become rivals to the General Conference."— *Origin and History*, vol. 3, p. 30.

Such was the situation when the brethren met again in conference session in Battle Creek in the spring of the year 1901.

CHAPTER SEVENTEEN

The 1901 Conference
of Reorganization

THE historic General Conference session held in the spring of the year 1901 called together 216 delegates from North America and overseas fields. Approximately 1,500 expectant Adventists poured into the city of Battle Creek from widely scattered parts of the United States. The world membership of the denomination at that time was rather substantial—more than 75,000. Membership growth had been extraordinary. In the two years elapsing since the 1899 session the records reveal a net increase of 12,504 members, an amount nearly double the gain of the two preceding years.

The material marks of progress coincided with the expansion in members. Tithe paid in the two years throughout the entire field amounted to $1,000,915.13, an increase over the former biennial period of $205,341.89. Donations and offerings amounted to $115,008.45—this to carry forward overseas work, a gain of $23,240.31 over the amount contributed during the former two-year period.

With 238 new churches organized since 1899 and 68 missionaries dispatched from the shores of America to foreign lands, the report for the past biennial period looked bright. Yet in spite of the signs of progress in the world work of the church, some of the delegates—those most thoroughly acquainted with top church administration—were apprehensive of the approaching session. The many prayers ascending to God from the lips of preachers and laymen betokened concern and uneasiness.

THE 1901 CONFERENCE OF REORGANIZATION

It was known that Ellen White, the Lord's messenger, had returned to the United States from Australia and that most likely she would be present at this conference. What would she say to the brethren about the changes needed in the organization of the Lord's work? For more than a decade she had called for a spreading of responsibility in administrative procedures and the government of institutions. What was painfully obvious was the fact that not much had been done to implement this instruction.

As we come to the 1901 General Conference session we witness the control of the church in the hands of a few men. But what is most heartening is that this meeting witnessed an emancipation from the tight reins of such government. There evolved a more representative form of church polity with distribution of authority, drawing in many men of ability serving on newly created boards, conferences, and mission committees.

The 1901 General Conference witnessed the providential leadings of God in the affairs of His church day by day through the busy meetings and committees of the three-week session. In all of this the guiding hand of the Lord's messenger, Ellen G. White, was felt.

A study of the 488-page *General Conference Bulletin* for 1901 reveals the counsel's overwhelming involvement with reorganization. The pages carry fascinating accounts of what proved to be the most important and successful session of the church held up until that time.

It would be well to say, however, that the absorbing concern with reorganization was not so complete that reports from the world field were neglected or inspirational meetings forgotten. The daily program, as given on page 29, was as follows:

"5:30- 6:30 A.M. Social meeting
"9:00-10:00 A.M. Bible study
"10:30 A.M.-12:20 P.M. Business proceedings

181

"3:00- 5:00 P.M. General business
"6:00- 6:50 P.M. Divisional prayer meeting
"7:00- 8:15 P.M. Preaching"

The Bible studies were well attended. The sermons were timely. John Harvey Kellogg's vitalizing health lecture in the Tabernacle, illustrated with stereopticon slides, captivated his audience. Mrs. White's devotional talks were hopeful and as usual deeply spiritual.

But we must now try to understand why the 1901 General Conference session was so deeply significant to the maturing church. The following year would witness the destruction by fire of the Battle Creek Sanitarium and the Review and Herald publishing house. Why? The answer suggests a basic problem, the solution of which should have been resolved earlier—the spreading out of interests from Battle Creek with the diffusion of light to other places, and the drawing into positions of responsibility of men fully consecrated to God.

A backward look will remind the reader that the General Conference organization was brought about at Battle Creek in May of 1863. At that time there were 3,500 Seventh-day Adventists in North America living in the Central and New England States. A president, secretary, and treasurer were chosen; a General Conference Committee of three was elected. This was an exceedingly simple plan in the structure of organization.

In the years that followed, the work of the denomination grew rapidly. Publishing work developed. The health work was begun and institutions were established. The church's health ministry eventually developed into the International Medical Missionary and Benevolent Association. A college at Battle Creek was opened, to be followed by other colleges in the East and West and overseas.

Sabbath school work was carried on under what developed into the International Sabbath School Association. Home missionary work, beginning with tract distribution, later was organized as the International Tract Society. Certain issues in the United States led the church into the religious liberty field. From this activity the National Religious Liberty Association was organized. With the inception and development of a foreign mission program, a Foreign Mission Board was set up.

These were individual, independent organizations, represented by independent corporations, manned, of course, by Seventh-day Adventists, but not integral parts of the conference organization as we know them today. The various branches of the work were not thought of or directed as departments, but as independent entities.

The institutional interests at our headquarters in Battle Creek grew very rapidly, and businessmen were drawn in to head up these activities. The General Conference Committee was increased to five, then seven, nine, and finally to thirteen. But these increases came very largely from the men at headquarters in Battle Creek, many of them tied in very closely with the business side of the work.

Strong movements were in the ascendancy for centralizing the various features of denominational work. It was natural that those at headquarters should feel they were prepared to give the wisest and best management to even the minute details of Seventh-day Adventist interests around the world.

But as the work of the denomination broadened, these details multiplied to the point where church leaders in Battle Creek were unable to cope with them properly. Business interests increased, and spiritual fervor waned. There was a failure in some spheres to heed the counsels God sent to alert the workers to their dangers and to guard the work.

A large part of the time of the employees of the Review and Herald office was devoted to commercial printing, at times harmful in character, and oftentimes to the neglect of evangelistic literature. The cause of God was marred by self-interest on the part of some workers. Discouragement ensued. It was during this period that many of the startling messages addressed to the Seventh-day Adventist ministry, now found in the book *Testimonies to Ministers,* were penned and sent to the leaders in Battle Creek.

To the work that was growing in other parts of the world field this situation meant a sad neglect. There was a failure to provide the funds needed, and our missionary workers were not properly sustained and they sometimes suffered want. Moves that obviously should be made must await instruction from Battle Creek. Workers were being dispatched to the world field by three Seventh-day Adventist organizations—the General Conference, the Foreign Mission Board, and the International Medical Missionary and Benevolent Association. The denomination was not then operating on a carefully planned budget as it is today, and the finances were uncertain and usually insufficient. Money was being borrowed with which to operate the foreign mission program.

With three organizations sending out workers and directing the work, there was confusion. The leading men of the church, so wrapped up in the interests at headquarters, had insufficient time to deal with the problems of the expanding work. This was very disheartening to those who were laboring in distant lands. Because of this situation and the difficulty of conducting a work so far from the Battle Creek headquarters, a move was under way in Europe to organize a European General Conference.

The medical missionary program, under the able leadership of Dr. John Harvey Kellogg, had grown rapidly into a large and strong program. By the year 1901 those employed in medical work numbered 2,000, while those employed by the denomination for conference, evangelistic, and other lines of work numbered only 1,500. The 2,000 medical workers were directed by the International Medical Missionary and Benevolent Association and not by the General Conference or the local conference committees.

Little wonder that it was with misgivings that the delegates gathered for the General Conference session scheduled to open Tuesday morning, April 2, 1901, in the Seventh-day Adventist Tabernacle in the city of Battle Creek. They were fearful of the outcome of the session. The denomination had outgrown its original organization and had reached a crisis no one knew how to meet. But a wise Providence had planned well for this meeting.

The day before the formal opening of the session, Mrs. White met with a special group of leaders in the Battle Creek college library. Present at this meeting were members of the General Conference Committee, conference presidents, institutional managers, doctors, teachers, and editors. To this group of responsible leaders Sister White unburdened her heart. Except for a brief statement about the importance of health reform and an appeal for loyalty to God in all things, the contents of her talk concerned reorganization. She urged upon this responsible group of men the necessity of bringing about immediate changes in the management of our conference and institutional affairs. She said in part:

"The work has been increasing; it has been growing. The light that I have had from the Lord has been expressed over and over again, not to as many as there are here today, but to different individuals. The plans upon which God wishes us to work have been laid down.

"Never should the mind of one man or the minds of a few men be regarded as sufficient in wisdom and power to control the work and say what plans shall be followed. The burden of the work in this broad field should not rest upon two or three men. We are not reaching the high standard which, with the great and important truth we are handling, God expects us to reach.

"Over and over again men have said, 'The voice of the conference is the voice of God; therefore everything must be referred to the conference. The conference must permit or restrict in the

185

various lines of work.' As the matter has been presented to me, there is a narrow compass, and within this narrow compass, all the entrances to which are locked, are those who would like to exercise kingly power. But the work carried on all over the field demands an entirely different course of action. . . .

"We have heard much about everything moving in the regular lines. When we see that the 'regular lines' are purified and refined, that they bear the mold of the God of heaven, then it will be time to endorse these lines. But when we see that message after message given by God has been received and accepted, yet no change has been made, we know that new power must be brought into the regular lines. The management of the regular lines must be entirely changed, newly organized. There must be a committee, not composed of half a dozen men, but of representatives from all lines of our work, from our publishing houses, from our educational institutions, and from our sanitariums, which have life in them, which are constantly working, constantly broadening. . . .

"God desires that His work shall be a rising, broadening, enlarging power. But the management of the work is becoming confused in itself. Not that anyone wishes to be wrong or to do wrong, but the principles are wrong. These principles are so foreign to God's principles that God cannot bless those who work upon them. What must be done is to bring in other minds. . . .

"God calls for a decided change. Do not wait until the conference is over, and then gather up the forces to see what can be done. Let us see what can be done now. Find out what power and intelligence there is that can be brought into the conference. Let all unite in taking hold of the work intelligently. This is what is needed.

"Every institution should have a voice in the working of the cause in which it has an interest. God wants us to come to the place where we shall be united in the work, where the whole burden will not be laid on two or three men. . . .

"When the cause was younger my husband used to counsel with men who had sound judgment. The work was much smaller then than it is now, but he did not feel able to manage it alone. He chose counselors from among those bearing responsibility in all parts of the work. And after counseling together, these men would go back to their work feeling a still greater responsibility to carry the work forward in right lines, to uplift, to purify, to solidify, so that the cause of God might move forward in strength."—Manuscript 43, 1901.

For an hour and a half Ellen White spoke. The men listened and pondered what they heard.

The next morning at nine o'clock in the Battle Creek Tabernacle the conference opened. The president of the General Conference, G. A. Irwin,* was in the chair and called the meeting to order. Two hundred and sixteen delegates presented themselves with their credentials. For the first time in ten years Ellen G. White was in the assembly. For nine years she had been engaged in pioneer work in Australia and New Zealand.

The first item of business was the admission of four newly organized local conferences to the General Conference (Queensland; S. Australia; Ontario, Canada; and Cumberland). Then the president gave his address, in which he reviewed the progress of the work over the preceding two years of his administration and concluded with the declaration:

"Ours is a momentous time, and this is a momentous occasion. The wisdom of no human agent is sufficient for the planning and devising that needs to be done."—*General Conference Bulletin,* April 3, 1901, p. 23.

His address complete, the chairman declared: "The conference is now formally opened. What is your pleasure?"

Mrs. White pressed to the front, ascended the steps to the rostrum, stood at the pulpit and began to speak. Only those who have had the privilege of seeing and hearing Sister White in one of these large and important gatherings of God's people can fully appreciate what her presence meant to a session. When she arose to speak, all were aware that she had a message from God for His people. She spoke with a firm, well-supported voice. All throughout the great Tabernacle heard her well.

---

* Elder Irwin took A. G. Daniells' place as president of the Australian Union Conference when Elder Daniells was asked at this session to assume the position of leadership.

In her very first remarks she brought the attention of all the delegates to the unfulfilled duties of reorganization awaiting them in this session:

"I feel a special interest in the movements and decisions that shall be made at this conference regarding the things that should have been done years ago, and especially ten years ago when we were assembled in conference and the Spirit and power of God came into our meeting, testifying that God was ready to work for this people if they would come into working order. The brethren assented to the light God had given, but there were those connected with our institutions, especially with the Review and Herald office and the conference, who brought in elements of unbelief, so that the light that was given was not acted upon. It was assented to, but no special change was made to bring about such a condition of things that the power of God could be revealed among His people.

"The light then given me was that this people should stand higher than any other people on the face of the whole earth, that they should be a loyal people, a people who would rightly represent truth. The sanctifying power of the truth, revealed in their lives, was to distinguish them from the world. They were to stand in moral dignity, having such a close connection with heaven that the Lord God of Israel could give them a place in the earth.

"Year after year the same acknowledgment was made, but the principles which exalt a people were not woven into the work. God gave them clear light as to what they should do, and what they should not do, but they departed from that light, and it is a marvel to me that we stand in as much prosperity as we do today. It is because of the great mercy of our God, not because of our righteousness, but that His name should not be dishonored in the world."—*Ibid.*

As was Mrs. White's custom, she placed primary emphasis upon the need for spiritual life pervading the ministers and people of the church. She pointed out the privilege of the Advent people to stand high above the world, sanctified by the truth, and having a close connection with Heaven. Then she turned to the immediate situation, as is indicated by the following statements gleaned from this address:

188

"Every soul in every conference, in every part of the Lord's vineyard, has the privilege of knowing the truth. But truth is not truth to those who do not practice it. Truth is only truth to you when you live it in the daily life, showing the world what those people must be who are at last saved. . . .

"Why, I ask you, are men who have not brought self into subjection allowed to stand in important positions of truth and handle sacred things? . . .

"The principles of heaven are to be carried out in every family, in the discipline of every church, in every establishment, in every institution, in every school, and in everything that shall be managed. You have no right to manage unless you manage in God's order. Are you under the control of God? Do you see your responsibility to Him? . . .

"Oh, my very soul is drawn out in these things! Men who have not learned to submit themselves to the control and discipline of God are not competent to train the youth, to deal with human minds. It is just as much an impossibility for them to do this work as it would be for them to make a world.

"That these men should stand in a sacred place, to be as the voice of God to the people, as we once believed the General Conference to be—that is past.* What we want now is a reorganization. We want to begin at the foundation and to build upon a different principle. . . .

"Here are men who are standing at the head of our various institutions, of the educational interests, and of the conferences in different localities and in different States. All these are to stand as representative men, to have a voice in molding and fashioning the plans that shall be carried out. There are to be more than one or two or three men to consider the whole vast field. The work is great, and there is no one human mind that can plan for the work which needs to be done. . . .

"According to the light that has been given me—and just how it is to be accomplished I cannot say—greater strength must be brought into the managing force of the conference. . . .

"God wants you to be converted, and may He help, that this work may go forward. He is a power for His people when they come into order. There must be a renovation, or reorganization; a

---

* See *Testimonies*, volume 9, pages 260, 261, a statement read before the delegates at the General Conference session in Takoma Park in the spring of 1909.

power and strength must be brought into the committees that are necessary. . . .

"If we will take hold of the Master, take hold of all the power He has given us, the salvation of God will be revealed."—*General Conference Bulletin,* April 3, 1901, pp. 24-26.

Thus the very serious nature of the situation that had developed was fearlessly and clearly delineated not only in these few key sentences but in the entire address. Help from God was promised if they would take hold of Him. There must be a change. This change was called for in one of the most solemn messages ever delivered to the church in General Conference assembled. The delegates must study, pray, and devise adequate solutions to the problems.

Would business proceed as usual? What would they do?

"Her words," wrote A. W. Spalding, "were not the orders of a taskmaster; they were the counsel of a commissioned servant of God who had earned the respect and reverence of a people she had helped to guide from the beginning."—*Origin and History,* vol. 3, p. 35.

A solemn silence pervaded the General Conference assembly as Ellen White moved away from the pulpit, where for an hour she had stood, and made her way to a chair. G. A. Irwin, the chairman, then stepped forward, and in response said:

"These are certainly very plain words that we have listened to, and it seems to me they come in very timely, right in the commencement of our conference. We notice the burden of the testimony was reorganization. . . . I, for one, want to accept the testimony that has been borne."—*General Conference Bulletin,* April 3, 1901, p. 27.

A. G. Daniells, a man in his prime, and one who for the past thirteen years had labored in New Zealand and Australia, now asked for the floor and told of the meeting the preceding day in which similar counsel had been given. He declared:

THE 1901 CONFERENCE OF REORGANIZATION

"We all feel that our only safety lies in obedience, in following our great Leader. We feel that we should begin at the very beginning of this work at this meeting, and just as nearly as we know how, build on His foundation.

"After the instruction had been given to us the matter was considered, and it was thought by many present that a change of conference management should be introduced at the beginning of the conference. I may say that I was acting as chairman of the meeting, and so, in behalf of the meeting, I am presenting the conclusions that we reached. In behalf of the meeting that I have referred to, I wish to introduce the following motion:

" 'I move that the usual rules and precedents for arranging and transacting the business of the conference be suspended, and that a general committee be hereby appointed, to consist of the following persons: the presidents and secretaries of the General Conference, of the General Conference Association, of the European and Australasian union conferences; of the Review and Herald, Pacific Press, and Echo publishing companies; of the Foreign Mission Board, Medical Missionary and Benevolent Association; of Battle Creek, Healdsburg, and Union colleges; and the following named persons: J. N. Loughborough, S. N. Haskell, A. T. Jones, W. W. Prescott, and such other persons as may be necessary to represent the important enterprises and interests connected with the work of the Seventh-day Adventists throughout the world, the same to be named by the committee when organized, and this committee to constitute a general or central committee, which shall do such work as necessarily must be done in forwarding the work of the conference, and preparing the business to bring before the delegates.'

"In the instruction given us this morning, committees were referred to, and we were told that these should be constructed of men who represent the varied interests throughout the great, wide world; that they should come together and carefully counsel regarding the matters to come before the conference and the methods of work that are to be carried forward. The committee named here aims to embrace these organizations and institutions, and fields in all parts of the world. I sincerely trust that God will give us wisdom and understanding and light from heaven to carry forward this work. I believe—I *know*—that victory is for us, and I believe that God has begun to work out that victory.

"And if we will throw away our preconceived opinions and will step out boldly to follow the light that He gives us, whether we can see clear through to the end or not—if we walk in the light we have, go just as far as we can today, God will give us further light; He will bring us out of bondage into glorious liberty. He will not lead us into confusion, brethren. He will lead us into order, and the right kind of order—order that He Himself establishes, and order that will in no way circumscribe or hinder His work, but will carry it forward with power and great rapidity.

"Now our people all over the world have their eyes turned to this occasion today. Hundreds of prayers are going up in behalf of this meeting. They have been ascending, and God has begun to answer already; and, brethren, let not one of us stand in the way of God's working out a complete deliverance and bringing entire victory.

"Oh, I am so glad we have a definite, certain voice to speak to us; and I am so glad that all through this meeting we can receive instruction and help. It seems to me that now is the time, brethren, to take hold of this matter of reorganization, and throw aside precedents, tradition, and everything that has so bound us, so we may get hold of the right thing. May God help us for His own name's sake."—*Ibid.*

Elder Daniells' motion was seconded by S. N. Haskell. Remarks were made by several speakers. The question was called, and the motion was carried unanimously.

All previous plans for the business of the conference were laid aside and the work of reorganization was begun.

Reports from the various parts of the world field, sermons, Bible studies, and devotional meetings filled the next few days as the large representative committee tackled its rather nebulous task of guiding the conference and bringing about a reorganization. Changes had been called for by the Lord, and changes had to be made. Steps must be taken that would distribute the responsibilities to men nearer where the work was being done.

CHAPTER EIGHTEEN

Changes and Triumphs in 1901

FORTUNATELY, as the delegates assembled in Battle Creek for the 1901 General Conference session and approached the task of reorganization, they had before them the knowledge of what had been done in Australia. Sister White had been in that field as the interests of the cause had grown. As noted earlier, at the time of the visit of Elder O. A. Olsen to Australia in 1894, A. G. Daniells and W. C. White, with the encouragement and in close counsel with Sister White, had led out in developing a form of organization that would bind the local conferences together in a union conference. This organization also drew together the various interests, such as the Sabbath school work, tract missionary work, and medical missionary work, into the union conference as departments, and not as separate organizations. This plan had worked very successfully. In Europe also, a plan had been developed, drawing local conferences and missions together into a form of union conference.

Elder Daniells, with his implicit trust in the messages of the Spirit of prophecy and his recent experience in leading in the organization of the work in Australia, was the man of the hour. It was logical that he should be called to stand at the head of the large committee of seventy-five, which came to be known as the committee on counsel. The first steps taken, after reviewing the general needs and the directions in which the work should move, were to set up subcommittees. First, a committee of eleven on organization, with W. C. White as the chairman, was appointed. Other committees were appointed—on education, on colporteur work, on publishing, on missionary work, et cetera. But it was the committee on organization especially that from day to day brought its reports to the conference as a whole. An early proposal was that union conferences following the territorial lines of the "districts" be formed throughout the North American and European fields.

This was carried out in a practical way by considering a request from several conferences and missions of the Southern field that they be allowed to organize into a union conference, with its president a member of the General Conference Committee. Elder O. A. Olsen and others spoke in favor of this plan. The reader will recall that he had called in 1892 and 1895 for just some such plan, and in 1897 the General Conference had given authorization for such. A constitution was drawn up, and the Southern Union Conference was formed and officers elected.

A full week passed before the basic action embodying reorganization was framed and presented to the conference in these words:

" '5. That the General Conference Committee be composed of representative men connected with the various lines of work in the different parts of the world.

" '6. That the General Conference Committee, as thus constituted, should take the place of all the present boards and committees, except in the case of the essential legal corporations.

" '7. That the General Conference Committee consist of twenty-five members, six of whom shall be chosen by the Medical Missionary Association, and nineteen by the General Conference. That five of these members be chosen with special reference to their ability to foster and develop the true evangelical spirit in all departments of the work, to build up the ministry of the word, and to act as teachers of the gospel message in all parts of the world; and that they be relieved from any special business cares, that they may be free to devote themselves to this work.

" '8. That in choosing this General Conference Committee,

the presidents of the union conferences be elected as members.' "
—*General Conference Bulletin,* April 11, 1901, p. 185.

The change proposed was a sweeping one. It indicated that the various independent and separate international organizations—the Sabbath School Association, the Religious Liberty Association, the Foreign Mission Board, et cetera— were now to be blended into the General Conference and that the committee was to be a much larger group with much wider representation. The medical missionary work, which had grown so strong, was to be integrated, with a definite representation on the General Conference Committee.

It took several days of earnest, prayerful discussion and consideration before the conference was ready to take an action on such a sweeping reorganization. At a critical time in the discussion Sister White stepped in and spoke directly to the point, exposing the vital involvements, e.g., in the matter of the organization of union conferences. She said:

"I am thankful that there is to be a time when the mists will be cleared away. I hope that this time has begun here. We want the mists here to be cleared away. I want to say that from the light given to me by God there should have been years ago organizations such as are now proposed. When we first met in conference it was thought that the General Conference should extend over the whole world. But this is not in God's order. Conferences must be organized in different localities, and it will be for the health of the different conferences to have it thus. This does not mean that we are to cut ourselves apart from one another, and be as separate atoms. Every conference is to touch every other conference, and be in harmony with every other conference. . . .

"New conferences must be formed. It was in the order of God that the union conference was organized in Australasia. The Lord God of Israel will link us all together. The organizing of new conferences is not to separate us. It is to bind us together."—*Ibid.,* April 4, pp. 68, 69.

From day to day throughout the conference session the various districts into which our work in North America had been loosely drawn were organized into union conferences. Constitutions were drawn up and accepted, and officers were elected. The various international auxiliary organizations as the Sabbath School Association, et cetera, took actions looking forward to their absorption into the General Conference.

It was a thrilling meeting of earnest, prayerful study, discussion, and action. There was no bitterness or holding back. The thought expressed by Elder Daniells at the close of Ellen White's address, in which she pointed out that God was calling for a reorganization, was kept in the minds of all: "We all feel that our only safety lies in obedience, in following our great Leader. We feel that we should begin at the very beginning of this work at this meeting, and just as nearly as we know how, build on His foundation."

For three long weeks the delegates labored carefully, patiently, earnestly. A new constitution for the General Conference was drawn up and adopted. It embodied the steps in reorganization painstakingly arrived at. When it came time to close the conference on Tuesday, April 23, it was evident that great changes had taken place. It was clear to all that the message from the lips of Ellen White calling for a reorganization had been heeded. The organization of union conferences provided for the men close to the problems to carry the burdens of the work close at hand. The General Conference now bound together the various union conferences, missions, and interests of a worldwide work, with an executive committee of twenty-five men representing the whole world field. Everyone seemed pleased and confident.

A farewell service was called for three o'clock on April 23, the closing day of the session. It was to be a missionary farewell service. A group of missionaries were present who expected to go to other lands. But it turned into a meeting of gratitude for God's special blessing witnessed at the conference. By suppertime it was clear that more time was needed, so an evening meeting was arranged. Many of the workers spoke, and one who pressed in early was J. N. Loughborough, who was also present when the General Conference was first organized in a one-day session in 1863. He observed:

"When we have heeded the light that He has given, the cause has gone straight every time; and the difficulties in the way have been when we have not strictly heeded the instruction that God has given.

"I was thinking, during the progress of this meeting, of our experiences in the early sixties, when the matter of organization was up. I have been greatly moved to witness in this meeting the same spirit coming in, in the reorganization, that was manifested in the organization at first. I have wondered for several years what that expression in the Testimony meant cautioning against tearing down this that God had established, when it said that this order was going to stand, strengthened and established. I know today what it means. I can see something of what it means to have that organization strengthened and established. I thank God for what I have seen here in this work of reorganization during this conference. I thank God that I have this privilege of meeting with you here in this conference. And I thank God that so many are moving out to go to distant lands."—*Ibid.*, April 25, p. 460.

Ellen White spoke at length at this meeting, and among other remarks she observed:

"Wrongs—serious wrongs—have been committed in Battle Creek. I did not know how we would get along at this meeting. The Lord gave me instruction regarding this. I was referred to an incident in the life of the prophet Elisha."

Then she recounted the appearance of the angels at Dothan, and continued:

"God presented this to me, and I did not know what it meant. I did not understand it. I pondered over it, and then as the lesson was fulfilled I began to grasp its meaning. I do not know that I would ever have seen the significance had it not been fulfilled right here. Who do you suppose has been among us since this conference began? Who has kept away the objectionable features that generally appear in such a meeting? Who has walked up and down the aisles of this Tabernacle?—the God of heaven and His angels. And they did not come here to tear you to pieces, but to give you right and peaceable minds. They have been among us to work the works of God, to keep back the powers of darkness, that the work God designed should be done should not be hindered. The angels of God have been working among us. . . .

"We have been trying to organize the work on right lines. The Lord has sent His angels to minister unto us who are heirs of salvation, telling us how to carry the work forward. . . .

"I was never more astonished in my life than at the turn things have taken at this meeting. This is not our work. God has brought it about. Instruction regarding this was presented to me, but until the sum was worked out at this meeting, I could not comprehend this instruction. God's angels have been walking up and down in this congregation. I want every one of you to remember this, and I want you to remember also that God has said that He will heal the wounds of His people.

"Press together, press together. Let us be united in Christ."—*Ibid.*, pp. 463, 464.

The general tenor of the scores of testimonies borne is represented in that of Elder Cornell McReynolds, who at this meeting became president of the newly organized Southwestern Union Conference, when he said:

"This is the best conference I have ever attended. I have been able to recognize the Spirit of God in all our meetings. The blessed Spirit has come in and instructed and led us. I praise the Lord from the depths of my soul for the privileges and blessings that I have received."—*Ibid.*, p. 467.

In his closing remarks the newly chosen leader of our worldwide work, A. G. Daniells, said:

"God has answered the thousands of prayers that have gone up to Him during the last six months, that this might be a conference of peace. God has answered those prayers in a signal manner. Praise His holy name. I sincerely pray that this harmony and union may continue forever."—*Ibid.*, p. 474.

And so the great conference of 1901 came to a close as the Tabernacle clock struck the hour of ten, April 23, 1901. In a startling way the Lord had called for a reorganization of the work of the denomination, and in response to the call the work had been reorganized.

From the facts here presented it is apparent that many of the counsels and reproofs given by the Lord's messenger to the leaders in Battle Creek during the last decade of the nineteenth century were called for by situations quite different from the question of righteousness by faith. Many of the messages of the servant of the Lord dealt with wrong policies and the wrong attitudes and actions of certain men. Mrs. White lifted the danger signal and pointed out situations that had to be corrected in order to meet the mind of God. And when the brethren in leadership acted, however belatedly, and moved into line with providential workings in the reorganization of the work, the blessings of the Lord were multiplied upon His people.

Soon after the 1901 conference session, back in her Elmshaven home, in California, Sister White spoke again of God's mighty work for His people at the Battle Creek Conference where reorganization was effected. In the following words she opened her front-page *Review* article:

"During the General Conference the Lord wrought mightily for His people. Every time I think of that meeting a sweet solemnity comes over me, and sends a glow of gratitude to my soul. We have seen the stately steppings of the Lord our Redeemer. We praise His holy name, for He has brought deliverance to His people."—*Review and Herald,* Nov. 26, 1901, p. 761.

Her recognition that reforms had been effected at the conference session was expressed subsequently many times. In one instance she wrote a personal letter to one of our workers reproving him for following a course which, she said, might have been proper had reforms not taken place:

"Your course would have been the course to be pursued if no change had been made in the General Conference. But a change has been made, and many more changes will be made and great developments will be seen. . . .

"It hurts me to think that you are using words which I wrote prior to the conference. Since the conference great changes have been made.. . . .

"A terribly unjust course has been pursued in the past. A want of principle has been revealed. But in pity to His people God has brought about changes. . . . The course of action which before the conference might have been a necessity is no longer necessary; for the Lord Himself interposed to set things in order. He has given His Holy Spirit. I am confident that He will set in order the matters that seem to be moving wrong."—Letter 54, 1901.

At the General Conference of 1909 A. G. Daniells, in his president's address, reported on the progress in reorganization during the preceding eight years. His statement sets forth the extensiveness of the changes that were called for and made:

"The growth and extension of our cause demonstrates more clearly each year the value of thorough organization and the meaning of the instruction that came to us through the Spirit of prophecy at the conference of 1901 with reference to reorganization. We were not told to *dis*-organize, but to *re*-organize. There was no intimation that the general plan of organization adopted by our denomination was wrong, but it was pointed out that our plans of administration were too narrow—that the circle was too small, and that the responsibilities of the cause were resting upon the shoulders of too few. We were, therefore, counseled to enlarge the circle of administration, and to distribute the responsibilities of management among a larger number.

"Immediate steps were taken to carry out this instruction. Since then the membership of the General Conference Committee has been increased from thirteen to forty. At that time there were but two union conferences, now there are twenty-one, located in nearly all parts of the world. Within their territories are included many important mission fields. To the committees in charge of these union conferences have been transferred countless details of administration which previously came to the General Conference Committee. During the same period fifty-seven local conferences have been added to the forty-five that had been organized up to 1901.

"In order to still further distribute responsibilities, a number of administrative departments have been created to take the oversight of special lines of work. There are now seven of these, known as the Sabbath School, Publishing, Medical, Educational, Religious Liberty, Young People's Missionary Volunteer, and North American Foreign departments. . . .

"Thus the reorganization that has been effected since the conference of 1901 has drawn into the administrative circle more than five hundred persons who were not there before, and the results show that this change has greatly increased the efficiency of the management of the work."—*General Conference Bulletin,* May 13, 1909, p. 8.

In 1903 at the General Conference session held at Oakland, California, further steps were taken in organization to correct a weakness which by that time had become quite apparent.* This related to the election of the officers of the General Conference. According to the constitution as adopted in 1901, the delegates attending a General Conference session were empowered to elect the General Conference Committee, and this committee was in turn to organize itself, electing its own officers. While there was not much discussion of this point, it was recognized at the time that this could mean that a man might be chairman for only one year. This provision doubtless came about as a rather extreme evidence of the desire to get far away from any "kingly power."

Somehow the flaw in such a plan was not seen at the time. This provision took out of the hands of the delegates attending a General Conference session the vital responsibility of electing the leaders of the church. This was now left in the hands of a committee of twenty-five. That some of the delegates attending the session of 1901 were not clear on this point is evidenced in their insistence that before that session closed the committee elect the chairman and announce their decision. This was done. Elder A. G. Daniells was thus chosen. The

* See Appendix C, p. 318.

201

delegates in 1901 did not discern at this point the extent the chairman would be crippled in his work, having no established tenure of office and no direct mandate from the delegates attending the General Conference session.

Furthermore, at no time had the messages from Ellen G. White called for the abolition of the office of "president of the General Conference"; rather, from earliest days her messages recognized such an office in the church. In a letter from Australia written to conference presidents in August, 1896, she declared: "It is not wise to choose one man as president of the General Conference." What follows indicated that she understood that the work devolving upon the president of the General Conference had grown too large for one man to carry and others should stand by his side to assist. What is more, she stated that "the president of the General Conference should have the privilege of deciding who shall stand by his side as counselors." (See *Testimonies to Ministers*, pp. 342, 343.)

After careful consideration at the 1903 session this matter was cared for by making constitutional provision for the election of the officers of the General Conference by the delegates attending the General Conference sessions.

Also, by the year 1903 the departments of the General Conference were quite well organized. In keeping with the work of reorganization begun in 1901, constitutional provision was also now made to enlarge the General Conference Committee by drawing the secretaries of these departments into this, the administrative committee of the church. This helped pave the way for the advance in the work reported by Elder Daniells at the session of 1909 as quoted above.

Four years after the call for reorganization was made, the following assuring message was given:

"The Lord has declared that the history of the past shall be rehearsed as we enter upon the closing work. Every truth that He has given for these last days is to be proclaimed to the world.

202

Every pillar that He has established is to be strengthened. We cannot now step off the foundation that God has established. We cannot now enter into any new organization; for this would mean apostasy from the truth."—Ellen G. White manuscript 129, 1905; in *Selected Messages,* book 2, p. 390.

When any arise asserting that God had rejected the leadership of the denomination because of the messages of reproof to men who had held positions of trust, we would point them to statements from Sister White's pen that indicate her confidence in the continuation of the organized work and in the men chosen to fill responsible positions after the General Conference of 1901. The following statements are typical of her attitude:

"In this perilous time the Lord has given us men of His choice to stand as the leaders of His people. If these men will keep humble and prayerful, ever making Christ their confidant, listening to and obeying His words, the Lord will lead and strengthen them. God has chosen Elder Daniells to bear responsibilities, and has promised to make him capable by His grace of doing the work entrusted to him. The responsibilities of the position he occupies are great, and the tax upon his strength and courage is severe; and the Lord calls upon us to hold up his hands, as he strives with all the powers of mind and body to advance the work. The Lord desires every church to offer prayer for him as he bears these heavy responsibilities. Our brethren and sisters should not stand ready to criticize and condemn those who are bearing heavy burdens. Let us refuse to listen to the words of censure spoken regarding the men upon whom rest such weighty responsibilities. . . . I know that Elder Daniells is the right man in the right place."—*Special Testimonies,* Series B, No. 2, p. 41 (July 23, 1904).

And the next year at the General Conference session held in Takoma Park, Washington, D.C., she declared:

"I have been given message after message for those who were standing at the head of the work here, for Elder Daniells and Elder Prescott, and for all connected with them in the work. The blessing of the Lord came upon me as I would write to them, saying, Be of good courage in the Lord. He is leading and guiding. He will bless you as you move forward. He will be your helper."—From an address before the General Conference at Takoma Park, May 16, 1905, in *Review and Herald,* May 25, 1905, p. 15.

Many a time Ellen White referred to the church as being highly esteemed by God and Christ, even though it is defective and imperfect. This was repeatedly stated in 1893 when some were teaching that the remnant church had become Babylon. It is significant that after the notable conference of 1901 similar statements were repeated. At a Sabbath morning service, November 22, 1902, she confidently said:

"We should remember that the church, enfeebled and defective though it be, is the only object on earth on which Christ bestows His supreme regard. He is constantly watching it with solicitude, and is strengthening it by His Holy Spirit. Will we, as members of His church, allow Him to impress our minds and to work through us to His glory?"—Manuscript 155, 1902; see *Selected Messages,* book 2, p. 396.

Again in 1910 she wrote: "Nothing in this world is so dear to God as His church. With jealous care He guards those who seek Him."—Letter 136, 1910; see *Selected Messages,* book 2, p. 397.

And the Lord has fulfilled His promises, and will continue to do so until the end.

CHAPTER NINETEEN

Crisis in the Publishing Work

O NE of the growing evils against which the Lord sent warning after warning to the leaders in Seventh-day Adventist publishing houses during the latter part of the last century and the early part of the present one was the demoralizing character of much of the commercial work that was being done on Seventh-day Adventist presses.

When these publishing houses were established the church was small and its demands for literature did not call for the full utilization of the publishing facilities and personnel necessary to manufacture Adventist books and periodicals. It was logical that commercial work should be solicited as a means of meeting the financial needs of this line of work. The practice was consistent, acceptable, and indeed seemed necessary.

At first, the amount of commercial work turned out for worldly business interests was rather insignificant. But with the passing of the years, as the public became acquainted with the fine quality of work done in these institutions, the volume of this class of work increased steadily, until it accounted for a large share of the annual output of Adventist publishing houses. This, naturally, called for an expansion of institutional buildings and for additional equipment. Often the pressure of commercial printing was so heavy that the production of church publications was neglected. This, to a great degree, was defeating the very purpose for which these publishing plants had been established.

However, the most serious objection to the commercial

printing that was flowing from the presses in an increasingly large volume was the questionable, demoralizing, and soul-destroying character of many of the books, pamphlets, and papers that were printed. But certain cautions were sounded. Commercial work, as such, need not be excluded from Adventist publishing houses at all times and in all cases.

The policy that should govern in this matter was clearly enunciated by God's servant:

"It is not necessary that the commercial work should be entirely divorced from the publishing houses, for this would close the door against rays of light that should be given to the world. And connection with outside parties need be no more detrimental to the workers than was Daniel's work as a statesman a perversion of his faith and principles. But whenever it is found to interfere with the spirituality of the institution, let the outside work be excluded. Build up the work that represents the truth. Let this always come first, and the commercial work second. Our mission is to give to the world the message of warning and mercy."—*Testimonies,* vol. 7, p. 163 (1902).

She stated further:

"In no case are the publishing institutions to be devoted chiefly to commercial work."—*Ibid.,* p. 162.

"When this work is given the first place, those connected with the publishing houses lose sight of the purpose for which they were established, and their work deteriorates.

"There is danger that managers whose spiritual perception is perverted will enter into contracts to publish questionable matter merely for the sake of gain. As the result of taking in this work, the purpose for which the offices of publication were established is lost sight of, and the institutions are regarded very much as any other commercial enterprise would be. In this God is dishonored.

"In some of our publishing houses the commercial work necessitates a constant increase of expensive machinery and other facilities. The outlay thus demanded is a heavy tax on the resources of the institution, and with a large amount of work there is required not only an increase of facilities, but a larger force of workers than can be properly disciplined."—*Ibid.*

In His mercy the Lord sent numerous messages, both oral and written, to warn against the perils of commercial work. The spirit and the character of these messages is revealed in a letter that Mrs. White wrote from Australia on December 19, 1891, to the workers in the office of the Pacific Press in California:

"I have a word from the Lord to you who are handling sacred things, and yet who do not appreciate the value of eternal realities and have not spiritual discernment to understand the work that you are doing. The Spirit of God is grieved because works of a worldly character, which are calculated to charm the senses, to fill the mind with that which can only be compared to wood, hay, and stubble, are multiplied in the office of publication. These books are read with eagerness, and they contain no spiritual nourishment, whereby the soul can acquire more strength, give no true idea of Christian life, or instruction in regard to the common duties of life. The atmosphere they breathe is one that is detrimental to solemn Christian experience.

"Were Christ upon the earth today He would cleanse the office of many things that are not in accordance with our high profession, as He cleansed the temple of its unholy traffic. It is written, 'My house shall be called an house of prayer, but ye have made it a den of thieves.' Let everyone begin to cleanse his own soul temple, and thus cooperate with Christ in the work of purifying the office.

"Let not books be placed before the workers which, if they do not mislead and corrupt the mind, will still give to the mind a disrelish for the Word of God which brings to view matters of eternal interest. Let the truth of God be subject for contemplation and meditation. The Bible is God's letter to man in which is instruction as to how to become rich in heavenly graces, to secure for the believer the life that shall measure with the life of God."—Letter 31, 1891.

In her statement written earlier, but published in 1902 in *Testimonies,* volume 7, pages 161-168, Mrs. White pinpointed the issue:

"When our publishing houses do a large amount of commercial work, there is great danger that an objectionable class of literature

207

will be brought in. Upon one occasion when these matters were brought to my attention, my Guide inquired of one occupying a responsible position in a publishing institution; 'How much do you receive in payment for this work?' The figures were placed before Him.

"He said: 'This is too small a sum. If you do business in this way, you meet with loss. But even should you receive a much larger sum, this class of literature could be published only at a great loss. The influence on the workers is demoralizing. All the messages that God shall send them, presenting the sacredness of the work, are neutralized by your action in consenting to print such matter.' . . .

"Books upon Indian warfare and similar topics, published and circulated as a money-making scheme, might better never be read. There is satanic fascination in such books. The heartsickening relation of crimes and atrocities has a bewitching power upon many youth, exciting in them the desire to bring themselves into notice by the most wicked deeds. . . . The horrible details of crime and misery need not to be lived over, and none who believe the truth for this time should act a part in perpetuating their memory."

Frankly and with candor she declared that—

"love stories and frivolous, exciting tales constitute another class of books that is a curse to every reader. . . .

"We have no permission from the Lord to engage either in the printing or in the sale of such publications, for they are the means of destroying many souls. I know of what I am writing, for this matter has been opened before me. Let not those who believe the message for this time engage in such work, thinking to make money. The Lord will put a blight upon the means thus obtained; He will scatter more than is gathered.

"There is another class of literature, more defiling than the leprosy, more deadly than the plagues of Egypt, against which our publishing houses need unceasingly to guard. In accepting commercial work, let them beware lest matters presenting the very science of Satan be admitted into our institutions. Let not works setting forth the soul-destroying theories of hypnotism, spiritualism, Romanism, or other mysteries of iniquity find a place in our publishing houses.

"Let nothing be handled by the employees that will sow one

seed of doubt in regard to the authority or purity of the Scriptures. Upon no consideration let infidel sentiments be placed before the youth, whose minds so eagerly grasp anything new. At the very highest figures that might be paid, such work could be published only at infinite loss."

Then Mrs. White asked some pointed questions:

"Think you that Jesus will stand in the publishing establishment to work through human minds by His ministering angels; think you that He will make the truth coming from the presses a power to warn the world, if Satan is allowed to pervert the minds of the workers right in the institution? Can God's blessing attend the publications coming from the press, when from the same press are sent forth satanic heresy and delusion? 'Doth a fountain send forth at the same place sweet water and bitter?' James 3:11. . . .

"When matters containing errors that counteract the work of God are printed in our houses of publication, God holds accountable not only those who allow Satan to lay a trap for souls, but those who in any way cooperate in the work of temptation.

"My brethren in responsible positions, beware that you do not harness your workers to the car of superstition and heresy. Let not the institutions ordained by God to send out life-giving truth be made an agency for the dissemination of soul-destroying error. . . .

"We are brought into connection with the world, not that we may be leavened with the world's falsehood, but that as God's agencies we may leaven the world with His truth."—*Ibid.*, pp. 165-168.

In November, 1901, seven months after the memorable General Conference of 1901, a startling message from the Lord through Mrs. White, addressed to "The Managers of the Review and Herald," was read to the board.* It stated plainly that unless the leaders of the institution would repent and heed the counsels of the Lord the judgments of God would fall upon the institution:

"God's design in the establishment of the publishing house at Battle Creek was that from it light should shine forth as a lamp that burneth. This has been kept before the managers. Again and

---

* Letter 138, Oct. 16, 1901.

again they have been told of the sacredness of God's office of publication and of the importance of maintaining its purity. But they have lost true understanding and have united with the force of the enemy by consenting to print papers and books containing the most dangerous errors that can be brought into existence. They have failed to see the evil influences of such erroneous sentiments on typesetters, proofreaders, and all others engaged in the printing of such matter. They have been spiritually asleep. . . .

"I have received a letter from Elder Daniells regarding the addition of another building to the Review and Herald office. The answer I make to this is: No, no, no. Instead of making any additions to the buildings already erected, cleanse the office of the trash of satanic origin, and you will gain room in every way. . . .

"I feel a terror of soul as I see to what a pass our publishing house has come. The presses in the Lord's institution have been printing the soul-destroying theories of Romanism and other mysteries of iniquity. The office must be purged of this objectionable matter. . . .

"You have given matter containing Satan's sentiments into the hands of the workers, bringing his deceptive, polluting principles before their minds. The Lord looks upon this action on your part as helping Satan to prepare his snare to catch souls. God will not hold guiltless those who have done this thing. He has a controversy with the managers of the publishing house. I have been almost afraid to open the *Review*, fearing to see that God has cleansed the publishing house by fire.

"The Lord has instructed me that those who cannot see the wickedness of cooperating with Satan by publishing his falsehoods might better seek some work in which they will not ruin our youth, body and soul. There is danger that the standard of truth and righteousness will be so lowered that God will bring His judgments upon the wrongdoers. . . .

"The work of printing and circulating stirring appeals for the truth, which should have been placed first, to which the time and the talent of the workers should have been devoted, has received little or no attention. The commercial work, some of it of a most objectionable character, has gradually assumed the supremacy. This work has absorbed the energies which should have been devoted to the publication of literature of the purest quality and the most elevating character. Time has been wasted, talent misapplied, and money misappropriated. The work which ought to have been done has been left undone. Satan's sentiments have been exalted. His theories have been printed by presses which should have been used to prepare the truth of God for circulation. Men have coveted promotion when their principles were under the ban of God's displeasure. Loss is infinitely better than dishonorable gain. . . .

"The light I have is: Refuse to print another line of this pernicious matter. Those who have had to do with its introduction into the publishing house need to repent before God in contrition of soul, for His wrath is kindled against them. Let this class of work be forever excluded from our publishing houses. Give more time to the publication and circulation of the books containing present truth. See that your work in this line reaches perfection. Do all in your power to diffuse throughout the world the light of heaven. . . .

"Unless there is a reformation, calamity will overtake the publishing house, and the world will know the reason."—*Ibid.*, vol. 8, pp. 90-96.

It did.

CHAPTER TWENTY

God Speaks by Fire

FOURTEEN months later the threatened judgment fell upon the Review and Herald publishing house. During the night of December 30, 1902, the main building was reduced to ashes by a seemingly unquenchable fire.* This calamity was even a worse tragedy than the fearful fire that burned to the ground the main building of the Battle Creek Sanitarium the night of February 18. The leaders had had opportunity to reflect upon the meaning of that disaster and yet nothing was done to remove the causes for these judgments.

But now they were startled to action. With the message of God's threatening judgments now recalled, and while the ashes of the great publishing house were still warm, the Review and Herald board met on Sunday, January 4, just four days after the fire, and adopted the following resolutions:

"First, That we agree that we do not expect to resume commercial work in the institution;

"Second, That our only interest is to care for the institution in reference to our denominational interests."—*Minutes of a meeting of the Review and Herald Board held on January 4, 1903.*

When the news of the Review fire reached Ellen G. White, she wrote from St. Helena, California, on January 5, 1903, to the brethren in Battle Creek a message that may be found in *Testimonies*, volume 8, pages 97-101. We quote in part:

---

*See *Review and Herald*, Jan. 6, 1903, p. 12, and Dec. 8, 1977.

"Today I received a letter from Elder Daniells regarding the destruction of the Review office by fire. I feel very sad as I consider the great loss to the cause. I know that this must be a very trying time for the brethren in charge of the work and for the employees of the office. I am afflicted with all who are afflicted. But I was not surprised by the sad news, for in the visions of the night I have seen an angel standing with a sword as of fire stretched over Battle Creek. Once, in the daytime, while my pen was in my hand, I lost consciousness, and it seemed as if this sword of flame were turning first in one direction and then in another. Disaster seemed to follow disaster because God was dishonored by the devising of men to exalt and glorify themselves.

"This morning I was drawn out in earnest prayer that the Lord would lead all who are connected with the Review and Herald office to make diligent search that they may see wherein they have disregarded the many messages God has given.

"Some time ago the brethren at the Review office asked my counsel about the erection of another building. I then said that if those who were in favor of adding another building to the Review and Herald office had the future mapped out before them, if they could see what would be in Battle Creek, they would have no question about putting up another building there. God said: 'My word has been despised; and I will turn and overturn.'

"At the General Conference held in Battle Creek in 1901, the Lord gave His people evidence that He was calling for reformation. Minds were convicted, and hearts were touched; but thorough work was not done.* If stubborn hearts had been broken in penitence before God there would have been seen one of the greatest manifestations of the power of God that has ever been seen. But God was not honored. The testimonies of His Spirit were not heeded. Men did not separate from the practices that were in decided opposition to the principles of truth and righteousness, which should ever be maintained in the Lord's work.

"The messages to the church of Ephesus and to the church in Sardis have been often repeated to me by the One who gives me instruction for His people. 'Unto the angel of the church of Ephesus write; . . . I know thy works, and thy labor, and thy patience, and how thou canst not bear them which are evil: and thou hast

---

* See "What Might Have Been," in *Testimonies,* vol. 8, pp. 104-106.

tried them which say they are apostles, and are not, and hast found them liars: and hast borne, and hast patience, and for my name's sake hast labored, and hast not fainted. Nevertheless I have somewhat against thee, because thou hast left thy first love. Remember therefore from whence thou art fallen, and repent, and do the first works; or else I will come unto thee quickly, and will remove thy candlestick out of his place, except thou repent.' Rev. 2:1-5.

" 'And unto the angel of the church in Sardis write: . . . I know thy works, that thou hast a name that thou livest, and art dead. Be watchful, and strengthen the things which remain, that are ready to die: for I have not found thy works perfect before God. Remember therefore how thou hast received and heard, and hold fast, and repent. If therefore thou shalt not watch, I will come on thee as a thief, and thou shalt not know what hour I will come upon thee.' Rev. 3:1-3.

"We are seeing the fulfillment of these warnings. Never have scriptures been more strictly fulfilled than these have been."—*Ibid.*

Mrs. White also described "the fiery sword . . . hanging over Battle Creek" that she had seen in vision:

"Men may erect the most carefully constructed, fireproof buildings, but one touch of God's hand, one spark from heaven, will sweep away every refuge. "It has been asked if I have any advice to give. I have already given the advice that God has given me, hoping to prevent the falling of the fiery sword that was hanging over Battle Creek. Now that which I dreaded has come—the news of the burning of the Review and Herald building. When this news came, I felt no surprise, and I had no words to speak. What I have had to say from time to time in warnings has had no effect except to harden those who heard, and now I can only say: I am so sorry, so very sorry, that it was necessary for this stroke to come. Light enough has been given. If it were acted upon, further light would not be needed.

"To our people, ministers and lay members, I am instructed to say: 'Seek ye the Lord while he may be found, call ye upon him while he is near: let the wicked forsake his way, and the unrighteous man his thoughts: and let him return unto the Lord,'—for many ministers and people are walking in strange paths,—'and he will have mercy upon him; and to our God, for he will abundantly pardon.' Isa. 55:6, 7.

"Let every soul be on the alert. The adversary is on your track. Be vigilant, watching diligently lest some carefully concealed and masterly snare shall take you unawares. Let the careless and indifferent beware lest the day of the Lord come upon them as a thief in the night. Many will wander from the path of humility, and casting aside the yoke of Christ, will walk in strange paths. Blinded and bewildered, they will leave the narrow path that leads to the city of God. . . .

"We need keen, sanctified perception. This perception is not to be used in criticizing and condemning one another, but discerning the signs of the times. We are to keep our hearts with all diligence, that we may not make shipwreck of faith."—*Ibid.*

"The fiery sword . . . hanging over Battle Creek" had fallen indeed. And in it all God was speaking to His people and providing them with opportunity to think through the meaning of the destruction. Wrote Ellen White:

"The destruction of the Review and Herald building should not be passed over as something in which there is no meaning. Everyone connected with the office should ask himself: 'Wherein do I deserve this lesson? wherein have I walked contrary to a "Thus saith the Lord," that He should send this lesson to me? Have I heeded the warnings and reproofs that He has sent, or have I followed my own way?' . . .

"When the Battle Creek Sanitarium was destroyed, Christ gave Himself to defend the lives of men and women. In this destruction God was appealing to His people to return to Him. And in the destruction of the Review and Herald office, and the saving of life, He makes a second appeal to them. He desires them to see that the miracle-working power of the Infinite has been exercised to save life, that every worker may have opportunity to repent and be converted."—*Ibid.*, pp. 101, 102.

There was considerable discussion in Battle Creek about the lessons to be learned from these two fires: first, the main building at the Battle Creek Sanitarium on the night of February 18, 1902, and then ten months later, on December 30, the manufacturing plant of the Review and Herald Publishing Association. The college, of course, had moved to Berrien Springs the year before. The only substantial Seventh-day Ad-

215

ventist institutional building left in the entire city was the Tabernacle.

"Were these judgments of God?" asked Arthur W. Spalding. Here is the church historian's reply:

"Was there a meaning in them? Some felt that they were judgments, and that they were meant to warn the Adventists to get out of Battle Creek. But others scoffed at the idea. 'I do not believe that our God is a god of vengeance,' said Lycurgus McCoy, chaplain of the sanitarium. 'That is a heathen idea, that when any calamity befalls it is because of the wrath of a god. I can tell you why the sanitarium burned and why the Review and Herald burned. They were magazines, so filled with combustibles that they would burn like tinder, and only a match or the crossing of wires was needed to set them off. I do not think God wanted them to burn. It was not an act of God but the negligence of men.'

" 'God's hand is in every occurrence,' answered W. W. Prescott, 'and how we relate ourselves to it determines whether we are heathen or Christian. The heathen says, "My god is angry with me: I will do what I can to appease him." But the Christian says, "My God is correcting me in love. I will answer to His discipline, and obey His will." '

" 'I do not believe, friends,' said A. G. Daniells, 'that this is heathenism. God has always disciplined His people like a Father; and when He permits calamities to come upon them, whatever the immediate cause, there is a meaning in them. And that meaning we must discover and heed. Now let us turn our steps, face about, and take the course that God directs.' "—*Origin and History,* vol. 3, p. 69.

The destruction of the sanitarium took place at a time distant enough from the Review fire to provide a pause for meditation and thought. God was speaking to His people. Had the time come to remove from Battle Creek? In the general removal to a new headquarters, a new center of world leadership, would there come a logical beginning again in new practices in publishing house procedures?

Friday morning, April 3, 1903—just three months after the Review and Herald fire—A. G. Daniells, president of the General Conference, addressing himself to Ellen G. White in the presence of the delegates gathered at Oakland, California, for the thirty-fifth session of the General Conference, discussed a resolution which called for removing the headquarters of the church from Battle Creek. This implied moving the publishing house, for the two were inseparably linked together. For forty years the offices of the General Conference had been in the publishing house. At the time of the fire they occupied a portion of the "West Building" just across the street from the factory and a building of the Review and Herald that served as the book depository. This building did not burn.

Turning to Mrs. White, he said:

"A resolution was introduced into the conference yesterday which some of the brethren wished me to place before you. It was not acted upon, but was left for further consideration today. The resolution was:

" 'That the General Conference offices or headquarters be moved from Battle Creek, Michigan, to some place favorable for its work on the Atlantic Coast.'

"It is a serious thing for us to move the headquarters of our General Conference. Battle Creek has been the headquarters for many years, ever since you and Elder White went there in 1853 [1855]. It is a serious thing to take this step. But some feel as if it ought to be done; that we will never secure the reformation called for; that we will never rise to do this work as God's people, to finish it in the earth, until we can break up some of the conditions that now exist, and thus set the work free. We have felt from what has occurred during the last two years, and the counsels you have given, that the time has come to move from that place. But we do not want to do this unless it is right, and we felt that we would like to place the matter before you, and receive any counsel and light you could give us."—*General Conference Bulletin*, April 6, 1903, p. 84.

Replying at considerable length, Mrs. White reviewed the counsels that she had given on previous occasions concerning the publishing house and urging our people to "get out of Battle Creek." She declared:

"I must say to our people that the Lord would have that institution [the Review and Herald] established in an entirely new place. He would have the present influences of association broken up. Will those who have collected in Battle Creek hear the voice speaking to them, and understand that they are to scatter out into different places, where they can spread abroad a knowledge of the truth, and where they can gain an experience different from the experience that they have been gaining?

"In reply to the question that has been asked in regard to settling somewhere else, I answer, Yes. Let the General Conference offices and the publishing work be moved from Battle Creek. I know not where the place will be, whether on the Atlantic Coast or elsewhere. But this I will say, Never lay a stone or a brick in Battle Creek to rebuild the Review office there. God has a better place for it. He wants you to work with a different influence, and connected with altogether different associations from what you have had of late in Battle Creek. . . .

"I ask you, brethren, shall we, because our books and papers have long borne the imprint of Battle Creek, again lay the foundation in the very place where our work has been destroyed by fire? . . .

"God would not have let the fire go through our institutions in Battle Creek without a reason. Are you going to pass by the providence of God without finding out what it means? God wants us to study into this matter, and to build upon a foundation in which all can have the utmost confidence."—*Ibid.*, pp. 84-87. (Also in *Review and Herald*, April 14, 1903, pp. 17, 18.)

Her statement closed with an appeal.

"May God help you to receive the words that I have spoken. Let those who stand as God's watchmen on the walls of Zion be men who can see the dangers before the people—men who can distinguish between truth and error, righteousness and unrighteousness.

"The warning has come: Nothing is to be allowed to come in that will disturb the foundation of the faith upon which we have been building ever since the message came in 1842, 1843, and 1844. . . . Brethren and sisters, God lives and reigns and works today. His hand is on the wheel, and in His providence He is turning the wheel in accordance with His own will. Let not men fasten themselves to documents, saying what they will do and what they will not do. Let them fasten themselves to the Lord God of heaven. Then the light of heaven will shine into the soul temple, and we shall see the salvation of God."—*General Conference Bulletin*, April 6, 1903, p. 88.

In his presidential address at the next biennial General Conference session held at Washington, D.C., in 1905, Elder A. G. Daniells reported:

"During the last biennial period, important changes have been made and movements set on foot which are certainly of vital interest to this cause, and which we feel sure will render it more effective service as the end approaches.

"In the Publishing Department some radical changes have been set on foot. One of these is the removal of the entire plant of the Pacific Press Publishing Company from the city of Oakland, California, to the rural district of Mountain View, forty miles in the country. Another is the decision and preparatory steps of the Echo Publishing Company [in Australia] to remove from the city of Melbourne to a country location in Victoria. And another is the winding up of the old Publishing Association of Battle Creek, Michigan, and the removal of the plant and business to a suburban location in the District of Columbia. The transfer is at present only partially made, but it is under way. . . .

"In eliminating commercial work, the entire investment and facilities of the plant, and all the time, energy, and ability of those in its employ can be devoted to our denominational work. . . .

"These changes are radical and vital enough, it would seem, to entirely revolutionize the Publishing Department of our cause. It is devoutly to be hoped that they will help to bring a revival of more earnest, determined efforts in behalf of a large distribution of our denominational literature, and a new and glorious era to this phase of our work."—*Review and Herald*, May 11, 1905, p. 7.

In the well-equipped Review and Herald publishing house built in Takoma Park, D.C., the modern presses turn night and day and the entire consecrated staff devotes its full time to the publishing of the literature of the church.

These were fiery times, and the movings of providence took shape in a still further disaster, this time on the West Coast. On the night of July 21, 1906, three months after the devastating San Francisco earthquake of April 18, the Pacific Press, newly established at Mountain View, was destroyed by fire. The institution was still licking its wounds from the mighty temblor that shook the coast when this further disaster struck.

Like the brethren in publishing leadership in Battle Creek, the western publishers paused to consider why the tragedy had come. They too had been the recipients of numerous cautions concerning the commercial work running through their presses. In an editorial in the *Signs of the Times,* published in the temporary printing office—the lead article entitled "What Do These Things Mean?" followed by the bold-faced line "The Earthquake, the Fire, Our Fire"—the editors searched about for the answer. One subtitle in this lead article asked, "But What of the Pacific Press?"

"Is this the judgment of God? Are there not lessons here? These questions are being asked in seriousness, in cynicism, in skepticism, tauntingly, mockingly.

"Of this seemingly awful calamity which came to a great publishing house we shall say, as we said of San Francisco's, God at least permitted it. The same dangers have ever menaced God's people that menace the world. The enemy of all righteousness surrounds them with the gilded baits of worldliness, enthralls them in cares and pleasures, and stupefies them with prosperity and desire for gain.

"They may in no way deal dishonestly. Their course and example in the world of commerce and manufacture, in trade and barter, may be exemplary in the highest degree. Men may have no evil thing to say of them. Yet, they may be using their energies, their talents, their means, their God-given powers, their influence, to promote and build up worldly enterprises, and thus become growingly indifferent to the claims which God has upon them. They may use the very facilities which God has bestowed upon them, to the neglect of God's work. They may do this honestly, mistakenly, believing it to be of indirect benefit to God's work; but indifference to God's claims on the part of His people is as bad as open, flagrant sin on the part of the world.

"In God's mercy to His people He must do more than warn. He must remove the means not used for Him; He must strip the human talents and energies of the facilities not used in His work, that His people may in humility learn that the King's business is paramount to all else; that God's work should be the business of His followers, first and last and all the time; that no work of any other character, honorable though it be, must be allowed to hinder or interfere with the work of God. If they ignore the lesson as San Francisco is ignoring it, if they say the calamity to building has naught to do with business or character, they will fail to learn the great lesson, and thus lose the blessing of sanctified service for God.

"Therefore with humbled heart we accept the lesson, the chastening from the hand of a merciful, patient, tender Father-teacher. And this lesson is not alone for the few workers here, though it is for them; it is for those who profess to be His commandment-keeping followers everywhere. Indifference to God's claims on the part of His professed children is as bad as open, chosen sin on the part of those who know Him not; and the real test of faith and character is not the coming or not coming of a calamity, but how men learn the lesson.

"God requires the whole heart, soul, mind, and strength. Yielding that to Him, all the calamities of earth are nothing. God's blessing and presence in the fiery furnace makes it safer than the throne of Babylon."—*Signs of the Times*, Aug. 29, 1906, p. 2.

Just as the board of the Review and Herald read in their disastrous fire God's message to make the interests of His cause first, and turned forever from commercial work, so did the stockholders and the board of directors of the Pacific Press, as plans were laid to rebuild the plant. All commercial work was discarded.

With firm determination that the publishing facilities of the church on the Pacific Coast should be dedicated solely to the proclamation of the third angel's message, the brethren in the West rebuilt and re-equipped their plant. God has honored their firm stand on a full devotion of the facilities to publishing the message.

221

CHAPTER TWENTY-ONE

Accusers of the Brethren

IF THE evils resulting from a failure of the church to follow closely the counsel of the Lord could be limited to the men and institutions as well as to the times in which they occurred, the historical narrative recording their failures would be sad enough, but influences for wrongdoing spread faster and work more havoc than can be known. As an example, think of how extremists and self-appointed reformers have built their arguments and their movements upon the events related to the years of crisis between 1888 and 1901.

Taking advantage of the messages of rebuke, admonition, and warning that had been coming at frequent intervals from the servant of the Lord just before and during the early 1890's, a few misguided, disgruntled, and unscrupulous individuals in the church in 1893 seized upon these Spirit of Prophecy messages, and by lifting portions out of their context, tried to make it appear that the Seventh-day Adventist Church had become Babylon, and that, therefore, all the honest in heart should "come out of her."

One man referred to as "Brother Stanton" by Ellen White, wrote a pamphlet titled "The Loud Cry of the Third Angel," which he circulated among Seventh-day Adventists. To show in a manner that has been employed many times since that the Adventist Church had become the mystic Babylon, Stanton gathered together extracts from the Ellen G. White writings that reproved church leaders, and this was offered as proof of the denomination's apostasy. One of these pamphlets fell into

222

the hands of the Lord's messenger. After reading it, she wrote its author a long letter from Napier, New Zealand, where she was then laboring. From this letter, dated March 23, 1893, I quote as follows:

"I address to you a few lines. I am not in harmony with the position that you have taken, for I have been shown by the Lord that just such positions will be taken by those who are in error. Paul has given us warning to this effect: 'Now the Spirit speaketh expressly, that in the latter times some shall depart from the faith, giving heed to seducing spirits, and doctrines of devils.'

"My brother, I learn that you are taking the position that the Seventh-day Adventist Church is Babylon, and that all that would be saved must come out of her. You are not the only man the devil has deceived in this matter. For the last forty years, one man after another has arisen, claiming that the Lord has sent him with the same message; but let me tell you, as I have told them, that this message you are proclaiming is one of the satanic delusions designed to create confusion among the churches. . . .

"My brother, if you are teaching that the Seventh-day Adventist Church is Babylon, you are wrong. God has not given you any such message to bear. Satan will use every mind to which he can attain access, inspiring men to originate false theories or go off on some wrong tangent, that he may create a false excitement and thus divert souls from the true issue for this time. I presume that some may be deceived by your message, because they are full of curiosity and desire for some new thing.

"It makes me feel sad indeed that you should be deceived in any way by the suggestions of the enemy, for I know the theory that you are advocating is not truth. In advancing the ideas you do, you will do great injury to yourself and to others. Do not seek to misinterpret, and twist, and pervert the *Testimonies* to substantiate any such message of error. Many have passed over this ground, and have done great harm. As others have started up full of zeal to proclaim this message, again and again, I have been shown that it was not truth."—*Review and Herald,* Sept. 12, 1893, p. 579; in *Testimonies to Ministers,* pp. 58-60.

This was plain language from an inspired writer and left no room for doubt as to the true source of Brother Stanton's information about the Seventh-day Adventist Church. He was

223

justly rebuked for teaching that the very movement that God had raised up to carry His final message to the world is Babylon. This deceived man was also reproved for having twisted the *Testimonies* to substantiate his erroneous views. Mrs. White, until the time of her death in 1915, was a powerful protagonist in the defense of the church movement that she had given her life to help create and develop.

In this letter to Brother Stanton, Mrs. White also averred that God is not leading offshoots but a church, a chosen people. Note carefully her words:

" 'God has a church upon the earth who are His chosen people, who keep His commandments. He is leading, not stray offshoots, not one here and one there, but a people. The truth is a sanctifying power; but the church militant is not the church triumphant. There are tares among the wheat. "Wilt thou then that we . . . gather them up?" was the question of the servant; but the master answered, "Nay; lest while ye gather up the tares, ye root up also the wheat with them." The gospel net draws not only good fish, but bad ones as well, and the Lord only knows who are His.

" 'It is our individual duty to walk humbly with God. We are not to seek any strange, new message. We are not to think that the chosen ones of God who are trying to walk in the light compose Babylon. The fallen denominational churches are Babylon. Babylon has been fostering poisonous doctrines, the wine of error. This wine of error is made up of false doctrines, such as the natural immortality of the soul, the eternal torment of the wicked, the denial of the pre-existence of Christ prior to His birth in Bethlehem, and advocating and exalting the first day of the week above God's holy and sanctified day. These and kindred errors are presented to the world by the various churches, and thus the Scriptures are fulfilled that say, "For all nations have drunk of the wine of the wrath of her fornication." It is a wrath which is created by false doctrines, and when kings and presidents drink this wine of the wrath of her fornication, they are stirred with anger against those who will not come into harmony with the false and satanic heresies which exalt the false sabbath, and lead men to trample underfoot God's memorial.' "—*Ibid.*, p. 579; in *Testimonies to Ministers*, pp. 61, 62.

Months later on June 11, 1893, in a letter addressed to W. F. Caldwell, an associate of Brother Stanton, Sister White wrote, from Wellington, New Zealand, a letter setting forth the same principles as stated in her letter to Stanton, but in somewhat different language, as follows:

"The Lord has not given you a message to call the Seventh-day Adventists Babylon, and to call the people of God to come out of her. All the reasons you may present cannot have weight with me on this subject, because the Lord has given me decided light that is opposed to such a message.

"I do not doubt your sincerity or honesty. I have written long letters at different times to those who were accusing the church of Seventh-day Adventists of being Babylon, that they were not handling the truth. You think individuals have prejudiced my mind. If I am in this state, I am not fitted to be entrusted with the work of God. But this matter has been brought before my mind in other cases where individuals have claimed to have messages for the Seventh-day Adventist Church, of a similar character, and the word has been given me, 'Believe them not.' 'I have not sent them, and yet they ran.' . . .

"God is leading out a people. He has a chosen people, a church on the earth, whom He has made the depositaries of His law. He has committed to them sacred trust and eternal truth to be given to the world. He would reprove and correct them. The message to the Laodiceans is applicable to Seventh-day Adventists who have had great light and have not walked in the light. It is those who have made great profession, but have not kept in step with their Leader, that will be spewed out of His mouth unless they repent. The message to pronounce the Seventh-day Adventist Church Babylon, and call the people of God out of her, does not come from any heavenly messenger, or any human agent inspired by the Spirit of God. . . .

"Jesus is coming in to give the individual members of the church the richest blessings, if they will open the door to Him. He does not once call them Babylon, nor ask them to come out. But He says, 'As many as I love, I rebuke and chasten' (with messages of reproof and warning) (Rev. 3:19). These reproofs I am not ignorant of. I have given warnings because the Spirit of the Lord has constrained me to do so, and have uttered reproofs because the Lord has given me words of reproof. I have not shunned to declare the whole counsel of God, which has been given me for the church."—Letter 16, 1893; in *Selected Messages,* book 2, pp. 63-67.

Mrs. White encouraged Seventh-day Adventists to hope in the goodness of the Lord while at the same time drawing next to Him in humility. The letter continues:

"I will say in the fear and love of God, I know the Lord has thoughts of love and mercy to restore and heal them of all their backslidings. He has a work for His church to do. They are not to be pronounced Babylon, but to be as the salt of the earth, the light of the world. They are to be the living messengers to proclaim a living message in these last days. . . .

"Again I say, The Lord hath not spoken by any messenger who calls the church that keeps the commandments of God, Babylon. True, there are tares with the wheat; but Christ said He would send His angels to first gather the tares and bind them in bundles to burn them, but gather the wheat into the garner. I know that the Lord loves His church. It is not to be disorganized or broken up into independent atoms. There is not the least consistency in this; there is not the least evidence that such a thing will be. Those who shall heed this false message and try to leaven others will be deceived and prepared to receive advanced delusions, and they will come to nought.

"There is in some of the members of the church, pride, self-sufficiency, stubborn unbelief, and a refusing to yield their ideas, although evidence may be piled upon evidence which makes the message to the Laodicean church applicable. But that will not blot out the church that it will not exist. Let both tares and wheat grow together until the harvest. Then it is the angels that do the work of separation.

"I warn the Seventh-day Adventist Church to be careful how you receive every new notion and those who claim to have great light. The character of their work seems to be to accuse and to tear down. . . .

"Let the believers heed the voice of the angel who has said to the church, 'Press together.' In unity is your strength. Love as brethren, be pitiful, be courteous. God hath a church, and Christ hath declared, 'The gates of hell shall not prevail against it' (Matt. 16:18). The messengers the Lord sends bear the divine credentials."—*Ibid.;* see *Selected Messages,* book 2, pp. 67-69.

A few months before writing to the two misguided brethren in question, Ellen White wrote, under date of December 23, 1892, from Melbourne, Australia, a heart-warming message to the delegates assembled in Battle Creek for the thirtieth session of the General Conference, February 17-March 6, 1893 (*General Conference Bulletin,* 1893, pp. 408, 409; *Testimonies to Ministers,* pp. 15-19, 31). In this letter she spoke of:

1. *God's supreme regard for His church*

"I testify to my brethren and sisters that the church of Christ, enfeebled and defective as it may be, is the only object on earth on which He bestows His supreme regard. While He extends to all the world His invitation to come to Him and be saved, He commissions His angels to render divine help to every soul that cometh to Him in repentance and contrition, and He comes personally by His Holy Spirit into the midst of His church."

2. *The church as His own fortress in this world*

"Consider, my brethren and sisters, that the Lord has a people, a chosen people, His church, to be His own, His own fortress, which He holds in a sin-stricken, revolted world; and He intended that no authority should be known in it, no laws be acknowledged by it, but His own."

3. *The large confederacy of Satan—his church*

"Satan has a large confederacy, his church. Christ calls them the synagogue of Satan because the members are the children of sin. The members of Satan's church have been constantly working to cast off the divine law, and confuse the distinction between good and evil. Satan is working with great power in and through the children of disobedience to exalt treason and apostasy as truth and loyalty. And at this time the power of his satanic inspiration is moving the living agencies to carry out the great rebellion against God that commenced in heaven."

4. *The beautiful church robed for final conflict against the enemy*

"At this time the church is to put on her beautiful garments— 'Christ our righteousness.' There are clear, decided distinctions to be restored and exemplified to the world in holding aloft the commandments of God and the faith of Jesus. The beauty of holiness is to appear in its native luster in contrast with the deformity and darkness of the disloyal, those who have revolted from the law of God. Thus we acknowledge God, and recognize His law, the foundation of His government in heaven and throughout His earthly dominions.

"His authority should be kept distinct and plain before the world; and no laws are to be acknowledged that come in collision with the laws of Jehovah. If in defiance of God's arrangements the world be allowed to influence our decisions or our actions, the purpose of God is defeated. However specious the pretext, if the church waver here, there is written against her in the books of heaven a betrayal of the most sacred trusts, and treachery to the kingdom of Christ. The church is firmly and decidedly to hold her principles before the whole heavenly universe and the kingdoms of the world. . . . The church is to be fed with manna from heaven, and to be kept under the sole guardianship of His grace. Clad in complete armor of light and righteousness, she enters upon her final conflict."

5. *Ample facilities for the church*

"To His church, Christ has given ample facilities, that He may receive a large revenue of glory from His redeemed, purchased possession. The church, being endowed with the righteousness of Christ, is His depository, in which the wealth of His mercy, His love, His grace, is to appear in full and final display. The declaration in His intercessory prayer, that the Father's love is as great toward us as toward Himself, the only-begotten Son, and that we shall be with Him where He is, forever one with Christ and the Father, is a marvel to the heavenly host, and it is their great joy. The gift of His Holy Spirit, rich, full, and abundant, is to be to His church as an encompassing wall of fire, which the powers of hell shall not prevail against. In their untainted purity and spotless perfection, Christ looks upon His people as the reward of all

228

His suffering, His humiliation, and His love, and the supplement of His glory—Christ, the great center from which radiates all glory. 'Blessed are they which are called unto the marriage supper of the Lamb.' "

6. *Confidence in the church and its Leader*

In reviewing our past history, having traveled over every step of advance to our present standing, I can say, Praise God! As I see what God has wrought, I am filled with astonishment, and with confidence in Christ as leader. We have nothing to fear for the future except as we shall forget the way the Lord has led us.

We are now a strong people, if we will put our trust in the Lord; for we are handling the mighty truths of the word of God. We have everything to be thankful for. If we walk in the light as it shines upon us from the living oracles of God, we shall have large responsibilities, corresponding to the great light given us of God.

These words, written a scarce four years after the Minneapolis Conference, are indeed significant. Whatever may have taken place there did not for a moment discourage Ellen White. "We have everything to be thankful for," she declared.

During this same year, 1893, Sister White furnished for the *Review and Herald* a number of articles in which she sounded solemn warnings against those who were bringing false charges against God's remnant church.* The Spirit of prophecy pointed out the false and misleading positions set forth by those who were teaching that God's remnant people constitute Babylon. Faithfully the Lord's messenger told of God's tender regard for His church. In fascinating language she portrayed Christ's love for His church, His labors to purify it from sin, and His operations in leading it in the great task of giving His last message to a perishing world. The Lord's assurance was given that the remnant people of God would triumph at last.

So we can see that God did not at any time during the stormy period of crisis following the Minneapolis meeting of 1888 regard His remnant church as Babylon. On the contrary, He regarded it

---

* Republished in full in *Testimonies to Ministers*, pp. 19-23, 32-62.

then, as He still does and always will, [as she wrote in 1902]; as the most precious thing in all the world—"the only object on earth on which Christ bestows His supreme regard."—*Selected Messages*, book 2, p. 396.

During the last fifteen years of Ellen White's life the thought that the Seventh-day Adventist Church was the object of Christ's supreme regard was repeated again and again:

"I am instructed to say to Seventh-day Adventists the world over, God has called us as a people to be a peculiar treasure unto Himself. He has appointed that His church on earth shall stand perfectly united in the Spirit and counsel of the Lord of hosts to the end of time."—Letter 54, 1908.

"Nothing in this world is so dear to God as His church."—Letter 136, 1910; in *Selected Messages,* book 2, p. 397.

Significantly and confidently, Ellen White wrote of the church on May 6, 1907:

"While there have been fierce contentions in the effort to maintain our distinctive character, yet we have as Bible Christians ever been on gaining ground."—Letter 170, 1907; in *Selected Messages,* book 2, pp. 396, 397.

How can anyone in the face of this history and unequivocal statements from the pen of Sister White that we have presented, assert that she indicated that God had forsaken the leadership of His people? The very purpose of God in sending messages to His church is often overlooked, and that which should constitute the strongest basis for confidence by some is used as the means of undermining confidence. The fact that God sent messages of warning and reproof indicated clearly that He had His hand on the work.

The fact that to the close of her life Ellen White continued her connection with the organization, bearing many messages of counsel, encouragement, instruction, and reproof to the leaders is another indication that the messages given were not intended to signify that the Lord had left the movement. Recalling that in the very heart of the message to the Laodicean church are the words, "As many as I love, I rebuke and chasten," we see the acceptance of light followed by God's rich blessing.

We conclude this chapter with a brief expression of confidence found in Ellen G. White's last messages addressed to the General Conference in session. This was in 1913, and unable to attend, Ellen White wrote her message to the delegates:

"I am encouraged and blessed as I realize that the God of Israel is still guiding His people, and that He will continue to be with them, even to the end."—*General Conference Bulletin,* May 27, 1913; in *Selected Messages,* book 2, p. 406.

CHAPTER TWENTY-TWO

Rumblings of Opposition After 1901

THE opposition to the message of righteousness by faith and to Elders Jones and Waggoner which took shape in Minneapolis in 1888 and which was carried into some areas of the field, gradually subsided within a few years. The historical record makes this clear. It is apparent also that many of those who at first had been foremost objectors, both at the denominational headquarters in Battle Creek and elsewhere, sincerely confessed their mistake and thereafter supported the message by their own personal witness of Christian realities. Others, having persisted in their hostility, became separated from their brethren and from the work of God, and some of the recalcitrants separated from the church altogether.

Faithful Stephen Haskell, in a letter to Ellen G. White written April 22, 1894, spoke of the necessity which demanded that her "influence uphold Eld. Waggoner and A. T. Jones for these number of years." Continuing, he explained that "this was absolutely necessary." Then he went on to say, significantly, "The whole country has been silenced against criticizing them to any extent. That battle has been fought, and the victory gained."

This was the testimony of a man who had taken the right position all the way through and who judged the years intervening between 1888 and 1894 as years of conflict and finally with "the victory gained."

It would be too much, though, to say that the victory was complete, that every man, woman, and child was converted, that every minister and layman was won over to complete and lasting surrender to God, that there was a total church-wide renewal of spiritual life in Christ Jesus, our Lord.

This was not the case after 1888, nor was it so after 1901, nor has it ever been the case in the experience of the church up until now. Human nature being what it is, it would be natural for the battle to be fought over and over again, individually and collectively. It is so even today, for it is this constant faith in Jesus exercised while we live in the flesh that constitutes the struggle of the Christian life. It is the humbling of human nature, the acceptance of the divine element of strength. Indeed, Ellen White wrote in 1894 to A. R. Henry: "The only true knowledge of the message of the righteousness of Christ, the only true test, is personal acceptance of it."—Letter 31a, 1894.

In answer to the question, "What is justification by faith?" she declared:

"It is the work of God in laying the glory of man in the dust, and doing for man that which it is not in his power to do for himself. When men see their own nothingness, they are prepared to be clothed with the righteousness of Christ."—*Review and Herald,* Sept. 16, 1902, p. 5.

Two years after Minneapolis the servant of God got at the heart of the problem when she spoke of righteousness by faith as "experimental knowledge." "Our hope is to be constantly strengthened by the knowledge that Christ is our righteousness" (*Testimonies,* vol. 5, p. 742). This represents day-by-day renewal of faith in God.

And there were many then who were not thus renewed. In the year 1904 Ellen White wrote as follows:

"In the lives of many of those whose names are on the church books there has been no genuine change. The truth has been kept in the outer court. There has been no genuine conversion, no positive work of grace done in the heart. Their desire to do God's will is based upon their own inclination, not upon the deep conviction of the Holy Spirit. Their conduct is not brought into harmony with the law of God. They profess to accept Christ as their Saviour, but they do not believe that He will give them power to overcome their sins. They have not a personal acquaintance with a living Saviour, and their characters reveal many blemishes."—*Review and Herald,* July 7, 1904, p. 7.

So in the matter of this delicate personal experience of righteousness by faith in which it is so easy imperceptibly to backslide, it can be said that victory is final only when life itself is done. And in any review of the situation in the Seventh-day Adventist Church since 1888 or 1901, it is necessary to keep these facts clearly in mind.

As we now examine the historical record and look at the General Conference sessions, we see that except for the meeting of 1888, righteousness by faith was not an issue in the great gatherings of the church. The doctrine was understood to be part of the third angel's message. Bible studies on this subject were presented again and again at large Seventh-day Adventist gatherings. In the 1901 meeting the committee members elected at that time were, as far as we can discover, men who fully believed in this doctrine, though some may not have entered fully into the personal experience of surrender and faith.

In order to obtain as accurate a picture as possible of the situation after 1901 we have consulted the Ellen G. White letter and manuscript files and have read hundreds of letters written by Mrs. White to denominational leaders, field and institutional workers, and lay members from that time until the time of her death in 1915.

We have also surveyed carefully the stream of letters from the pen of A. G. Daniells, General Conference president from 1901 till 1922, to the Elmshaven office in California. Some of these letters were addressed to Sister White and others to her son, W. C. White, who was a member of the General Con-

234

ference Committee, and who had been for many years one of Elder Daniells' chief counselors.

In addition to examining all of this valuable correspondence we have gone through the periodical files of the church and have consulted still other sources of information.

In this searching inquiry not only have we observed some negative attitudes, but we have found many heartening indications of full acceptance. In all of this voluminous material we have found only three references to any active opposition to the blessed truth of righteousness by faith. These references, all of which are confined to the early part of the period in question, and which were concerned mostly with local manifestations, we shall now consider, as follows:

1. A 1902 letter addressed to the "Dear Brethren and Sisters of the Iowa Conference." In this message Ellen White said:

"I am sorry that so many are doubtful in regard to justification by faith, and that some are standing in opposition to the light that God has given on this subject. . . .

"Christ's righteousness has been misrepresented by some in positions of responsibility, who, supposing they were doing God's service, have done things which show that they are spiritually blind. Men have been overbearing and imperious in spirit, and their wrong course of action, their lack of principle, will cause them to be denounced by the Lord as surely as the Pharisees were denounced. The woes that fell on the Pharisees will as verily fall on all who are engaged in a *like* work, unless they repent. . . .

"My dear brethren and sisters in Iowa, determine to reveal Christ's righteousness more fully than you have revealed it in the past; determine to show that you are not of this world, but of the kingdom of heaven. You are in danger of losing a rich experience. Will you not cultivate the grace of Christ in your hearts? Let not selfishness, springing from self-love, separate you from one another and from God. Bind yourselves to one another by the cords of Christian benevolence. If faithful you will hear from the Saviour's lips the words, 'Well done, thou good and faithful servant: . . . enter thou into the joy of thy Lord.' "—Letter 134, 1902.

This searching letter had the desired effect. I can testify from personal knowledge that the opposition soon disappeared. Not long after this incident I became a minister in the Minnesota Conference, just across the northern boundary of the Iowa Conference. Both of these conferences belonged to the same union conference, and I had the privilege of attending a union session and some workers' meetings in Iowa, and became well acquainted with all of our workers in that prosperous State. In my association with these dedicated Christian men I never heard one of them, either in a meeting or in a private conversation, utter a single word against the doctrine of righteousness by faith. It was no longer an issue.

2. In January and February of the year 1902 three articles dealing with the book of Galatians, written by William Brickley, a layman of Kimball, Minnesota, appeared in the *Review and Herald* and created some agitation. A. G. Daniells wrote of this in a letter to George I. Butler, dated April 11, 1902:

"Just before the Week of Prayer a series of articles appeared from one Brother Brickley, on Galatians. They were openly and squarely against the message that came to this people at Minneapolis and that has been embraced by thousands of our people and openly and repeatedly endorsed by the Spirit of prophecy. These articles have caused a great deal of trouble and dissatisfaction among our brethren in different States.

"Many of our ministers were perfectly astonished that the *Review* would publish them. They could not believe that they had been read by the editor, and so wrote him. Some of them gave due warning that if the *Review* continued to publish such theology it would be necessary for the State conference committees to take their stand against the *Review,* and use their State papers and other local facilities to place the situation truly and fairly before their brethren. I stand in a position to know that serious injury has been wrought by those articles. And I know that the *Review* could not stand with our brethren if it continued that course."

Three days later Elder Daniells wrote W. C. White a letter in which he passed on to him similar information. He also mentioned the fact that in a personal interview with Uriah Smith he had raised the question of how these unfortunate articles were permitted to get into the paper.

If the reader is tempted to pass judgment upon Elder Smith for having permitted the publication of these articles, he would do well to remember that he was nearing the end of his life (he died March 6, 1903) and that because of his rapidly failing health he was unable to spend much time in the office to oversee his work.

3. In a letter of April 14, 1902, to W. C. White, Elder Daniells wrote a brief paragraph about a situation he had found in the Northwest. This paragraph reads as follows:

"I feel somewhat concerned about this matter. I am surprised to find scattered all through these Northwestern States men who are deep in the fog over this question. As surely as we live, they are still under the old covenant, the covenant of works. Matthew Larsen seems to be the leader of this faction. He is traveling about wherever he can, sowing this evil seed. Not only the older men who were at work when Brother Butler, Brother Morrison, and others fought this battle, but some of the younger fellows who are coming on, have imbibed these old heresies from the men in the field who are still unconverted to this new light."

About a month after writing the lines just quoted, Elder Daniells wrote another letter to W. C. White, dated May 12, 1902, and referred again to the same situation as follows:

"I am deeply convinced that something ought to be done to place a flood of light in the homes of our people. I know of no better book to do this, outside of the Bible, than Brother Waggoner's book."

The book to which Elder Daniells alluded was *The Everlasting Covenant,* by J. H. Waggoner. It would appear from this that the main issue at that time and in that part of the field was over the covenants. This issue had also been one of the bones of contention in Minneapolis in 1888.

How many copies of Elder Waggoner's book may have

been distributed, and what else may have been done to fill the homes and hearts of the workers and members with light, we do not know, but whatever was done must have been done effectively, for in all our searching we have not found in any letter or paper any mention of any further opposition in that section of the field or in any other part of the wide world.

During my fifty-five years in the Seventh-day Adventist ministry I have come in contact with our workers and members all around the world. I have associated with our ministers in nearly every land where our work is established. I have heard them preach, listened to their theological discussions, eaten at their gracious tables, and slept in their friendly homes. I have attended Adventist camp meetings, annual meetings, conference and mission sessions, workers' meetings, and other gatherings, and I can truthfully say that in all this association with church workers and people of different races, nations, and tongues, I have never heard a worker or a lay member—in America, Europe, or anywhere else—express opposition to the message of righteousness by faith. Neither have I known of any such opposition having been expressed by Seventh-day Adventist publications.

So much at least for the negative side of the historical picture. And in the manner in which church leaders came to grips with the negative teachings, we see a strong, continuing support for the positive.

CHAPTER TWENTY-THREE

To Prepare the Way
of the Lord

WE NOW turn from the negative to the positive. What are the facts on the affirmative front? Has the truth regarding righteousness by faith been fully received and proclaimed by Seventh-day Adventists during the decades that have passed since the 1901 General Conference session? Perhaps the whole truth could be told in the context of A. W. Spalding's observations on the constant challenge and demands and conflicts developed by this teaching:

"The eighties and the nineties saw the revival and restatement in power of the indispensable, prime doctrine of Christianity, that justification and sanctification are through the reception of Christ in the life. That teaching was sorely needed then; and even though sent through imperfect channels, it became an inspiring message which rescued the church from the danger of legalism, and opened minds to the sublime reaches of the gospel. The last decade of the century saw the church developing, through this gospel, into a company prepared to fulfill the mission of God." —*Origin and History*, vol. 2, pp. 302, 303.

So it is correct to say that the message has been declared, both from the pulpit and through the press, and by the lives of thousands upon thousands of God's dedicated people who have learned the result of spiritual life in Christ. Anyone who takes the time to examine Seventh-day Adventist books, papers, pamphlets, and tracts will discover that this glorious truth has been printed time and time again. To illustrate this I turn first to representative books by Ellen G. White. We would note first of all that Mrs. White in setting forth this simple basic gospel truth, did not devote a book solely to this topic. In an 1893 pamphlet, "Justified by Faith," she presented the subject clearly and well. See *Selected Messages,* volume 1, pages 389-398. But in most of her books the doctrine is dealt with in one form or another, and these books have been sold by the hundreds of thousands throughout the world.

The monumental book *The Great Controversy,* the 1888 edition, which was published six months before the Minneapolis meeting, constitutes a most dramatic theological presentation on righteousness by faith because it is told largely in the setting of Reformation history and therefore highlights the sharp conflict between Rome's pernicious doctrine of salvation by works and Luther's glorious proclamation of the Pauline teaching of justification through faith in Christ alone. The 1911 edition of the same book by Ellen White continues to proclaim this central teaching of the gospel in more than thirty languages.

In the year 1892 *Steps to Christ* appeared. More than 24 million copies of this book have been printed in a total of eighty-four languages. This volume is the most widely circulated and the most frequently translated of Mrs. White's books, and it is only one of a long list of her works containing this precious truth of righteousness by faith. All the following books from the Spirit of prophecy present the Bible teaching of righteousness by faith in Christ. The list is only partial, and we mentioned books already alluded to in chapter five:

> *Testimonies for the Church,* in nine volumes (1855-1909)
>
> *Bible Sanctification,* now *The Sanctified Life* (1881 and 1889)
>
> *The Great Controversy* (1888)
>
> *Patriarchs and Prophets* (1890)
>
> *Steps to Christ* (1892)
>
> *Thoughts From the Mount of Blessing* (1894)

The Desire of Ages (1898)
Christ's Object Lessons (1900)
The Acts of the Apostles (1911)
Gospel Workers (1915)
Prophets and Kings (1917)
Testimonies to Ministers and Gospel Workers (1923)
Selected Messages, book 1 (1958)

Representative books by Seventh-day Adventist authors that have issued from denominational presses in North America—not to mention those published in other lands—and that have dealt with the subject of righteousness by faith, are many. We shall mention only a few:

Daniel and the Revelation, by Uriah Smith
Bible Readings for the Home Circle, a compilation.
The Coming of the Comforter, by L. E. Froom
The Way to Christ, by W. H. Branson
Our Firm Foundation (in two volumes), by a group
Drama of the Ages, by W. H. Branson
The Seventh-day Adventist Bible Commentary (in seven volumes)
How Men Are Saved, by W. H. Branson
Christ Our Righteousness, by A. G. Daniells*
By Faith Alone, by Norval F. Pease
Fruitage of Spiritual Gifts, by L. H. Christian
Origin and History of the Seventh-day Adventist Church, by A. W. Spalding
Seventh-day Adventists Answer Questions on Doctrine, by a group
His Cross and Mine, by Meade MacGuire
What Jesus Said, by H. M. S. Richards
Preachers of Righteousness, by R. A. Anderson

---

* This book was written in response to an action of the members of the Ministerial Association Advisory Council held in Des Moines, Iowa, October 22, 1924.

In certain of these books only a few paragraphs deal with the subject of righteousness by faith, but in others whole chapters are devoted to it, and in some instances the entire book is consecrated to the great theme of salvation through Christ—a theme that embraces the glorious truth of righteousness by faith.

In the periodical files of the church many articles dealing with the doctrine of righteousness by faith appear from the pens of a number of authors. Most of these articles appear under such titles as "Justification by Faith," "Sanctification by Faith," "Redemption," "How Men Are Saved," "The Plan of Salvation," "Christ Our Righteousness," "The Righteousness of the Saints," "The Wedding Garment," "The Law and the Gospel," "The Law and Grace," et cetera. Many of these excellent statements are from the pen of Ellen White, for as long as she lived, an article from her pen appeared nearly every week in the *Review and Herald* and the *Signs of the Times,* and often in the *Instructor,* and sometimes in the union papers. In most of these articles some phase of the message of righteousness by faith shines forth to instruct and gladden the reader.

Wrote Elder A. G. Daniells in 1926:

"In harmony with the primary purpose of providing a 'compilation of the writings of Mrs. E. G. White on the subject,' exhaustive research was made through all the writings of the Spirit of prophecy as held in trust by us as a people, in bound volumes and also in printed articles appearing in the files of our denominational papers, covering a period of twenty-five years from 1887 to 1912. So vast was the field of study opened up, so marvelous and illuminating the hidden gems of truth which came to light, that I became amazed and awed at the solemn obligation resting upon me, of rescuing these gems from their obscurity, and placing them, in a cluster of brilliancy and beauty, where they would win rightful recognition and acceptance in the glorious finishing of the work entrusted to the remnant church."—*Christ Our Righteousness,* 1941 ed., p. 5.

Through the years since 1901 and before, Seventh-day Adventists have published numerous tracts on righteousness by faith, and from time to time this theme has been covered in Sabbath school lessons. The various phases of salvation through faith in Christ have been taught with power and clarity over the radio for a number of years and more recently on television. This subject has been made prominent in different courses of Bible correspondence lessons. Adventist pastors and evangelists have announced this vital truth from church pulpits and public platforms, with hearts aflame with love for Christ. And through the monthly journal, *The Ministry*, Seventh-day Adventist preachers and writers have constantly been urged to make Jesus Christ and His righteousness as the Saviour, the center of all their teaching.

This emphasis has not been more prominent than the importance of the subject merits. If anything, it has not been so great as this precious theme deserves.

Many Seventh-day Adventists still seem ignorant of this all-important doctrine. Much of this lack of awareness results from their failure to read Adventist books and periodicals presenting the gospel in clear, forceful language. As an instance we would cite a series of seven editorials by D. A. Delafield, dealing with righteousness by faith, which appeared in 1950 in the *Review and Herald*. We quote from the opening article:

"The greatest deception that has ever fastened itself upon the human mind is that righteousness consists of the profession of religion and participation in public and private forms of worship. God had instructed the Jews in certain acts of worship which were given to encourage faith in the plan of salvation, but these were not intended to be the sum and substance of religious experience.

"Religious forms might serve to add shape and beauty to the true worship of God, as the skeleton and muscles add form and grace to the human figure. Yet they can never provide spiritual life any more than the bones and muscle can supply life and energy to the body. To find true life and power, every believer must look outside of himself and outside of the forms of his religion to Christ and His righteousness, in which alone salvation from sin can be found.

"It is difficult for the heart of man to see and understand its deep spiritual poverty and its need for genuine heart religion. Unconsciously we feel 'too wise to need instruction, too righteous to need salvation, too highly honored to need the honor that comes from Christ.'—*The Desire of Ages,* p. 279.

"This self-righteousness is a common and a grave danger to spiritual life in our time, when religion is marked by the form without the power as much as in the days when the Pharisees confronted Christ with the question about fasting.

"If we are to receive the new wine and become partakers of the righteousness of Christ, we must, first of all, become new bottles. This suggests complete surrender of ourselves to God and change of heart and mind. It is the only way to a holy life and it is the place to begin.

"We are told: 'In order to obtain the righteousness of Christ, it is necessary for the sinner to know what that repentance is which works a radical change of mind and spirit and action. The work of transformation must begin in the heart, and manifest its power through every faculty of the being; but man is not capable of originating such a repentance as this, and can experience it alone through Christ, who ascended up on high, led captivity captive, and gave gifts unto men. . . .

" 'He who would become a child of God must receive the truth that repentance and forgiveness are to be obtained through nothing less than the atonement of Christ. Assured of this the sinner must put forth an effort in harmony with the work done for him, and with unwearied entreaty he must supplicate the throne of grace, that the renovating power of God may come into his soul. Christ pardons none but the penitent, but whom He pardons He first makes penitent. The provision made is complete, and the eternal righteousness of Christ is placed to the account of every believing soul.'—ELLEN G. WHITE, *Justified by Faith* (tract), pp. 8, 9.

"By faith we may come to the Saviour with our load of selfishness and find pardon and a new life."—*Review and Herald,* May 4, 1950, p. 3.

We fear that to many church members the message of righteousness by faith has become a dry theory instead of a living reality in their daily experience.

They have neglected the light that God in His love and mercy has caused to shine upon them. They have failed to exchange the worthless garments of their own self-righteousness for the spotless robe of Christ's righteousness. In the sight of God their poor souls are naked and destitute. Unless they heed the counsel of the True Witness to buy of Him the white raiment, that the shame of their nakedness may not appear, they will soon be rejected by their Lord.

What we need today is a trumpet blast that will awaken us all to the solemn and imperative necessity of constantly being covered with the immaculate robe of Christ's righteousness. Wrote Ellen White:

"The thought that the righteousness of Christ is imputed to us, not because of any merit on our part, but as a free gift from God, is a precious thought."—*Gospel Workers*, p. 161.

"The sweetest melodies that come from God through human lips . . . [are] justification by faith, and the righteousness of Christ. —*Testimonies*, vol. 6, p. 426.

"The righteousness of Christ, as a pure white pearl, has no defect, no stain, no guilt. This righteousness may be ours."—*Review and Herald*, Aug. 8, 1899, p. 501.

However—

"The enemy of God and man is not willing that this truth should be clearly presented, for he knows that *if the people receive it fully, his power will be broken.*"—*Gospel Workers*, p. 161. (Italics supplied.)

But there will be an awakening such as the church has never known before—a spiritual resurrection from death in trespasses and sins. To know, as Ellen White and other pioneers knew, the sweetness and charms of Jesus' love is to know what is essential for the church in this last hour. This is the third angel's message. Wrote A. G. Daniells:

"A serious question arose in the minds of some who heard the message of Righteousness by Faith presented at the Minneapolis Conference, as to the relation that message bore to the third angel's message. In their perplexity, a number wrote to Mrs. E. G. White for an expression of her views on this question.

"Regarding this inquiry and her reply, we have her published statement, as follows:

" 'Several have written to me, inquiring if the message of justification by faith is the third angel's message, and I have answered, "It is the third angel's message in verity." '—*Review and Herald*, April 1, 1890.

"There is more in this statement than a brief, clear, positive answer to a question. It has a deep, vital meaning. It sounds a serious warning, and makes an intelligent, earnest appeal to every believer in the third angel's message. . . .

"Justification by faith, it is affirmed, is 'the third angel's message in verity.' The words 'in verity' mean, *in fact, in reality, in very truth.* That means that the message of justification by faith and the third angel's message are the same in purpose, in scope, and in results."—*Christ Our Righteousness* (1941 ed.), p. 64.

Declared Ellen White:

"Justification by faith and the righteousness of Christ are the themes to be presented to a perishing world."—Letter 24, 1892.

Seventh-day Adventists must proclaim these glorious truths to people everywhere today—just before Christ appears with "power and great glory"—for with prophetic insight wrote the messenger of the Lord:

"The message of Christ's righteousness is to sound from one end of the earth to the other to prepare the way of the Lord. This is the glory of God, which closes the work of the third angel."—*Testimonies*, vol. 6, p. 19.

"There will be no future probation in which to prepare for eternity. It is in this life that we are to put on the robe of Christ's righteousness. This is our only opportunity to form characters for the home which Christ has made ready for those who obey His commandments."—*Christ's Object Lessons*, p. 319.

"Only those who are clothed in the garments of His righteousness will be able to endure the glory of His presence when He shall appear with 'power and great glory.' "—*Review and Herald,* July 9, 1908, p. 8.

Wrote Elder Daniells:

"In its truest sense, righteousness by faith is not a *theory;* it is an *experience,* a vital change which takes place in the believer in Christ. It gives the sinner a new standing before God. It is the essence of Christianity, for we read:

" 'The sum and substance of the whole matter of Christian grace and experience is contained in believing on Christ, in knowing God and His Son whom He hath sent.' 'Religion means the abiding of Christ in the heart, and where He is, the soul goes on in spiritual activity, ever growing in grace, ever going on to perfection.' (*Review and Herald,* May 24, 1892.)"—*Christ Our Righteousness,* p. 74.

The work of God in the earth is still unfinished. The finishing touches will be made by God Himself when the last saint is robed in that spotless garment woven in the loom of heaven in which there "is not one thread of human devising." Each of us may wear such a robe and wear it forever.

Ellen G. White
Sermons at Minneapolis

✦✦✦

A Living Connection With God

Morning talk by Ellen G. White
Minneapolis, Minnesota, October 11, 1888

I AM thankful, brethren and sisters, that God has spared me to come to this meeting. I have been sick nigh unto death; but prayer was offered by those assembled at the Oakland camp meeting, and the Lord heard them. It was not by my faith, for I had none, but they exercised faith in my behalf, and the Lord gave me strength to bear my testimony to the people in Oakland, and then I started, as it were, at a venture to come on this journey. I had but one sinking spell on the way, but the Lord helped me, and when we reached Kansas City I went out to the campground where they were holding their meeting and spoke to the people. In this I realize and know that the Lord has strengthened me, and He shall have all the glory.

Now as we have assembled here we want to make the most of our time. I have thought again and again that if we would only make the most of the precious opportunities God has given us, they would do us so much more good; but we too often let them slip away, and we do not realize that benefit from them which we should.

My mind has been directed to the words of the apostle Paul. He says, in the twentieth of Acts, beginning with verse 17: "And from Miletus he sent to Ephesus, and called the elders of the church. And when they were come to him, he said unto them, Ye know, from the first day that I came into Asia, after what manner I have been with you at all seasons, serving the Lord with all humility of mind, and with many tears, and temptations, which befell me by the lying in wait of the Jews: and how I kept back nothing that was profitable unto you, but have shewed you, and have taught you publickly, and from house to house, testifying both to the Jews, and also to the Greeks, repentance toward God, and faith toward our Lord Jesus Christ."

I have thought again and again, brethren and sisters, if we were Bible believers as well as Bible readers, and would carry out just what God has given us, we would be far better than we are at the present time.

But we do not realize that it is the loving voice of God speaking to us from His Word. We are to think everything of it and take it home to our hearts. Then Paul goes on to say, in verse 24, "Neither count I my life dear unto myself, so that I might finish my course with joy, and the ministry, which I have received of the Lord Jesus, to testify the gospel of the grace of God." "Wherefore I take you to record this day, that I am pure from the blood of all men. For I have not shunned to declare unto you all the counsel of God" (verses 26, 27). What a testimony is that— "free from the blood of all men."

Now here is the exhortation: "Take heed therefore unto yourselves, and to all the flock, over the which the Holy Ghost hath made you overseers, to feed the church of God, which he hath purchased with his own blood." Now what is the necessity of watching them? Why says he, "For I know this, that after my departing shall grievous wolves enter in among you, not sparing the flock" (verses 28, 29).

Brethren, if we would be [in earnest] the power of the Holy Ghost would attend our efforts, and we would see a different state of things among us. We are placed in trust with the most solemn truths ever committed to mortals, but the course of some is of such a character that God cannot answer their prayers. Their prayers are offensive to His holiness, and should He hear and answer their prayers they would be confirmed in a wrong course, and others would be led away from the straight paths. Why cannot we take the truth God has revealed and weave it into our very life and character? If we have the spirit of Christ in our hearts we will have a burden for the perishing souls around us as Paul had, and we will leave such an impression upon the young men and women who claim to believe the truth that they will feel that there are important responsibilities resting upon them. They will feel that their faith must be increased and that they must take up the work lying directly in their pathway, and be a blessing to others—humble, diligent, obedient; and when they meet their associates it will be to talk of Jesus. They will carry Jesus into their homes and testify to all of His mercy.

If Christ is formed within, the hope of glory, you will put away all vanity and foolish speaking. You will be sanctified through the truth. You will so labor for God that you can have an approving conscience in your ministerial work, and you can say with the devoted Saint Paul that you are clean from the blood of all men. But you cannot say this unless you are constantly gaining wisdom and knowledge from God as the branch draws nourishment from the living vine, unless His Holy Spirit is resting upon you and you are taking Jesus into your heart, thinking and talking of Jesus, and doing His work wherever you are. This is the only way that we can work successfully in these last times. Christ was Himself the example we should follow, not merely in outward form, but as He was in purity, self-denial, meekness, and love. So we

249

should follow Him in the world. His humiliation, His reproach, His crucifixion, and His cross He gave to His disciples. He also gave to them the glory that was given Him. He said, "He that believeth on me, the works that I do shall he do also; and greater works than these shall he do; because I go unto my Father."

Brethren, it is a positive necessity that we come up to a higher and holier standard. We must meet the difficulties in our Christian warfare as Paul met them when the Jews were lying in wait for him. We shall have to come through trying places, for there will be spies watching on our track and lying in wait for us. We shall not only be brought before councils, but we shall be thrust into prison, and we must be in that advanced position of faith that we shall know God and the power of His grace, where we can lift up holy hands to Him without wrath and doubting; and we must learn how to believe that God hears us.

I know that God hears the prayers of His people. I know that He answers them. But He cannot bless us while we are cherishing selfishness; and what saith the Scriptures? "If I regard iniquity in my heart, the Lord will not hear me." But if we put away all self-exaltation, all self-righteousness, and come into living connection with God, the righteousness of God will be imputed to us. "As far as the east is from the west, so far hath he removed our transgressions from us."

The wisdom from above is abiding with us just so surely as we ask Him for it. The Lord has not forsaken us, but it is our sins and our iniquities that have separated us from God. We want in the name of Jesus to break down the barriers between our souls and God and then the peace of Christ will abide in our hearts by faith. We want to present ourselves in all humility before God, and get rid of everything like pride, selfishness, evil surmising, evil speaking, and all iniquity. Jesus will not take His abode in the heart where sin is enthroned. We want less of self and more of Jesus. We want to learn how to believe—that it is simply taking God at His word—but it is impossible to learn this unless we place ourselves in that position where we will be submissive to God. Our will must be on God's side, not on the side of Satan. The result of proving the forgiving love of God is to be perfectly reconciled to God's will. Then the human will and the divine become united. Every faculty must be kept in its place, all consecrated to God; every faculty working in God's order, performing His will and purpose.

We need not feel anxious and troubled, as though the work was in our hands alone to manage. The Lord is standing at the helm. The Infinite has His hand on the machinery. If we humbly do our work with fidelity, the Lord will take care of the results. Have faith in God. This faith will enable us to have perfect trust and to look upon every movement in God's own light. Nothing that is taking place or that can take place need to excite in us fearful apprehensions, for God the great Master

Worker has charge of His own work; and if man will not interfere, but leave the work to God's own control, He will do this work well. Now, Christ would have you who minister in sacred things to be holy as He is holy. Do not forget that your power is in God. Be sure that if God has called you to open His Word to the people, He has called you to purity and goodness.

You should have a clear apprehension of the gospel. The religious life is not one of gloom and of sadness, but of peace and joy coupled with Christlike dignity and holy solemnity. We are not encouraged by our Saviour to cherish doubts and fears and distressing forebodings; these bring no relief to the soul and should be rebuked rather than praised. We may have joy unspeakable and full of glory. Let us put away our indolence and study God's Word more constantly. If we ever needed the Holy Ghost to be with us, if we ever needed to preach in the demonstration of the Spirit, it is at this very time. If we will not work without it now, we shall have it in every emergency in the future, and be prepared for what is coming upon the earth. We need to dwell more upon present truth and the preparation essential in order that sinners may be saved. If the Spirit of God works with our efforts, we shall be called out not only to present repentance in its true light but pardon also, and to point to the cleansing fountain where all pollution may be washed away.

We have a far more solemn work resting upon us in preaching the gospel of Christ than we have imagined. If we have the truth abiding in the heart, we shall be growing up to the full stature of men and women in Christ Jesus. Let us think of these things more earnestly. Let there be no more cramping of the intellect. There are greater wonders to be opened to our senses, consistent with the progress of the work. The mystery of revelation challenges investigation, for there are mines of truth to be opened to God's people. We must put off self-righteousness, we must reach loftier heights. God will direct the soul action if we seek the righteousness of Christ so that God can be pleased with our efforts. We want none of self and all of Jesus. The baptism of the Holy Ghost will come upon us at this very meeting if we will have it so. Search for truth as for hidden treasures. The key of knowledge needs to be held in every hand that it may open the storehouse of God's treasury, which contains stores of precious gems of truth. When a man is craving for truth from God's Word, angels of God are by his side to lead his mind into green pastures.

If the truth rested with greater weight upon ministers of God, they would not handle the Word of God deceitfully. They seem to have a burden for souls while speaking to the people, but when out of the desk they are destitute of spirituality. Be afraid of such. They preach but do not practice. They show by their manner that the truth has not sanctified their souls and what they have said has had no weight upon them. God's laborers will carry the burden of souls with them. God will not work with the man who preaches the claims of God in the desk and gives a lie to the truth out of the desk. We want to be clean from the blood of all men, that the blood of souls will not be found upon us, that we can say with Paul, "I am pure from the blood of all men."

Let us commence right here in this meeting and not wait till the meeting is half through. We want the Spirit of God here now; we need it, and we want it to be revealed in our characters. We want the power of God here, and we want it to shine in our hearts. Brethren, let us take hold of the work as never before. Let us inquire, How is it with my soul? Is it in that condition that it will be well with me? Shall Christ come and find me as I now am? May God help us to be clean in spirit, pure and holy in all manner of conversation and godliness.—Manuscript 6, 1888.

+ + +

Tell of God's Love and Power

Sermon by Ellen G. White
Minneapolis, Minnesota, October 13, 1888

Text: "Behold, what manner of love the Father hath bestowed upon us, that we should be called the sons of God: therefore the world knoweth us not, because it knew him not." 1 John 3:1.

(First page of sermon missing)

HOW CAN we understand God? How are we to know our Father? We are to call Him by the endearing name of Father. And how are we to know Him and the power of His love? It is through diligent search of the Scriptures. We cannot appreciate God unless we take into our souls the great plan of redemption. We want to know all about these grand problems of the soul, of the redemption of the fallen race. It is a wonderful thing that after man had violated the law of God and separated himself from God, was divorced, as it were, from God—that after all this there was a plan made whereby man should not perish, but that he should have everlasting life.

After the transgression of Adam in Eden it was Christ whom God gave to us, not that we might be saved in our sins, but that we might be saved from our sins, that we should return to our loyalty to God and become obedient children. As we yield our minds, our souls, our bodies, and our all to the controlling Spirit of God, it is then that the Spirit of truth is with us and we can become intelligent in regard to this great plan of redemption.

It is true that God gave His only-begotten Son to die for us, to suffer the penalty of the [broken] law of God. We are to consider this and dwell upon it. And when our minds are constantly dwelling upon the matchless love of God to the fallen race, we begin to know God, to become acquainted with Him, to have a knowledge of God, and of how Jesus Christ, when He came to our world, laid aside His royal robes and His kingly crown and clothed His divinity with humanity. For our sakes He became poor that we through His poverty might be made rich. The Father sent His Son here, and right here on this little atom of a world were enacted the grandest scenes that were ever known to humanity.

All the universe of heaven was looking on with intense interest. Why? The great battle was to be fought between the power of darkness and the Prince of light. Satan's work was to magnify his power constantly. Where was his power? He claimed to be the prince of the world and he exercised his power over the inhabitants of the world. Satan's power was exercised in such a masterly manner that they would not acknowledge God. Satan wanted that the children of men should get such an idea of his wonderful work that they would talk of his masterly power. In doing this he was all the time placing God in a false light. He was presenting Him as a God of injustice, and not a God of mercy. He was constantly stirring up their minds so that they would have an incorrect view of God.

How was God to be rightly represented to the world? How was it to be known that He was a God of love, full of mercy, kindness, and pity? How was the world to know this? God sent His Son, and He was to represent to the world the character of God.

Satan has come right in and placed himself between God and man. It is his work to divert the human mind, and he throws his dark shadow right athwart our pathways, so that we cannot discern between God and the moral darkness and corruption and the mass of iniquity that is in our world. Then what are we going to do about the matter? Shall we let that darkness remain?—No. There is a power here for us that will bring in the light of heaven to our dark world. Christ has been in heaven and He will bring the light of heaven, drive back the darkness, and let the sunlight of His glory in. Then we shall see, amid the corruption and pollution and defilement, the light of heaven.

We must not give up at the defilement that is in the human race and ever keep that before the mind's eye. We must not look at that. What then are we to do? What is our work?—To behold "what manner of love the Father hath bestowed upon us." Do not let the blighting influences that are flooding the world be the picture that is before the mind, but hold up the purity and love of God. Do not hang in memory's hall pictures of all the corruption and iniquity that you can bundle to-

253

gether. No, do not do it. It discourages the mind. A discouraged man is good for nothing. Just get the mind off these dark pictures by talking of God's love, and you may hang memory's halls with the brightest pictures that you can imagine.

We want to keep the perfect Pattern before us. God was so good as to send a representation of Himself in His Son Jesus Christ, and we want to get the mind and heart to unfold and reach upward. Just as soon as Adam and Eve fell, their countenances fell at the sight of their miserableness. We may see our wretchedness, and we should pray that God will reveal our own hearts to us; but we should pray also that He will reveal Himself to us as a sin-pardoning Redeemer. Let yours be the prayer, Reveal Thyself to me, that in Thy matchless grace I may lay hold on the golden link, Christ, which has been let down from heaven to earth, that I may grasp it and be drawn upward.

Brethren, you have all seen on the bosom of the lake the beautiful white lily. How anxious we have been, how we have wished and worked, that we might get that blossom. No matter how much scum and debris and filth there is around it, yet that does not destroy our desire for the lily. We wonder how the lily can be so beautiful and white where there is so much filth. Well, there is a stem that strikes down to the golden sands beneath and gathers nothing but the purest substance that feeds the lily until it develops into the pure and spotless flower as we see it.

Should not this teach us a lesson? It ought to. It shows that although there is iniquity all around us we should not approach it. Do not talk of the iniquity and wickedness that are in the world, but elevate your minds and talk of your Saviour. When you see iniquity all around you it makes you all the more glad that He is your Saviour, and we are His children. Then, shall we look at the iniquity around us and dwell upon the dark side? You cannot cure it; then talk of something that is higher, better, and more noble. Talk of those things that will leave a good impression on the mind, and will lift every soul up out of this iniquity into the light beyond.

Now, we may go into a cellar and stay there and look around into its dark corners, and we can talk of the darkness and say, "Oh, it is so dark here," and keep talking about it. But will it make it any lighter? Oh no! What are you going to do? Come out of it; come out of the dark into the upper chamber where the light of God's countenance shines brightly.

You know our bodies are made up of the food assimilated. Now, it is the same with our minds. If we have a mind to dwell on the disagreeable things of life, it will not give us any hope, but we want to dwell on the cheery scenes of heaven. Says Paul, "Our light affliction, which is but for a moment, worketh for us a far more exceeding and eternal weight of glory."

While we were in Switzerland I had many letters from a sister whom I dearly love and highly esteem. In every one of these letters were the most gloomy pictures. She seemed to be dwelling on everything objectionable. Soon after I received these letters I prayed the Lord that He would give her help to turn her mind from the channel that it was running in. That night I had a dream presented to me three times. I was walking in a beautiful garden, and Sister Martha ———— was by my side. As soon as she came into the garden I said, "Martha, do you not see this beautiful garden? See, here are the lilies, the roses, and the pinks." "Yes," she said, as she looked up and smiled. Soon I looked to see where she was. I was looking at the lilies, the roses, and the pinks, and did not see her. She was in another part of the garden, and was grasping a thistle. Then she was pricking her hands on the bramblebushes. She said they hurt her hands, and she asked, "Why do they keep all these thistles and these briers in the garden? Why do they let them stay here?"

Then there appeared before us a tall, dignified man who said, "Gather the roses, the lilies, and the pinks; discard the brambles and touch them not." Then I awoke, and when I went to sleep I dreamed the very same thing again. Three times I had the same dream, and I arose—because I could not sleep—and wrote to Sister Martha the dream I had had.

Now, said I, God does not want you to gather up everything objectionable; He wants you to look at His wonderful works and at His purity. He wants you to take a view of His matchless love and His power, to look up through the beauties of nature to nature's God. Said I, This [dream] represents your case exactly. You are dwelling on the dark side. You are talking of those things that give no light and bring no joy into your life. But you must turn your mind from these things to God. There are enough roses, pinks, and lilies in the garden of God's love so that you need not look at the briers, the thistles, and the brambles. Now, I did not see these things, because I was delighting myself with the flowers and all the beauties of the garden.

Now, that is what we want to do, brethren. We want to have our minds on the encouraging things. We want to have our minds on the new country to which we are to be introduced. Our citizenship is not of this world, but it is above, and we want to consider what characters we should possess in order to become inhabitants of that better world and associates of the saints of God in heaven.

Sister Martha took it, and her soul was lifted above discouragement. Now, I do not want Satan to succeed in throwing his dark shadow across your pathway. I want you to get away from that shadow. The Man of Calvary will throw the light of His love across your pathway and dispel the darkness. He is able to do it and will do it, for He is Lord of all. Somebody has thrown His light around you; it is Jesus Christ.

THIRTEEN CRISIS YEARS

I remember when my sister Sarah, now sleeping in the grave, who attended me in my first travels, was in discouragement. She said, "I had a strange dream last night. I dreamed somebody opened the door and I was afraid of him; and as I continued to look at him he increased in size and filled the whole space from the floor to the ceiling, and I continued to grow more and more afraid. Then I thought that I had Jesus, and I said, 'I have Jesus; I am not afraid of you.' Then he began to shrink and shrink until you could scarcely see him, and he went out of the door."

It taught her a lesson. She said, "Ellen, we talk a great deal more of the power of the devil than we have any right to. It pleases him, and his satanic majesty is honored; he exults over it, and we give him honor in doing this; but," she said, "I am going to talk of Jesus, of His love, and tell of His power." And so she brought her soul right out of darkness and discouragement into light, and she bore a living testimony for God and heaven.

Now, I think our testimony would be a great deal better if we talked more of Jesus and His love and did not pay so much honor to the devil. Why should we not do it? Why not let the light of Jesus shine in our hearts?

I remember that when I was in Oakland there was a sister who was in great trouble. She said, "My mother troubles me. My father is a good man; but my mother has her eyes fixed on so many young couples where the husband is disloyal that she seems to think her husband and everyone else is disloyal. I do not know what she will do or drive him to. She thinks he is unfaithful, and she talks of it and dwells upon it till she brings all her misery on the rest of us, as though she were imposed upon, when there is no need of it at all."

Is not this the case with many of us? Do we not dwell on trifles and talk of them till our thoughts are changed to the same similitude? We can drive even our children to do wrong things by accusing them of wrongs of which they are not guilty. While we are to rebuke and exhort in all love, should we not also exalt Jesus and talk of His love?

"Behold, what manner of love the Father hath bestowed upon us, that we should be called the sons of God." It is one of Satan's devices that we should be picking up all these disagreeable things and that our minds should not be dwelling on God and His love. That is what Satan wants, that we should keep our minds occupied with these things of a revolting character that cannot bring peace, joy, and harmony into the life—nothing but discouragement—and that we should not represent Jesus Christ.

Now, Christ left us His work when He went away, and He said, "Lo, I am with you alway, even unto the end of the world." We are not left alone in the hands of the devil. Do you think our heavenly

Father would leave us alone to carry on the work of redemption and bringing up the fallen race, that He would leave us in a world flooded with evil with no help, no support, after He had endured the agonies of the cross? Do you think He will leave us now?—No! Says the Saviour, "Lo, I am with you alway, even unto the end of the world." And again, "If I go away I will come again." "If ye shall ask any thing in my name, I will do it." This is on the condition that we keep His commandments. Is not this a blessed promise? Why do we not talk of it more and praise God for it? Here are the precious promises of the Word of God to us, and why do we not take them?

Now I want to read to you something about this love of God, and what we ought to do in order that we shall bring joy into our own hearts. Paul says, "For this cause we also, since the day we heard it, do not cease to pray for you, and to desire that ye might be filled with the knowledge of his will in all wisdom and spiritual understanding." Not in order that we might have a taste, but that we might be filled. "That ye might walk worthy of the Lord unto all pleasing, being fruitful in every good work, and increasing in the knowledge of God. Strengthened with all might, according to his glorious power, unto all patience and longsuffering with joyfulness."

If we have a sense of the goodness of God in sending His Son to die for sinful man, and if we keep that interwoven into our experience and riveted in the mind, we shall have such love for those for whom Christ died that there will be no [desire for] supremacy. It is Satan that brings in these differences. While we are worshiping God there will be no hatred, no envy, no evil surmising. Brethren, we have no time for these. We cannot think of them. There is something else before us. It is the eternal weight of glory, the plan of salvation. We ought to understand it from beginning to the close, that we may present it justly to the world.

What is our work here? We are to take hold of the work just where Christ left it. What was His work? To reveal the Father to us. What is our work? To reveal Christ to the world. How can we do this? By talking of the devil? Oh no, we have a better work to do. We want to talk of the crucified and risen Saviour. Oh, what a terrible thing it would be for any of us to profess to be followers of Jesus Christ and then make a botch of it, and He find us with characters all stained with defilement. What a fearful responsibility rests upon us! How is Christ to be revealed to the world, unless it is through those who take hold on His merits, who believe in Jesus Christ, to the saving of their souls? He cleanseth me. He cleanseth me from the defilement of sin. And here let the sound be heard of what Christ has done for me. There is liberty for the sons of God. There is a wide place for my feet to stand on, and we may have the fullness of the love of God in our hearts.

I thank God that Christ has died for me and that I have been

257

brought through a terrible ordeal of sickness and suffering of mind. It seemed as though the enemy cast a cloud of darkness between me and my Saviour, and for twelve days it seemed that I could think of nothing but my sufferings. When I came to Oakland my heart was so weak and feeble that it seemed that a stone was lying on it. Not a particle of joy was there in it; not an emotion of gladness could I realize. But was I to think that heaven was closed to me? No! I must take the Bible, and I took the Bible and walked right out by faith, and the darkness separated from me.

When I awake in the night I begin to pray. Some three weeks ago I awoke and said, "O God, have mercy on me." I had no more than spoken when a voice by me seemed to say, "I am right by you, I have not left you." This was everything to me, and it may be just the same to you. Jesus says, I am right by you, dwelling with you, you are not alone at all. That was just the joy I experienced, and it was worth more than mountains of gold to me. I have learned to trust my Saviour, and I want to tell you that I have a Saviour, and He lives; and because He lives I shall live also.

Our lives are hid with Christ in God, and when He who is our Life shall appear, we shall appear with Him in glory. You do not need to be discouraged. Christ came to save His people from their sins. The devil will come to you and tell you that you are a sinner and cannot be saved. But Christ says He came to save sinners, and there you can meet the devil every time. Christ can pardon your sins. He says, "Come now, and let us reason together . . . : though your sins be as scarlet, they shall be as white as snow; though they be red like crimson, they shall be as wool."

Oh, I want you to take the rich promises of God and hang memory's halls with them. What more could you want than that promise? We have the assurance that a mother can forget her nursing child but He will not forget us. Oh, I want the promises of God to be the living pictures on memory's walls, that you can look at them. Then your heart can be filled with His grace and you may exalt Jesus and crown Him Lord of all. That is your privilege.

Now I want to read Colossians 1:12: "Giving thanks unto the Father, which hath made us meet to be partakers of the inheritance of the saints in light." There is something to be patient and long-suffering over— "who hath delivered us from the power of darkness." Yes, we should talk of deliverance, not of bondage; we should be joyful and not cast down. "And hath translated us into the kingdom of his dear Son." Why can we not act as subjects of His kingdom? May the love of Christ burn on the altar of our hearts, and may you love Christ as your Saviour, and your brethren as yourself.

"In whom we have redemption through his blood, even the forgiveness of sin." Now we want to act like individuals who are redeemed by the blood of Christ; we are to rejoice in the blood of Christ and in the forgiveness of sins. That is what we are to do, and may God help us to get our minds off the dark pictures, and think on those things that will give us light.

Now I want to read another scripture: "Be careful for nothing." What does that mean? Why, don't cross a bridge before you get to it. Don't make a time of trouble before it comes. You will get to it soon enough, brethren. We are to think of today, and if we do well the duties of today, we will be ready for the duties of tomorrow. "But in every thing by prayer and supplication with thanksgiving let your requests be made known unto God." Thanksgiving is to be brought in. "And the peace of God, which passeth all understanding, shall keep your hearts and minds through Christ Jesus." Then we are not given over into the hands of the devil; we have a loving heavenly Father, and He has given His Son to bear our iniquity.

Now what is next? "Finally, brethren." Now, this is to each of you. It comes along down the line to our times. "Finally, brethren, whatsoever things are true, whatsoever things are honest, whatsoever things are just, whatsoever things are pure, whatsoever things are lovely, whatsoever things are of good report; if there be any virtue, if there be any praise, think on these things." Shall we do it? Shall we turn over a page in our religious experience and train and educate the mind so that it will not take these things that are disagreeable and think on them? Shall we think on these things that give us no power, or shall we let our minds dwell on those things that will give us a better feeling toward our brethren and elevate our souls to God? Now, there are many things that we need to bring into our lives and characters. May God help us that we may take these things to our hearts and think of them, that our minds may be elevated above earthly things.

We have seen of the grace of God since we met you last. Since last spring I have visited Lemoore, Fresno, and Selma. I was at the Selma camp meeting. During my stay there I was introduced to a tall man—over six feet tall—and well proportioned. When he took my hand he seemed much affected and said, "I am so glad to meet you; I am thankful that I can speak with you." After going into the tent a brother came in and said, "That man has a history." Then he went on and told how a year before he had been converted; how he had once kept the Sabbath but had gone back, and how he claimed that he never had been converted. Then after he gave up the truth he went back into the company of hard cases, and Satan took complete possession of him. Two or three were linked with him in his wickedness—men who would not want it to be known that they were in such business. They stole and did wickedness in every way.

He was not a licentious man; he had a wife and he respected her. She was a Sabbathkeeper, and he would not allow a word to be said against her. This was the position he took; he loved her, but not enough to stop his evil course. He did not care for the spoil of his robberies, but did it for the enjoyment he found in it. Well, Elder [E. P.] Daniels was holding meetings, and he was speaking on confession. What was said seemed to take hold of this man's mind, and he could not resist. He seemed to turn white, and then left the tent. He could not stand it. He went out and then he came back again. This he did three times; he looked as if he were going to faint away.

After the meeting had closed he said, "I must talk to you, sir." He told Elder Daniels his condition and said, "Is there any hope for me? I am a lost man; I am undone; I am a sinner. Will you pray for me? I dare not leave this place to go home for fear the Lord will cut me down in my sins." He said he could not stay in the tent, and went out again and again, but did not dare remain outside for fear the power of the devil should fasten on him and that would be the last of him.

They prayed for him, and the man was converted right there. The defiant look was gone; his countenance was changed. "Now," said he, "I have a work to do. I stole thirty-one sheep from that man in Selma, and I must go and confess to him." Elder Daniels was afraid to have it known for fear they would shut him up. He said he would rather go to prison and stay there than to think that Christ had not forgiven his sin. So he started, with a young man who before this was engaged with him in thefts, to go and see the man. He met the man on the road and stopped him. The man commenced to shake like an aspen leaf. He was an infidel. Well, he got on his knees before them in the road and begged to be forgiven. The man asked, "Where did you get this? What has brought you into this state? I did not know that there was any such religion as this." They told him that they had been down to the camp meeting, and heard it preached there. "Well," said he, "I will go over to that meeting." . . .

They confessed to having burned houses and barns. And they went to the grand jury and confessed to having stolen here and there. Mind, they confessed to the authorities. They said, "We deliver ourselves up. Do with us as you see fit." So the case was considered in court, and they had a council over the matter. One suggested that they better put those men through. The judge looked at him and said, "What, put him through? Put a man through that God is putting through? Would you take hold of a man that God is taking hold of? Whom God's forgiving power has taken hold of? Would you do that? No, I would rather have my right arm cut off to the shoulder." Something got hold of those men so that they all wept as children.

The report of that experience went everywhere. People thought that there was a power in this truth that was in nothing else—a power that shows that Jesus lives. We have seen the power of His grace manifested in many cases in a remarkable manner.

Now, whenever we can see anything encouraging, put it in the paper, and talk about it. Why talk of Satan's great power and his wonderful works, and say nothing of the majesty and goodness and mercy of our God which falls to the ground unnoticed? Pick these up, brethren, with consecrated hands, pick them up. Hold them high before the world. Talk of the love of God and dwell upon it; thank Him for it. Open the doors of your hearts and show forth your gratitude and love. Clear away this rubbish which Satan has piled before the door of your heart and let Jesus come in and occupy. Talk of His goodness and power.

You know how it was with Moses. He felt that he must have an answer to his prayer. He realized the responsibility of leading the people out of Egypt, but he did not go and pick up everything objectionable and dwell on it. He knew they were a stiff-necked people, and he said, "Lord, I must have Thy presence"; and the Lord said, "My presence shall go with thee." You remember Moses went into the wilderness and stayed forty years, during which time he put away self, and that made room so that he could have the presence of God with him.

He thought if he could have the presence of God's glory it would help him to carry on this great work. He says, "Shew me thy glory." Now that was a man of faith, and God did not rebuke him. God did not call it presumption, but He took that man of faith and put him into the cleft of the rock and put His hand over the rock and showed him all the glory that he could endure. He made His goodness to pass before him, and showed him His goodness, His mercy, and His love. If we want God's glory to pass before us, if we want to have memory's halls hung with the promises of love and mercy, we want to talk of His glory and tell of His power. And if we have dark and miserable days we can commit these promises to memory and take our minds off discouragement. It would please the devil to think he has bothered us; but we want to talk of Jesus and His love and His power, because we have nothing better to talk of.

Now, brethren and sisters, let us hope in God. Let gratitude enter into our hearts, and while we may have to bear plain testimony to separate from sin and iniquity, we do not want to be hammering upon that string forever. We want to lift up these souls that are cast down; we want them to catch that love of God and know that He will put His everlasting arms beneath them. Brethren and sisters, we want to look up; not down, but upward, upward, lifting the soul higher and still higher. I want these blessings and I will not rest satisfied until I am filled with all the fullness of God. Nothing can be greater than that, can it?

We want to be in that position where we shall perfect a Christian character and represent Jesus Christ to the world. Christ was sent as our pattern and shall we not show that we have all His love and kindness and all His charms? And the love of Jesus Christ will take possession of our characters and our lives, and our conversation will be holy, and we will dwell on heavenly things.

I believe that Jesus is interested in all this assembly. He is here today. He says, "Where two or three are gathered together in my name, there am I in the midst of them." He is with you and that to bless. We want the blessing, and why should we not have it? We are to meet the moral darkness that is in the world, and we must meet it as Christ did. We must reveal Christ to all who are around us. When we do this work we are abiding in Christ and Christ is abiding in us, not only when we speak of Him, but He is with us all the time to help us on every point, to press back the power of moral darkness.

"Fear not, little flock; for it is your Father's good pleasure to give you the kingdom." He is not your enemy, He is your best Friend, and He wishes us to show to the world that we have a God. He wants us to show that we have Jesus with us, and He is stronger than the strong man armed. Therefore, let us elevate our minds and our conversation and seek for heaven and heavenly things. God help us when we are in this position, that we shall not be seeking after earthly things, but that we shall be charmed with the things of heaven. We want to "behold, what manner of love the Father hath bestowed upon us, that we should be called the sons of God: therefore the world knoweth us not, because it knew him not. Beloved, now are we the sons of God, and it doth not yet appear what we shall be: but we know that, when he shall appear, we shall be like him; for we shall see him as he is."

I look over this congregation, and you look like discouraged men, like men who have been fighting with the powers of darkness; but courage, brethren! There is hope! "It doth not yet appear what we shall be: but we know that, when he shall appear, we shall be like him; for we shall see him as he is. And every man that hath this hope in him purifieth himself, even as he is pure."

Oh, I love Him. I love Him, for He is my love. I see in Him matchless charms, and oh, how I want that we shall enter in through the gates into the city. Then shall every crown be taken off from every head and cast at the feet of Jesus our blessed Redeemer. He has purchased it for me; He has purchased it for you, and we shall acknowledge Him Lord of all. And we shall cast all our honor at His feet and crown Him Lord of all. We shall shout, "Glory to God in the highest." I wish we would learn to praise Him more. "Whoso offereth praise glorifieth" God. I wish you would talk of it. I wish you would educate your hearts and lips to praise Him, to talk of His power and glory. I wish you would tell of His power. When you do it you are elevating your Saviour, and when you lift that standard up against your enemy he will flee from you. God help us to praise Him more and to be found faultless.—Manuscript 7, 1888.

The Need of Advancement

Morning Talk
Minneapolis, Minnesota, October 18, 1888

I HOPE that at the beginning of this meeting our hearts may be impressed with the positive statement of our Saviour, "Without me ye can do nothing." We have a great and solemn truth committed to us for these last days, but a mere assent to and belief in this truth will not save us. The principles of the truth must be interwoven with our character and life. We should cherish every ray of light that falls upon our pathway, and live up to the requirements of God. We should grow in spirituality. We are losing a great deal of the blessing we might have at this meeting because we do not take advance steps in the Christian life as our duty is presented before us; and this will be an eternal loss.

If we had a just appreciation of the importance and greatness of our work, and could see ourselves as we are at this time, we should be filled with wonder that God could use us, unworthy as we are, in the work of bringing souls into the truth. There are many things that we ought to be able to understand, that we do not comprehend because we are so far behind our privileges. Christ said to His disciples, "I have yet many things to say unto you, but ye cannot bear them now." This is our condition. Would they not have been able to understand what He had to say to them if they had been doers of His word—if they had improved point after point of the truth which He had presented to them? But although they could not then understand, He told them that He would send the Comforter, who would lead them into all truth. We should be in a position where we can comprehend the teaching, leading, and working of the Spirit of Christ. We must not measure God or His truth by our finite understanding or by our preconceived opinions.

There are many who do not realize where they are standing, for they are spiritually blinded. "Examine yourselves, whether ye be in the faith; prove your own selves. Know ye not your own selves, how that Jesus Christ is in you, except ye be reprobates?" I trust that none of us will be found to be reprobates. Is Christ abiding in your hearts by faith? Is His Spirit in you? If it is, there will be such a yearning in your soul for the salvation of those for whom Christ has died that self will sink into insignificance, and Christ alone will be exalted. Brethren and sisters, there is great need at this time of humbling ourselves before God, that the Holy Spirit may come upon us.

There are many who are content with a superficial knowledge of the truth. The precious truths for this time are brought out so clearly in our publications that many are satisfied, and do not search the Scriptures for themselves. They do not meditate upon the statements made, and bring every proposition to the law and to the testimony, to see if their ideas correspond to the Word of God. Many do not feel that it is essential for them to compare scripture with scripture, and spiritual things with spiritual; and therefore they do not grow in grace and in the knowledge of the truth, as it is their privilege to do. They accept the truth, without any deep conviction of sin, and present themselves as laborers in the cause of God when they are unconverted men. One says, "I want to do something in the cause of truth"; another says, "I want to enter the ministry"; and as our brethren are very anxious to get all the laborers they can, they accept these men without considering whether their lives give evidence that they have a saving knowledge of Christ. No one should be accepted as a laborer in the sacred cause of God until he makes manifest that he has a real, living experience in the things of God. One reason why the church is in a backslidden state is that so many have come into the truth in this way, and have never known what it is to have the converting power of God upon their souls.

There are many ministers who have never been converted. They come to the prayer meeting and pray the same old lifeless prayers over and over; they preach the same dry discourses over and over, from week to week and from month to month. They have nothing new and inspiring to present to their congregations, and it is evident that they are not eating the flesh and drinking the blood of the Son of man, for they have no life in them. They are not partakers of the divine nature; Christ is not abiding in their hearts by faith.

Those who profess to be united to Christ should be laborers together with God. The people of God are to warn the world and to prepare a people to stand in the day of wrath when the Son of man shall come in the clouds of heaven. The members of the church of Christ should gather up the divine rays of light from Jesus and reflect them to others, leaving a bright track heavenward in the world. They are to be as the wise virgins, having their lamps trimmed and burning, representing the character of Christ to the world. We are not to be satisfied with anything short of this. We are not to be satisfied with our own righteousness, and content without the deep movings of the Spirit of God.

Christ says, "Without me ye can do nothing." It is this marked nothingness, so apparent in the labors of many who profess to be preaching the truth, that alarms us; for we know that this is an evidence that they have not felt the converting power of Christ upon their hearts. You may look from the topmost bough to the lowest branch of their work, and you will find nothing but leaves. God desires us to come up to a higher standard. It is not His will that we should have such a dearth of spirituality. There are some young men who say they have given themselves to the work, who need a genuine experience in the things of God before they are fit to labor in the cause of Christ. Instead of going without the camp, bearing reproach for Christ's sake; instead of seeking the hard places, and trying to bring souls into the truth, these beginners settle themselves in an easy position to visit those who are far advanced in experience. They labor with those who are more capable of teaching them than they are of teaching others. They go from church to church, picking out the easy places, eating and drinking, and suffering others to wait upon them. When you look to see what they have done, there is nothing but leaves. They bring in the report, "I preached here, and I preached there"; but where are the sheaves they have garnered? Where are the souls that have embraced the truth through their efforts? Where is the evidence of their piety and devotion? Those who are bringing the churches up to a higher standard, by earnest efforts as soldiers of Jesus Christ, are doing a good work.

Too often the churches have been robbed by the class I have mentioned, for they take their support from the treasury and bring nothing in return. They are continually drawing out the means that should be devoted to the support of worthy laborers. There should be a thorough investigation of the cases of those who present themselves to labor in the cause. The apostle warns you to "lay hands suddenly on no man." If the life is not what God can accept, the labors will be worthless; but if Christ is abiding in the heart by faith, every wrong will be made right, and those who are soldiers of Christ will be willing to prove it by a well-ordered life. There are many who enter the ministry, and their influence demoralizes the churches; and when they are rejected they take their dismissal as a personal wrong. They have not Christ in the soul as a well of water springing up unto everlasting life.

I want to exhort those who are in positions of responsibility to waken to their duty and not imperil the cause of present truth by engaging inefficient men to do the work of God. We want men who are willing to do hard service for the Lord. I remember visiting in Iowa when the country was new, and I saw the farmers breaking the new ground. I noticed that they had heavy teams, and made tremendous efforts to make deep furrows, but the laborers gained strength and muscle by the exercise of their physical powers. It will make our young men strong to go into new fields and break up the fallow ground of men's hearts. This work will drive them nearer to God. It will help them to see that they are altogether inefficient in themselves. They must be wholly the Lord's. They must put away their self-esteem and self-importance, and put on the Lord Jesus Christ. When they do this, they will be willing to go without the camp, and bear the burden as good soldiers of the cross. They will gain efficiency and ability by mastering difficulties and overcoming obstacles. Men are wanted for responsible positions, but they must be men who have given full proof of their ministry in willingness to wear the yoke of Christ. Heaven regards this class with approval.

I exhort you to have the eyesalve, that you may discern what God would have you do. There are too many Christless sermons preached. An array of powerless words only confirms the people in their backslidings. May God help us that His Spirit may be made manifest among us. We should not wait until we go home to obtain the blessing of Heaven. The ministers should begin right here with the people to seek God and to work from the right standpoint. Those who have been long in the work have been far too content to wait for the showers of the latter rain to revive them. We are the people who, like John, are to prepare the way of the Lord; and if we are prepared for the second coming of Christ, we must work with all diligence to prepare others for Christ's second advent, as did the forerunner of Christ for His first advent, calling men to repentance. The truth of God must be brought into the soul temple, to cleanse and purify it from all defilement. May God help us to search the Scriptures for ourselves, and when we are all filled with the truth of God, it will flow out as water from a living spring. We cannot exhaust the heavenly fountain, and the more we draw, the more we shall delight to draw from the living waters. O may we be converted! We want the ministers and the young men to be converted. We want to lift up the standard. Let all the people come up to the high calling of God in Christ Jesus. Let us pray that we may hunger and thirst after righteousness; for Jesus says, "Blessed are they which do hunger and thirst after righteousness: for they shall be filled."

—*Review and Herald,* Oct. 8, 1889.

+++

Have Light in Yourselves

Morning Talk

Minneapolis, Minnesota, October 19, 1888

WE HAVE most precious promises in the word of God, which ought to give us courage and confidence. They should enable us to come out of uncertainty and darkness, to come where we may know that the Spirit beareth witness with our spirit that we are the children of God. There is nothing wanting in the storehouse of our God.

Jesus has said, "Believe me, that I am in the Father, and the Father in me; or else believe me for the very works' sake. Verily, verily, I say unto you, He that believeth on me, the works that I do, shall he do also; and greater works than these shall he do; because I go unto my Father." The disciples of Christ are to do greater works than Jesus Himself has done. He says further: "Whatsoever ye shall ask in my name, that will I do, that the Father may be glorified in the Son." "If ye ask anything in my name, I will do it." Christ spoke these words for the comfort of all who should have faith in

266

Him, and it is our privilege to believe that God will do just as He has said He would.

It is not enough to say, "I believe;" we must exercise the living faith that claims the promises of God as our own, knowing that they are sure and steadfast. The enemy of our souls would be glad to steal away these precious promises from us, and cast darkness before our eyes, so that we should not be able to appropriate the good things that God means that we shall have. God is waiting to do great things for us as soon as we come into a right relation with Him; but if we hold ourselves in doubt and unbelief, the enemy can keep the control of our minds, and intercept the promises of God. Unbelief always results in a great loss to our souls. It was said concerning one place where Christ visited, "He did not many mighty works there because of their unbelief." Christ cannot work in our behalf if we do not manifest faith in Him. We should train our souls to have faith in God. But instead of this, how many there are who educate themselves to doubt. I have heard testimony after testimony in meeting in which there did not seem to be one word of genuine faith, but which cast a shadow over the whole congregation. It is not God's will that we should be in this position. Brethren and sisters, it is our privilege to walk in the light, as Christ is in the light. He is at our right hand to strengthen us, and He tells us that greater works than He has done shall we do, because He goes to the Father. He is ready to impart unto us the rich blessing and grace of God.

How shall we encourage you to have faith in God? You say, "How can I talk faith, how can I have faith, when clouds and darkness and despondency come over my mind? I do not feel as though I could talk faith; I do not feel that I have any faith to talk." But why do you feel in this way?—It is because you have permitted Satan to cast his dark shadow across your pathway, and you cannot see the light that Jesus sheds upon your pathway. But another says: "I am very frank; I say just what I feel, I talk just as I think." Is that the best way to do?—No; God wants us to educate ourselves so that we shall speak right words,—words that will be a blessing to others, that will shed rays of light upon their souls.

Suppose that at times we are destitute of the joy we should like to experience, can we not feel assured that the promises of God are still yea and amen in Christ Jesus? The promises of God do not rest upon feeling. They have a foundation as distinct from feeling as light is from darkness. We must learn to move from principle, and when we learn to do this, we shall move understandingly, and not be controlled by varying emotions.

Christ has said, "If ye abide in me, and my words abide in you, ye shall ask what ye will, and it shall be done unto you." Brethren, can you explain why we are not more efficient in ministering to others, and why we are not better able to help the church, than we were ten years ago? There is no reason why we should not be growing in efficiency and power to do the work of God. The Lord wants us to use every iota of the ability He has given us, and, if we do this, we shall have improved and increased ability to employ. God desires that we shall have a thorough understanding of the truth as it is in Jesus. We should dig in the mine of truth for the rich treasures of knowledge that are hidden in God's word. If we employ our talents in searching the Scriptures, and in imparting knowledge to others, we shall become channels of light. You should not allow the channel between God and your soul to become obstructed. You should not be moved by circumstances. You should refuse to listen to the suggestions of Satan, that he may not paralyze your efforts to do good.

What we need is Bible religion; for if Christ is abiding in us, and we in Him, we shall be continually advancing in the divine life. If we are connected with the Source of all wisdom and power, we shall not fail of becoming strong men and women in Christ Jesus. If we fully receive the truth of heavenly origin, we shall not fail of becoming sanctified through it; and when trials come we shall not go to complaining, as did the children of Israel, and forget the Source of our strength. We must gather up the divine rays of glory, not to hide our light by putting it under a bushel or under a bed, but to set it on a candlestick, where it will give light to others. We must put our talents out to the exchangers, that we may accumulate more talent to bring to Jesus. In this way we shall be growing Christians, and every word we speak will be ennobling and sanctifying. We should educate ourselves to speak in such a way that we shall not have cause to be ashamed of our words when we meet them in the judgment. We should seek to have our actions of such a character that we will not shrink from having our Saviour look upon them. Christ is here this morning; angels are here, and they are measuring the temple of God and those who worship therein. The history of this meeting will be carried up to God; for a record of every meeting is made; the spirit manifested, the words spoken, and the actions performed, are noted in the books of heaven. Everything is transferred to the records as faithfully as are our features to the polished plate of the artist.

We must fight the good fight of faith. Satan will try to sever the connection which faith makes between our souls and God. He will seek to discourage us by telling us that we are unworthy of the grace of God, and need not expect to receive this or that favor because we are sinners. These suggestions should not cut off our confidence; for it is written: "Jesus Christ came into the world to save sinners, of whom I am chief." There is no reason why we should not claim the promises of the Lord. There is no reason why we should not be light-bearers. There is no reason why you should not advance, why you should not become more and more intelligent in prayer and testimony, and make manifest that God hears and answers your petitions.

We should have more wisdom and confidence today than we had yesterday. Why are we so well satisfied with our feeble attainments? Why do we settle down content with our present deficient experience? We should not always be fed upon the milk of the word; we must seek for meat, that we may become strong men and women in Christ. God will give you everything that you are prepared for, everything that will minister to your strength. He will make peace with you if you lay hold of His strength. But He will not let His power drop upon you without effort on your part. You must cooperate with God in the work of salvation.

We need to grow in the knowledge of our Lord and Saviour Jesus Christ. We must educate ourselves to talk faith, to pray in faith, and to abstain from dropping one seed of doubt and discouragement. We desire that young men shall go forth from this conference to become experienced workers in the cause of God. Let the older ministers take heed that they make straight paths for their feet, that the lame be not turned out of the way. Let no watchman or shepherd of the flock place himself on judgment-seat, to criticize others, to pick flaws and find fault with the brethren. Oh, that everyone at this meeting would take his position on the Lord's side! We must have light in ourselves. Do not believe anything simply because others say it is truth. Take your Bibles, and search them for yourselves. Plead with God that He will put His Spirit upon you, that you may know the truth and understand its principles. If you gain an experience of this kind, there is nothing that will turn you from the truth. You will be like Daniel in the lions' den, and like Joseph in Pharaoh's prison.

From the light that God has given me, I can say that not half of those who profess to believe the present truth have a thorough understanding of the Third Angel's Message. Many believe the truth because they have heard it preached by someone in whom they had confidence. When our people search the word of God for themselves, we shall hear less murmuring than we hear today. We need that faith that will lead us to study the Bible for ourselves, and take God at His word.

Christ says: "Verily, verily, I say unto you, He that believeth on me, the works that I do shall he do also; and greater works than these shall he do; because I go unto my Father. And whatsoever ye shall ask in my name, that will I do, that the Father may be glorified in the Son. If ye shall ask anything in my name, I will do it. If ye love me, keep my commandments. And I will pray the Father, and he shall give you another Comforter, that he may abide with you for ever."

Brethren, you must take advanced steps. God wants every one of you to turn from your iniquity, and connect with Him, the Source of all wisdom and truth, that when you open your lips the words of Christ may flow forth. Shall we not let the Spirit of God come among us, and flow from heart to heart? The Spirit of God is here this morning, and the Lord knows how you will receive the words that I have addressed to you on this occasion.—*Signs of the Times*, November 11, 1889.

✦ ✦ ✦

Advancing in Christian Experience

Minneapolis General Conference
Sabbath, October 20, 1888

"SIMON PETER, a servant and an apostle of Jesus Christ, to them that have obtained like precious faith with us through the righteousness of God and our Saviour Jesus Christ: Grace and peace be multiplied unto you through the knowledge of God, and of Jesus our Lord, according as his divine power hath given unto us all things that pertain unto life and godliness, through the knowledge of him that hath called us to glory and virtue: whereby are given unto us exceeding great and precious promises: that by these ye might be partakers of the divine nature, having escaped the corruption that is in the world through lust. And beside this, giving all diligence, add to your faith virtue; and to virtue knowledge; and to knowledge temperance; and to temperance patience;

269

and to patience godliness; and to godliness brotherly kindness; and to brotherly kindness charity. For if these things be in you, and abound, they make you that ye shall neither be barren nor unfruitful in the knowledge of our Lord Jesus Christ. But he that lacketh these things is blind, and cannot see afar off, and hath forgotten that he was purged from his old sins. Wherefore the rather, brethren, give diligence to make your calling and election sure: for if ye do these things, ye shall never fall: for so an entrance shall be ministered unto you abundantly into the everlasting kingdom of our Lord and Saviour Jesus Christ. Wherefore I will not be negligent to put you always in remembrance of these things, though ye know them, and be established in the present truth" (2 Peter 1:1-12).

Now mark, it is these graces, this righteousness, that is to be constantly added; and if these things be in you and abound, they make you that you shall be neither barren nor unfruitful in the knowledge of the Lord Jesus Christ.

Now here is subject matter that we might dwell upon, and subject matter for many discourses; but we want to present merely a few ideas to your mind at this time, and we want you to see the necessity of progress. You cannot be a fruitful Christian and have a knowledge of our Lord and Saviour Jesus Christ unless you are a practical Christian, unless you are making progress all the time in divine life. This is all important. Many seem to think that as soon as they go down into the water and receive baptism, and their names are entered upon the church book, then the work is all done. They might have tasted of the knowledge of the world to come; they might have received the evidence that they are children of God; but they cannot retain it unless they go on making progress.

It is impossible for them to obtain a knowledge of Jesus Christ and of His light and knowledge unless they are advancing and are learners, adding grace to grace. If they do not bring into their households practical religion, they will soon lose it all; and they will go into the meeting and carry through a form, and pray and exhort, and perhaps hold some office in the church; but unless they are making advancement all the time there is a decided want, and they will swing back to their old position of ungodliness, just like any other sinner. It is important that we keep all the time adding grace to grace, and if we will work upon the plan of addition, God will work on the plan of multiplication; and just as fast as we add, God multiplies His graces unto us.

Those who live doing the works of the enemy, yet bearing the name of the Lord, are lying; they profess to believe the Bible, yet they are working right away from it in their lives and character. In the place of representing Jesus in the character that they shall give to the world, they represent the works of Satan, the works of darkness. Now any such names that may be on your church books, although they may give of their means to help to sustain the church, notwithstanding all that, they are stumbling blocks to the church every day they are in it.

Now, what we want to present is how you may advance in the divine life. We hear many excuses: I cannot live up to this or that. What do you mean by this or that? Do you mean that it was an imperfect sacrifice that was made for the fallen race upon Calvary, that there is not sufficient grace and power granted us that we may work away from our own natural defects and tendencies, that it was not a whole Saviour that was given us? or do you mean to cast reproach upon God? Well, you say, it was Adam's sin. You say, I am not guilty of that, and I am not responsible for his guilt and fall. Here all these natural tendencies are in me, and I am not to blame if I act out these natural tendencies. Who is to blame? Is God? Why did God let Satan have this power over human nature? These are accusations against the God of heaven, and He will give you an opportunity, if you want it, of finally bringing your accusations against Him. Then He will bring His accusations against you when you are brought into His court of judgment.

How is it that He is pleading, "I know all the evils and temptations with which you are beset, and I sent My Son Jesus Christ to your world to reveal to you My power, My mightiness; to reveal to you that I am God, and that I will give you help in order to lift you from the power of the enemy, and give you a chance that you might win back the moral image of God." God sent His Son, who was as Himself, one with the Father, and He bore insult and shame and mockery for us, and suffered at last the ignominious death upon Calvary. Satan met Him with opposition just as soon as He came into the world; but He met it all; He did not swerve a bit. Had it not been for the power that God gave Him, He could not have stood the assaults of the enemy; but He did, and although He had him to meet at every step, and was pressed step by step, yet here was the battle fought in this world with the powers of darkness.

Why was not the devil destroyed? Why do you ask such a question? Did not God know what was best? Would it not have destroyed confidence in God? Would it not have cast a reflection upon God if He had destroyed him, him that had taken hold of the very heart of the universe, and the world that was created? The only way to show the disposition of Satan was to give him a chance to develop himself as one who would be worthy of condemnation and death. So the God of heaven, while He did not destroy Satan, gave His Son to counteract the influence of Satan; and when He gave His Son He gave Himself, and here was the image of God that was brought to our world. What for? That we might become mighty with God.

Christ had to meet the enemy. What had he [Satan] been doing prior to Christ's coming to this earth? Why, he had been trying to gain the hearts of evil men and evil women. When Christ came to our world, Satan had been working with all the deceptive powers that he could command

271

with his angels to gain the hearts of evil men and women, and combined with Satan they will work on the children of disobedience; and it seems that when Christ made His appearance in our world that Satan had planted himself on the throne as the sovereign of this world. He had the control of human minds. He had taken the human bodies and wrought upon them so that they were possessed with demons. He wrought upon them so that the moral image of God was almost obliterated in them. He was weaving himself into the Jewish nation, and they were led captive and would not acknowledge Christ as the Son of God, notwithstanding the mighty evidences which accompanied Him.

Now Christ takes the field and commences to press back this power of moral darkness. In Luke He announces what His work is to be. "The Spirit of the Lord is upon me, because he hath anointed me to preach the gospel to the poor; he hath sent me to heal the brokenhearted, to preach deliverance to the captives, and recovering of sight to the blind, to set at liberty them that are bruised, to preach the acceptable year of the Lord" (Luke 4:18, 19). Even while Christ announced His mission and "all bare him witness, and wondered at the gracious words which proceeded out of his mouth," Satan was on the ground. And there is no meeting but that he is there, and as the truth is being impressed on minds, Satan presents the difficulties.

Christ said, "This day is this scripture fulfilled in your ears." But a state of unbelief arose and the questions began to come up, Is not this the son of Joseph and Mary? What is this that He claims? Is not this Joseph's son? We have seen Him walking with His father to the carpenter shop. "And he said unto them, Ye will surely say unto me this proverb, Physician, heal thyself: whatsoever we have heard done in Capernaum, do also here in thy country. And he said, Verily I say unto you, No prophet is accepted in his own country. But I tell you of a truth, many widows were in Israel in the days of Elias, when the heaven was shut up three years and six months, when great famine was throughout all the land; but unto none of them was Elias sent, save unto Sarepta, a city of Sidon, unto a woman that was a widow. And many lepers were in Israel in the time of Eliseus the prophet; and none of them was cleansed, saving Naaman the Syrian" (verses 23-27).

Now this widow was a heathen woman. God did not send Elijah to those who were in Samaria. Why? Because they had great light, blessings, and privileges, and did not live up to them. And because they had had this great light and had not lived up to it, they were the most hardhearted people in the world, the hardest to impress with the truth. They were not susceptible to the influences of the Spirit of God. There were many lepers in Israel, and none of them were cleansed save Naaman, the Syrian. What was the matter? He who had lived up to the light that he had was in a more favorable position before God than those on whom He had bestowed great light, power, and spiritual advantages, and yet their lives did not correspond to their advantages and privileges.

What did the people do [with Christ] in their madness? They "rose up, and thrust him out of the city." Could their eyes have been opened they would have beheld angels of God all around Him, that all heaven was engaged in this warfare between Christ and the prince of the powers of this world. They could have seen this, but their eyes were holden that they might not see it.

Here I want to tell you what a terrible thing it is if God gives light, and it is impressed on your heart and spirit, for you to do as they did. God will withdraw His Spirit unless His truth is accepted. But Christ was accepted by some; the witness was there that He was God. But a counterinfluence pressed in, and the evil angels were working through the congregation to raise doubts that would cause disbelief so that it would shut out every ray of light that God would permit to shine. No more could Christ do in such a place. You can see what a hold Satan had and what mistakes the people had made; they had not advanced, and because they had not advanced they had been working under the generalship of Satan and yet claimed that they were working under the generalship of God. But God had nothing to do with their unbelief and their rising up against Jesus Christ.

I wish you could see and feel that if you are not advancing you are retrograding. Satan understood this; he knew how to take advantage of the human mind, and he had taken advantage of the human family ever since they had first stood upon the field of battle against the powers of darkness. Christ knew what the warfare was to be.

Who was watching this warfare that was going on? Who was watching when Christ stood on the banks of Jordan and offered such a prayer as heaven had never listened to before, and a light like a dove broke forth from the heavens, and a voice was heard to say, "This is my beloved Son, in whom I am well pleased"? There were those who heard these things and spread the news everywhere among the Jews, and it went from one to the other, so this manifestation of God's power was not lost at that time.

What does that say to us? "This is my beloved Son, in whom I am well pleased." It says to you, I, God, have sent My Son into your world, and through Him is opened all heaven to fallen man. After the sin of Adam man was divorced from God, but Christ came in. He was represented through the sacrificial offerings until He came to our world. Here Christ offers this prayer, and what does it say to us? The human race is accepted in the Beloved. His long human arm encircles the race, while with His divine arm He grasps the throne of the Infinite, and He opens to man all of heaven. The gates are ajar today. Christ is in the heavenly sanctuary and your prayers can go up to the Father.

Christ says, If I go away, I will send you the Comforter, and when we have the Holy Spirit we have everything. We have knowledge, wisdom, power, and we have a connection with the God of wisdom. When heaven was opened to man, and God said, "This is my beloved Son, in whom I am well pleased," He said it to us. Your prayers, through faith in your substitute, Jesus Christ, are accepted. God accepts Christ, our substitute. He took human nature upon Himself and fought the battles that human nature is engaged in. He is connected with the divine and was to fight the battles with Satan.

Now, what we want you to see is the relation which you sustain to the work of God. What condescension God has shown that He should give His Son that we might defeat the powers of darkness! God was not the originator of sin, in order that He might rid the human race of sin. Here was the law of God, and He could not alter it a jot or tittle. It was a representation of His character. He could not change it because it is by that law that we are to be judged in the last day. It is no excuse to say that iniquity abounds, and that the law of God is done away or changed or altered. It is this that causes the existence of iniquity. This is the very work that Satan commenced in heaven, and he will carry it forward to the end. I ask you what position shall we take that we may be partakers of the divine nature? Why should we not see in that law the righteousness of Jesus Christ? Christ comes in and imputes to me His righteousness in His perfect obedience to that law.

Here the battle is before us. We see the battle, how Christ contended with the powers of darkness; and we see what He has done, and why the cross of Calvary had been erected between God and man. Then what? Man comes to Christ, and God and man are united at the cross, and here mercy and truth have met together, righteousness and truth have kissed each other. This is drawing man to the cross, where Christ died in behalf of man, to elevate the law of Jehovah, but not to lessen it one iota. Could He have done this, Christ need not have died. The cross of Calvary will stand in the judgment and testify to everyone the immutability and changeless character of the law of God, and not a word can be offered for sin in that day.

"And I, if I be lifted up from the earth, will draw all men unto me." What does that mean? The work must be carried on, and this little world was chosen in which to carry on this work. All the universe of heaven was interested in the great work. Every world that God has created is watching to see how the battle between the Lord of light and glory and the powers of darkness will end. Here is Satan, who has been seeking with all his power to shut out the true character of God, so that the world could not understand it, and under a garb of righteousness he works upon many who profess to be Christians, but they represent the character of Satan instead of the character of Jesus Christ. They misrepresent my Lord. They misrepresent the character of Jesus every time that they lack mercy, every time that they lack humility.

Satan, by instigating in man a disposition to transgress the law of God, mystifies the character of God. Someone must come to vindicate the character of God, and here is Christ, who stands as the representation of the Father, and He is to work out the salvation of the human race.

That wonderful plan of salvation will bear investigation. All heaven is interested in this work. Up to the time when Christ died, though He was human, He was without sin, and He must bear His trials as a human being. There was to be no miracle interposed for Him. There had been miracles wrought for Him, as at the time the people were going to cast Him over the brow of the hill. Miracles have been wrought for men who have been followed by mobs, when the angel of the Lord would take their arms and protect the servants of God against the work of Satan.

I knew something of this in my early experience. I know whereof I am speaking. [The reporter indicates that here Ellen White related the experience of her husband when an angel walked with him through an angry mob. Recorded in *Life Sketches . . . of James White and His Wife, Ellen G. White*, pp. 54, 55.]

All can testify that God has wrought in these cases; then just such things will take place with us as did with Christ. He was to work no miracle for Himself, but angels protected His life till the time came when He was to be betrayed by one of His disciples, till He was to give His life on Calvary's cross, and Satan stirred up the minds of men to think that the angels of heaven were indifferent. But every one was watching the contest with interest. From the moment that Christ knelt in prayer on the sod of Gethsemane till He died on the cross and cried out, "It is finished," the angels and all the universe of God looked on with the greatest interest. When those words were spoken, the plan was completed—the plan whereby Satan's power should be limited and broken, and whereby Christ should finally die. And when Christ rose from the dead His triumph was complete. Satan knew that his battle with Christ was lost, but yet he is at enmity with God.

It is man who has apostatized from God. Satan works on men's minds, trying to instill his devices into their minds and make them think that he is at last to be the sovereign of this world. But not so, for the God of heaven lives and reigns, and has children on the earth that He will translate to heaven without their seeing death, when He shall come with power and great glory. We want to ask, What excuse have you when this has been done in your behalf? Just as soon as the trial was ended and Christ was hanging on the cross, Satan thought he had gained the victory; but as soon as Christ arose that thought was uprooted forever for every world that God had ever created. It was final. Never again could he have the least power over the worlds or in heaven.

The justice of God was seen in that He gave Christ to die to save man, for the law condemned man to death; but the righteousness of Christ was brought in and imputed to him that he might be brought back to his loyalty to God. And when Christ's work was done, the news was heralded through the heavenly hosts.

When Jesus arose triumphant over the grave, and when He ascended from the Mount of Olivet, He was not only in sight of a few disciples, but many were looking on. There was a multitude of angels, thousands upon thousands who beheld the Son of God as He ascended on high. And as He approached the city of God their voices were raised and the highest angels sang, "Lift up your heads, O ye gates; and be ye lift up, ye everlasting doors; and the King of glory shall come in." The question arises, "Who is this King of glory?" Then the answer comes back, "The Lord of hosts, he is the King of glory." Then the gates are thrown back and the heavenly train enter in, and the angels would bow in adoration before the Son of God, but He waves them back. Not yet; He must first hear from the Father that the sacrifice has been accepted, and He says, I have a request. What is that request? That those whom Thou hast given Me be with Me where I am. Then comes the answer, Let all the angels worship Him; and they bow in adoration before Him, and they touch their golden harps, and raise their voices in praise, saying, Worthy is the Lamb that was slain, and lives again, a conqueror. And how the arches of heaven ring with rejoicing!

Now Christ is in the heavenly sanctuary. And what is He doing? Making atonement for us, cleansing the sanctuary from the sins of the people. Then we must enter by faith into the sanctuary with Him, we must commence the work in the sanctuary of our souls. We are to cleanse ourselves from all defilement. We must "cleanse ourselves from all filthiness of the flesh and spirit, perfecting holiness in the fear of God." Satan will come and tempt you and you will give way to his temptations. What then? Why, come and humble your hearts in confession, and by faith grasp the arm of Christ in the heavenly sanctuary. Believe that Christ will take your confession and hold up His hands before the Father—hands that have been bruised and wounded in our behalf— and He will make an atonement for all who will come with confession. What if you cannot understand about this matter? He says, "He that lacketh these things is blind, and cannot see afar off, and hath forgotten that he was purged from his old sins" (2 Peter 1:9).

Now brethren and sisters, I want you to see that you must "add to your faith virtue; and to virtue knowledge; and to knowledge temperance; and to temperance patience; and to patience godliness; and to godliness brotherly kindness; and to brotherly kindness charity. For if these things be in you, and abound, they make you that ye shall neither be barren nor unfruitful in the knowledge of our Lord Jesus Christ."

276

Now when you commence to work, Satan is going to work in an opposite direction; and if you are unkind and harsh, and if you are not seen in the house of God bearing your cross, you have not the knowledge of the Lord Jesus Christ; you do not discern Him in His love and matchless purity.

Many will say, I am saved, I am saved, I am saved. Well, have they been cleansed from all filthiness of the flesh and spirit? and can they cleanse themselves by the righteousness of the law? Jesus Christ came to this world, and there is His righteousness to impart to the children of men who are obeying the law of God. The whole world can say, I am saved, as well as any transgressor today. They can say, I believe on Christ that He is my Saviour, but why do they disregard His law which is the transcript of His character? When they disregard the law of Jehovah they disregard the Lord Jesus Christ.

Now, I want to say to you before closing, that we have a wonderful friend in Jesus, who came to save His people from the transgression of the law. What is sin? The only definition of sin is that it is the transgression of the law. Then here is Jesus Christ, who comes right in and imparts His righteousness to us; we cannot overcome in our own strength, but by faith in Him. If you will believe on Jesus Christ, you will have Him today. You must believe that He is your Saviour now, and that He imputes to you His righteousness because He has died, and because He has been obedient unto every requirement of that transgressed law of God. If you do this, you will have a saving knowledge of Jesus Christ. Adam and Eve lost Eden because they transgressed that law, but you will lose heaven if you transgress it.

We can be filled with all the fullness of God. Our lives may measure with the life of God. Then can we press back the powers of darkness. Glory to God in the highest! I love Him because He first loved me. I will magnify His name. I rejoice in His love, and when we shall enter in through the gates into the city it will be the highest privilege to cast my crown at His feet. Why? Because He gave me the victory, because He wrought out the plan of salvation. And when I look at the glory, and at the saints redeemed, just like a flash will I cast my crown at the feet of my Redeemer. It is His; it was He who purchased my redemption. Glory to God in the highest! Let us praise Him and talk of His mightiness and of what He will do for us. Let us keep His law and then He can trust us, for He has a law and He will reward obedience to that law; He will give us a crown of glory.

Now, brethren, we are almost home; we shall soon hear the voice of the Saviour richer than any music, saying, Your warfare is accomplished. Enter into the joy of thy Lord. Blessed, blessed, benediction; I want to hear it from His immortal lips. I want to praise Him; I want to honor Him that sitteth on the throne. I want my voice to echo and re-echo through the courts of heaven. Will you be there? Then you must educate your voice to praise Him on earth, and then you can join the heavenly choir and sing the song of Moses and the Lamb. God help us, and fill us with all fullness and power, and then we can taste of the joys of the world to come.—Manuscript 8, 1888.

✦ ✦ ✦

A Chosen People

Sermon by Ellen G. White at
Minneapolis, Minnesota, October 21, 1888

"YE ARE a chosen generation, a royal priesthood, an holy nation, a peculiar people; that ye should shew forth the praises of him who hath called you out of darkness into his marvellous light. . . . Dearly beloved, I beseech you as strangers and pilgrims, abstain from fleshly lusts, which war against the soul; having your conversation honest among the Gentiles: that, whereas they speak against you as evildoers, they may by your good works, which they shall behold, glorify God in the day of visitation" (1 Peter 2:9-12).

These words point out the high standard that we should maintain before the world. The God of heaven has done everything that He could do to win our allegiance. He made an infinite sacrifice that we might be brought out of darkness into His marvelous light.

Claiming possession of the world, Satan determined to get possession also of the minds of men. He comes to them with the advantages offered by the world, and says, "All these shall be yours if you will worship me." And many, lured on by the prize held out by him, bow at his shrine.

With a mighty arm and with wonderful manifestations of His power, God brought Israel out of Egypt. He made them His chosen people, and gave them His law. He said to them: "Thou art an holy people unto the Lord thy God. . . . Know therefore that the Lord thy God, he is God, the faithful God, which keepeth covenant and mercy with them that love him and keep his commandments to a thousand generations" (Deut. 7:6-9).

To us also have been spoken the words, "Ye are a chosen nation." Our work is to show forth the praises of Him who hath called us out of darkness into His marvelous light. How are we to do this? By showing to the world that we are a commandment-keeping people, walking in harmony with God's law. By never losing sight of His goodness and love, and by making everything in our lives subordinate to the claims of His Word. Thus we shall be representatives of Christ, showing forth in our lives a transcript of His character.

"But," one says, "I thought the commandments were a yoke of bondage." It is those only who break the law that find it a yoke of bondage. To those who keep the law it is life and joy and peace and happiness. The law is a mirror, into which we may look and discern the defects in our characters. Should we not be grateful that God has provided a means whereby we may discover our shortcomings?

There is no power in the law to save or to pardon the transgressor. What, then, does it do? It brings the repentant sinner to Christ. Paul declares, "I . . . have taught you publickly, and from house to house, testifying to the Jews, and also to the Greeks, repentance toward God and faith toward our Lord Jesus Christ" (Acts 20:20, 21). Why did he preach repentance? Because the law of God had been transgressed. Those who have broken the law must repent. Why did he preach faith in Christ? Because Christ is the One who has redeemed sinners from the penalty of the law. The law points to the remedy for sin—repentance toward God and faith in Christ.

Do you wonder that Satan wants to get rid of the law? He and all his agencies are striving to trample underfoot the commandments of Jehovah, and to erect a standard of their own. We are to show that God's chosen people will keep His commandments, refusing to swerve to the right or to the left in disobedience. They are to show that the truth of heavenly origin has done great things for them, that its converting power has taken hold of their souls.

Paul declares, "I had not known sin, but by the law. . . . I was alive without the law once: but when the commandment came, sin revived, and I died" (Rom. 7:7-9). The commandments remained the same, but Paul died.

In true conversion, the sinner is first convicted of his real condition. He realizes that he is a transgressor of God's law, and that the Lord has claims upon him which He will not relinquish. He sees that the connection between himself and God has been broken, but that if he repents of his transgression, confesses his sin, and takes hold by faith upon the grace of Christ, the connection that has been broken will be restored.

If God could have changed His law to meet man in his fallen condition, Christ need not have come to this world. Because the law was immutable, unchangeable, God sent His only-begotten Son to die for the fallen race. But did the Saviour take upon Himself the guilt of human beings and impute to them His righteousness in order that they might continue to violate the precepts of Jehovah? No, no! Christ came because there was no possibility of man's keeping the law in his own strength. He came to bring him strength to obey the precepts of the law. And the sinner, repenting of his transgression, may come to God and say, "O Father, I plead forgiveness through the merits of a crucified and risen Saviour." God will accept all who come to Him in the name of Jesus.

In order for man to obtain eternal life, divine power must unite with human effort, and this power Christ came to place within our reach. He says, "Without me ye can do nothing" (John 15:5). And He says again, "If ye shall ask any thing in my name, I will do it" (John 14:14). We have a right to lay hold of the arm of infinite power. When Christ came to the world, all heaven was poured out in this one great gift. God Himself came to us in Christ. "Have I been so long time with you, and yet hast thou not known me, Philip?" Christ said. "He that hath seen me hath seen the Father; and how sayest thou then, Shew us the Father?" (John 14:9).

My object in speaking these words to you today is to lead you to take your minds off the things of this world, and place them on the things of eternity. If your affections are set on things above, if in the daily life you are seeking to follow the perfect pattern, you need never be discouraged. The enemy may seek to cast his dark shadow between you and Christ, but your faith is to pierce the gloom. What are we in this world for? To represent Christ and to be a blessing to our fellow men. Christ is to be formed in us, the hope of glory. We are to live His life, that our lives may show forth to the world the love of God and the power of the gospel.

When God's people take their eyes off the things of this world, and place them on heaven and heavenly things, they will be a peculiar people, because they will see the mercy and goodness and compassion that God has shown to the children of men. His love will call forth a response from them, and their lives will show to those around them that the Spirit of God is controlling them, that they are setting their affections on things above, not on the things of the earth.

In thinking of heaven we may put our imagination to the utmost stretch, and think the loftiest thoughts that we are capable of thinking, and our minds will grow weary in the effort to comprehend the breadth and depth and height of the subject. It is impossible for our minds to take in the great themes of eternity. It is impossible for us even to make an effort to understand these things without the effort affecting our whole character for good, and having an uplifting influence on our minds. As we think of how Christ came to our world to die for fallen man, we understand something of the price that was paid for our redemption, and we realize that there is no true goodness or greatness apart from God.

Only by the light shining from the cross of Calvary can we know to what depths of sin and degradation the human race has fallen through sin. Only by the length of the chain let down from heaven to draw us up can we know the depths to which we had sunk. And it is only by keeping the unseen realties in view that we can understand anything of the wonderful theme of redemption.—Manuscript 17, 1888.

✦ ✦ ✦

Counsel to Ministers

Discourse, Minneapolis, Minnesota, October 21, 1888

"I AM the true vine, and my Father is the husbandman. Every branch in me that beareth not fruit he taketh away: and every branch that beareth fruit, he purgeth it, that it may bring forth more fruit. Now ye are clean through the word which I have spoken unto you. Abide in me, and I in you. As the branch cannot bear fruit of itself, except it abide in the vine, no more can ye, except ye abide in me. I am the vine, ye are the branches: He that abideth in me, and I in him, the same bringeth forth much fruit: for without me ye can do nothing. If a man abide not in me, he is cast forth as a branch, and is withered; and men gather them, and cast them into the fire, and they are burned. If ye abide in me, and my words abide in you, ye shall ask what ye will, and it shall be done unto you. Herein is my Father glorified, that ye bear much fruit; so shall ye be my disciples."

Brethren, I want to ask you a question. How can we come to God with full assurance of faith if we bear no fruit that testifies to a change wrought in us by the grace of God, no fruit that shows that we are in fellowship with Christ? How can we approach God in faith and be abiding in Christ and He in us when by our works we show that we are not bearing fruit?

What is the fruit we should bear? The fruit of kindly words and deeds. In God's Word we are told what are the works of the flesh and what the fruits of the Spirit. "The works of the flesh are manifest, which are these, adultery, fornication, uncleanness, lasciviousness, idolatry, witchcraft, hatred, variance, emulations, wrath, strife, seditions, heresies, envyings, murders, drunkenness, revellings, and such like: of the which I tell you before, as I have also told you in time past, that they which do these things shall not inherit the kingdom of God. But the fruit of the Spirit is love, joy, peace, longsuffering, gentleness, goodness, faith, meekness, temperance: against such there is no law." Is not this sufficiently plain? None of us need walk in uncertainty. "And they that are Christ's have crucified the flesh with the affections and lusts. If we live in the Spirit, let us also walk in the Spirit. Let us not be desirous of vain glory, provoking one another, envying one another."

In order to have true spiritual discernment, in order to be con-

281

scious of our own weakness and deficiency and our unlikeness to Christ, we need a close connection with God. Then we shall have a humble opinion of ourselves. We shall be meek and lowly in heart, walking prayerfully and carefully before God. We shall not boast ourselves beyond our measure.

In every age the gospel ministry has tended to the same end. But every minute specification is not revealed in the Word of God. He desires us to use our reason and experience, by their help adopting methods and plans which, under the existing circumstances, are for the benefit of the church and the schools and the other institutions which have been established. "By their fruits ye shall know them." If erroneous opinions are entertained, search the Scriptures with hearts which are humbled before God. Pray to the Lord, believing that He hears, and that He is a rewarder of those who diligently seek Him. If we will only believe, we shall receive the help we need.

The message "Go forward" is still to be heard and respected. The varying circumstances taking place in our world call for labor which will meet these peculiar developments. The Lord has need of men who are spiritually sharp and clear-sighted, men worked by the Holy Spirit, who are certainly receiving manna fresh from heaven. Upon the minds of such, God's Word flashes light, revealing to them more than ever before the safe path. The Holy Spirit works upon mind and heart. The time has come when through God's messengers the scroll is being unrolled to the world. Instructors in our schools should never be bound about by being told that they are to teach only what has been taught hitherto. Away with these restrictions.* There is a God to give the message His people shall speak. Let not any minister feel under bonds or be gauged by men's measurement. The gospel must be fulfilled in accordance with the messages God sends. That which God gives His servants to speak today would not perhaps have been present truth twenty years ago, but it is God's message for this time.

"Let no man deceive himself. If any man among you seemeth to be

---

* NOTE: These words were spoken October 21, 1888, to the workers in General Conference session who were giving thoughtful attention to the presentation of truths from God's Word. This was at a time when the absent and ailing president endeavored to restrict such study by a telegram urging that the brethren "stand by the landmarks." Ellen White ever encouraged careful Bible study, and indicated, as she did in 1892, that "the diligent, prayerful seeker for truth will find precious rays of light yet to shine forth from the word of God." She also at that time stated: "Many gems are yet scattered that are to be gathered together to become the property of the remnant people of God."—*Counsels on Sabbath School Work*, p. 34.

In her wholesome discussion of the question of "new light"—and all features of the question must be taken into consideration—she in 1885 said that "the only safety for any of us is in receiving no new doctrine, no new interpretation of the Scriptures, without first submitting it to brethren of experience. Lay it before them in a humble, teachable spirit, with earnest prayer; and if they see no light in it, yield to their judgment; for 'in the multitude of counselors there is safety.' "—*Testimonies*, vol. 5, p. 293.

She explained that the church is responsible for what is taught as the doctrines of the church. She made it clear, as she did in 1907, that "while it is true that the Lord guides individuals, it is also true that He is leading out a people, not a few separate individuals here and there, one believing this thing, and another that."—*Testimonies to Ministers*, p. 488. She warns that "men and women will arise professing to have some new light or some new revelation

wise in this world, let him become a fool"—in his own estimation—
"that he may be wise." An experience of this kind is needed here,
right with the men who have been forward to speak in this meeting.
"For the wisdom of this world is foolishness with God. For it is written,
He taketh the wise in their own craftiness. And again, The Lord knoweth
the thoughts of the wise, that they are vain. Therefore let no man
glory in men." Do consider this, I beseech you. "Thus saith the Lord,
Let not the wise man glory in his wisdom, neither let the mighty man
glory in his might, let not the rich man glory in his riches: but let him
that glorieth glory in this, that he understandeth and knoweth me, that
I am the Lord which exercise lovingkindness, judgment, and righteousness in the earth; for in these things I delight, saith the Lord."

Let men and women who are truly converted offer themselves in all
humility to the service of the Lord, for verily He hath need of them.
First, they must be emptied of all selfishness. They will be cleansed vessels unto honor. They will reflect the bright beams of the Sun of Righteousness to all with whom they come in contact. Partakers of the divine
nature, they will be savors of life unto life. They will not talk of the
faults of others, but will repeat the words of divine wisdom which have
penetrated and illuminated their hearts. They will be men who fear to
talk and make sport of God's messengers, but men who pray much.

"Where the Spirit of the Lord is, there is liberty. But we all, with
open face beholding as in a glass the glory of the Lord, are changed
into the same image from glory to glory, even as by the Spirit of the
Lord." John declares, "That which was from the beginning, which we
have heard, which we have seen with our eyes, which we have looked
upon, and our hands have handled, of the Word of life; . . . that which
we have seen and heard declare we unto you, that ye also may have
fellowship with us; and truly our fellowship is with the Father, and
with his Son Jesus Christ."

As John studied the life of Christ in the Word, he beheld as in a glass
the glory of the Lord, and he became changed into the same image,

---

whose tendency is to unsettle faith in the old landmarks. Their doctrines will not bear the test
of God's Word, yet souls will be deceived."—*Testimonies* (1885), vol. 5, p. 295.

The fundamental truths held by Seventh-day Adventists, born of diligent and faithful
Bible study, and attested by the miracle-working power of the Spirit of God, have stood through
the years. In 1900 Ellen White declared: "Eternal truth, which we have adhered to from the
beginning, is to be maintained in all its increasing importance to the close of probation."—
Ellen G. White letter 121, 1900.

The presentations of 1888, and subsequently, corrected the errors in the thinking of some,
and adjusted and led to a balanced emphasis of truth. This experience did not invalidate truth
we had earlier accepted. Genuine new light does not provide substitutes for, or cast a shadow
on, truth that has gone before. On this point Ellen White wrote in 1905, stating that "men will
arise with interpretations of Scripture which are to them truth, but which are not truth.
The truth for this time God has given us as a foundation of our faith. He Himself has
taught us what is truth. One will arise, and still another, with new light, which contradicts
the light that God has given under the demonstration of His Holy Spirit. . . . We are not to
receive the words of those who come with a message that contradicts the special points of
our faith."—*Selected Messages*, book 1, p. 161. And in this connection she declared that
"when the power of God testifies as to what is truth, that truth is to stand forever as the
truth."—*Ibid.* —WHITE TRUSTEES

from glory to glory, from character to character, till he was like that which he adored. He imitated the life in which he delighted. He knew the Saviour by an experimental knowledge. His Master's lessons were engraved on his soul. When he testified of the Saviour's grace, the simplicity of his language was eloquent with the love that pervaded his whole being. He had not a doubt nor a suspicion. He entered into no controversy, no wearisome contention.

In witnessing for Christ he declared what he knew, what he had seen and heard. There was no supposition, no guesswork, about what he said. And when insult was put upon Christ, when He was slighted, John felt the slight to the very depths of his being, and broke forth into indignation which was a manifestation of his love for Jesus. Christ had humbled Himself; He had taken man's nature; and few could see Him as John saw Him. But John had an advanced experience; the darkness had passed away. On him the true light was shining, and in his epistles he breaks forth against sin, presenting Christ as the One who could cleanse from all iniquity.

It was John's deep love for Christ that led him to desire always to be close by His side, and this position was awarded him. Jesus loves those who represent the Father, and John could talk of this love as no other of the disciples could. He reveals to his fellow men that which he knows by living experience it is his duty to reveal, representing in his character the character of Christ. The glory of the Lord was expressed in his face. The beauty of holiness which had transformed him shone with a Christlike radiance from his countenance.

Those who truly love God must manifest loving-kindness of heart, judgment, and righteousness to all with whom they come in contact; for these are the works of God. There is nothing Christ needs so much as agents who feel the necessity of representing Him. Evil speaking and evil thinking are ruinous to the soul. This has been current in this conference. There is nothing the church lacks so much as the manifestation of Christlike love. As the members of the church unite together in sanctified association, cooperating with Christ, He lives and works in them. Our eyes need the anointing with the heavenly eyesalve, that we may see what we are, and what we ought to be, and that power is provided in Christ sufficient to enable us to reach the high standard of Christian perfection.

We must keep Jesus our pattern ever before us. This is and ever will be present truth. It was by beholding Jesus and appreciating the virtues of His character that John became one with his Master in spirit. With spiritual vision he saw Christ's glory, the glory as of the only begotten of the Father, full of grace and truth; and he was changed from glory to glory into His likeness. And to him was committed the work of telling of the Saviour's love and the love His children should manifest for one another. "This is the message that ye heard from the beginning," he writes, "that we should love one another. . . . We know that we have passed from death unto life, because we love the brethren. He that loveth not his brother abideth in death. Whosoever hateth his brother is a murderer: and ye know that no murderer hath eternal life abiding in him. Hereby perceive we the love of God, because he laid down his life for us: and we ought to lay down our lives for the brethren. But whoso hath this world's good, and seeth his brother have need, and shutteth up his bowels of compassion from him, how dwelleth the love of God in him? My little children, let us not love in word, neither in tongue; but in deed and in truth."

"Beloved, let us love one another: for love is of God; and every one that loveth is born of God, and knoweth God. He that loveth not knoweth not God; for God is love. In this was manifested the love of God toward us, because that God sent his only begotten Son into the world, that we might live through him. . . . Beloved, if God so loved us, we ought also to love one another. . . . God is love; and he that dwelleth in love dwelleth in God, and God in him."

But although John dwells so particularly on love, he does not clasp hands with sin. Hear his words regarding the apostate from the faith, he who has had a knowledge of the truth but has departed from the faith, giving heed to seducing spirits. "Whosoever transgresseth, and abideth not in the doctrine of Christ, hath not God. He that abideth in the doctrine of Christ, he hath both the Father and the Son. If there come any unto you, and bring not this doctrine, receive him not into your house, neither bid him God speed: for he that biddeth him God speed is partaker of his evil deeds." Let all consider this.

John writes further, "He that saith, I know him, and keepeth not his commandments, is a liar, and the truth is not in him. But whoso keepeth his word, in him verily is the love of God perfected. . . . He that saith he abideth in him ought himself also so to walk, even as he walked."

The Lord has plain words for those who, like the Pharisees, make great boast of their piety but whose hearts are destitute of the love of God. The Pharisees refused to know God and Jesus Christ whom He had sent. Are we not in danger of doing the same thing as did the Pharisees and scribes?

But while reproof is to be given, it must be given in accordance with Christ's direction. The apostle Paul writes, "Brethren, if a man be overtaken in a fault, ye which are spiritual, restore such an one in the spirit of meekness; considering thyself, lest thou also be tempted." This work is given not only to ministers but to every individual member of the church. It is to be carried out in the family and in the church. Love and unity strengthen by exercise. Do not become impatient with your brother's faults and weaknesses. On another point you may well be disgusted with your own weakness. We are related to one another in the mysterious web of humanity. We are but threads which help to compose the great whole.

We see individuals committing errors, and we are pained because their lives are not in accordance with the Bible standard of righteousness. But we are not to become impatient. If we have the mind of Christ, we shall feel a burden for the welfare of him who has forgotten to be a doer of the Word. Do not speak of his errors to others. Follow the rule Jesus has given. Go to the wrongdoer alone first, and see if by words of wisdom you cannot save him.

The apostle James, inspired by Jesus Christ, lays down our duty in clear lines. "Brethren, if any of you do err from the truth, and one convert him; let him know, that he which converteth the sinner from the error of his way, shall save a soul from death, and shall hide a multitude of sins." We are Christ's witnesses, Christ's representatives. In his epistle to Titus, Paul charges him to set in order things that are wanting in the church. "Speak thou the things which become sound doctrine," he says. The teacher of truth is to educate all, both old and young. He is to exhort aged men to be "sober, grave, temperate, sound in faith, in charity, in patience. The aged women likewise, that they be in behaviour as becometh holiness, not false accusers, not given to much wine, teachers of good things; that they may teach the young women to be sober, to love their husbands, to love their children, to be discreet, chaste, keepers at home, good, obedient to their own husbands, that the word of God be not blasphemed." When those who profess to be servants of Christ do not walk circumspectly, God is dishonored and the truth is reproached.

"Young men likewise exhort to be sober minded. In all things shewing thyself a pattern of good works: in doctrine shewing uncorruptness, gravity, sincerity, sound speech, that cannot be condemned; that he that is of the contrary part may be ashamed, having no evil thing to say of you."

I have been pained to hear so much jesting and joking among old and young as they are seated at the dining table. I have inquired, Are these men aware that there is by their side a Watcher who is disgusted with their spirit and the influence which they exert, and is making a record of their words and actions? Will our ministers, young and old, countenance these things? Shall not we who name the name of Christ take heed to the words, "In all things shewing thyself a pattern of good works, in doctrine shewing uncorruptness, gravity, sincerity, sound speech, that cannot be condemned"? If the truth as it is in Jesus abides in our hearts, it will sanctify our lives. Our speech will not be evil. Obeying the truth we shall work the works of righteousness.

By our words and deeds we may reveal the power of the truth to transform the character. We may each reveal that we depend on Christ's righteousness, not upon our own manufactured righteousness. We may abide in Christ as the branch abides in the vine, having such a living connection with Him that it is a pleasure to work as He worked, to be a help and blessing to our brethren. We can work the works of Christ, doing those things that are pleasing in His sight.

In all you do, make Christ the center of attraction. Constantly look to Him who is your pattern, the Author and Finisher of your faith. Cultivate constant, fervent gratitude to God for the gift of His beloved Son. Represent Christ. Squander not your moral forces upon trifles, but earnestly improve the opportunities given you to reflect the light of the Sun of Righteousness. Cease to glorify man. Glory in Christ and the truth. You may crown Jesus with honor, for though so meek and lowly He was a daily conqueror over temptation. Every soul who is a partaker of the divine nature is an overcomer in His own behalf, and is victorious, having escaped the corruption that is in the world through lust.

We are laborers together with God; and not only are we to have respect unto the recompense of reward, but we are to labor zealously for the Redeemer's glory by bringing sheaves to the Master. Every soul saved will swell the triumphant anthems of praise which the redeemed will sing. In every fellow being we are to see the purchase of the blood of Christ. The Saviour's interest is identified with the interests of the souls He has ransomed by an infinite sacrifice.

My brethren and sisters, do we realize the importance of this subject? Why are we so listless? Why are we satisfied to remain so poorly fitted to work for the uplifting of humanity? Why is not every entrusted capability used for the Master? Why are so many contented with the feeble, lifeless condition of our churches? The heavenly universe is looking with amazement upon our Christless work. Neglect is seen in all our borders. Slipshod work is tolerated and passed by. How long shall this continue? Shall we not arise, and with determined, harmonious effort take up our responsibilities, laboring in Christ's lines with sanctified capabilities? Put away the controversial spirit which you have been educating yourselves in for years. Educate yourselves to pray to God in sincerity and truth. Sing with the spirit and understanding also. Much is expected of us.

What are our young men doing? Jesus is waiting to bind their hearts up with His great heart of love, to bind their interests with His own. He says to them, Young men, flee youthful lusts. Will you obey His voice? You are surely not doing this now. The truth is an inherent power, and if brought into the sanctuary of the soul, will draw men and women to Christ. It will win its way to human hearts. To those who look to Him Christ by His Holy Spirit reveals the beauty of truth. He shows Himself to be the sin-pardoning Saviour.

Young men, you may have the truth on your side. When your heart and all your faculties are brought under the influence of truth, when you bring the truth, with all its living, sanctifying principles, into your heart, you will have confidence to present it to others. Christ is then made unto you wisdom, and righteousness, and sanctification, and redemption. We are laborers together with God, and Christ is by your side. You are yoked up with Him, He leading and guiding. Such a worker is as a sharp sickle in the harvest field. He does not use his God-given powers in debating. That is Satan's line. Pointing to the cross of Calvary, he cries, "Behold the Lamb of God, which taketh away the sin of the world." He urges sinners to behold eternal realities. He holds the telescope before his eyes, that by faith he may discern these realities. Like Moses, he endures the seeing of Him who is invisible. He does not seek ease or amusement. He does not visit the churches to be petted and waited upon, to jest and joke. He knows that there is stern, earnest work to be done. Those who are truly converted do not waste the precious moments in foolish conversation and making a mock of their brethren. By words that have a weight of influence for good they give full proof of their ministry. They deny self and lift the cross, and follow Jesus the cross-bearer. They ardently desire to yoke up with Christ, to lift His burdens and partake of His sufferings.

Young men, Jesus calls you, saying, "Follow Me." Those who follow Him will not walk in darkness, for Christ is the light of life. Our older ministering brethren must drop some of their responsibilities or else they will go down in the silence of the grave. The aged standard-bearers may act as worthy counselors and living witnesses, but their younger and stronger brethren should bear the heavy burdens. John says, "I have written unto you, young men, because ye are strong, . . . and ye have overcome the wicked one." You whose eyes are not dimmed, whose brain power has not been worn by constant taxation, should plan, devise, and execute, treating the aged workers with tenderness, as fathers, and looking up to them as counselors and guides. Young workers should respect the age and experience of their older brethren.

The Lord desires us all to be learners in the school of Christ. Young and old have precious lessons to learn from the divine Teacher, and when these lessons are learned they are to impart them to others. God is presenting to the minds of men divinely appointed precious gems of truth, appropriate for our time. God has rescued these truths from the companionship of error, and has placed them in their proper framework. When these truths are given their rightful position in God's great plan, when they are presented intelligently and earnestly, and with reverential awe, by the Lord's servants, many will conscientiously believe because of the weight of evidence, without waiting for every supposed difficulty which may suggest itself to their minds to be removed. Others, not discerning spiritual things, will keep themselves in a combative frame of mind, opposing every argument that does not meet their ideas. Shall this miserable work cease?

Those who have not been sinking the shaft deeper and still deeper into the mine of truth will see no beauty in the precious things presented at this conference. When the will is once set in stubborn opposition to the light given, it is difficult to yield, even under the convincing evidence which has been in this conference. To controvert, to question, to criticize, to ridicule, is the education many have received and the fruit they bear. They refuse to admit evidence. The natural heart is in warfare against light, truth, and knowledge. Jesus Christ has been in every sleeping room where you have been entertained. How many prayers went up to heaven from these rooms?

Satan is fruitful in bringing up devices to evade the truth. But I call upon you to believe the words I speak today. Truth of heavenly origin is confronting Satan's falsehoods, and this truth will prevail. We do well to remember that Christ is the light of the world, and that fresh beams of light are constantly reflected from the Source of all light.

He who studies the truth, who prayerfully opens the eyes of his understanding to see and his heart to receive the bright beams of the Sun of Righteousness, will be in harmony with the messenger and the message God sends. All the opposition, all the prejudice, all the suggestions of the enemy, will never make the truth less precious or less true. Only when men yield to the subtilty of the enemy does the truth become darkness to them. But even though the truth is opposed and spoken against by those who should be blessed, strengthened, and made joyful by it, its value and brightness is not lessened; for the Lord's messengers will hold up the telescope to the spiritual eye, that the truth may be seen from all points, and its value appreciated.

A fair investigation will not fail to reveal wonderful things in God's Word. Every jot of resistance places the opposer in a darker shade. He does not want to see. He will not search God's Word. But opposition and resistance only serve to bring out truth in new, distinct lines. The more truth is spoken against, the brighter it will shine. Thus the precious ore is polished. Every word of slander spoken against it, every misrepresentation of its value, awakens attention and is the means of leading to closer investigation as to what is saving truth. The truth becomes more highly estimated. New beauty and greater value are revealed from every point of view.

Brethren, God has most precious light for His people. I call it not new light; but O, it is strangely new to many. Jesus said to His disciples, "A new commandment I give unto you, That ye love one another; as I have loved you." This was really an old commandment, which had been given in the Old Testament scriptures, but it had been lost. It had not been practiced. The command that they should love one another as Christ had loved them was indeed new to the disciples. But the revealing of this love would give to the world an unmistakable evidence that they were God's children.

I call upon the young men who are entering the work as ministers to take heed how they hear. Be careful how you oppose the precious truths of which you now have so little knowledge. Search the Scriptures for yourselves. You have altogether too limited knowledge of yourself. Know for yourselves what is truth. Do not take any man's words, any man's prejudices, any man's arguments, any man's theories. This has been done by ministers to the injury of their experience, and it has left them novices when they should be wise in the Scriptures and in the power of God. Take your Bibles, humble yourselves, and weep and fast and pray before the Lord, as did Nathanael, seeking to know the truth. Jesus' divine eye saw Nathanael praying, and answered his prayer.

I saw an angel of God inquiring of these men who have educated themselves as debaters, "How many prayers have you offered?" Oh, your levity, your speeches, are all written in the book. If you only knew how Christ has regarded your religious attitude at this meeting!

You must gain an experience for yourselves. I beg of you not to think that long sermons are an unmistakable evidence of your ministerial ability. Oh, there is something more to the ministry than sermonizing. Many, many discourses, like the offering of Cain, are profitless because Christless. Those who give them tire the people and fail to give them proper spiritual food.

Piety must be practiced in the home. Interested personal efforts must be made for those around you. Seek the Lord in private prayer. Ask Christ to do for you what you need to have done. He has been tempted in all points like as we are, and He knows how to succor those that are tempted. God calls upon you to leave the atmosphere of unbelief in which you have been dwelling, and place yourselves in an atmosphere of faith and confidence. Do your best. Do not seek wisdom from finite men, who may be bewildered by the temptations of Satan, who may plant the seeds of doubt rather than the seeds of faith. Go to Jesus, "who giveth to all men liberally, and upbraideth not." Has not His invitation reached your ears and touched your heart? He says, "Come unto me, all ye that labour and are heavy laden, and I will give you rest. Take my yoke upon you, and learn of me; for I am meek and lowly in heart: and ye shall find rest unto your souls. For my yoke is easy, and my burden is light."

Let no human hand place a yoke upon your neck. Take the yoke Christ gives. Learn of Him; for He is meek and lowly, and you will find rest. It is Christ's meekness and lowliness that you need. Go to the Lord with the faith, simplicity, and confidence of a little child. Tell Him the whole trouble, withholding nothing. Ask Him to teach you how to use your entrusted talents in the best way. Thus you may increase your talents. If you go out to labor in any portion of the Lord's great moral vineyard, take heed; keep watch over yourself, over your thoughts and words. Pray for an understanding heart, for a knowledge of how to humble yourself before the Lord. Ask for Christ's grace and efficiency, and you will not be left to labor alone. God gives every humble, devoted learner a clearer insight into the truth. He will give them precious souls as their hire.

I have been instructed that many go forth to preach who do not know how to labor for the salvation of sinners. They are not themselves consecrated to God. They need to be converted. Many have been dedicated to the sacred work of the ministry when, if close examination were made in regard to their religious experience, it would be seen that they need to seek most earnestly for the transforming grace of Jesus Christ before they can teach sinners how to seek in faith for pardon.

Those who would be laborers together with God must receive wisdom from the Great Teacher who is our example in all things, in order to present the truth in its simplicity. Learn of Christ. All pride, all selfishness, all self-importance, must be cut away from all teachers. All the *sang-froid,* which is so common, the theatrical gestures, all lightness and trifling, all jesting and joking, must be seen by the one who wears Christ's yoke to be "not convenient"—an offense to God and a denial of Christ. It unfits the mind for solid thought and solid labor. It makes men inefficient, superficial, and spiritually diseased.

He who believes the truth for this time will practice personal piety. The language of his heart will be, "Who is sufficient for these things?" Let every minister be sedate. As he studies the life of Christ he will see the necessity of walking circumspectly. Yet he may be, and will be, if connected with the Sun of Righteousness, cheerful and happy, showing forth the praises of Him who hath called him out of darkness into His marvelous light. The conversation will be pure, entirely free from all slang phrases.

If Christ is abiding in your heart, you will show meekness and gentleness and purity of thought. You will follow elevated, noble principles, because you have learned the lessons taught in the school of Christ. If you have not felt the need of learning every day in this school, it is time you did feel this need. Learn of Christ, and then go forth in the strength of Him who has said, "Lo, I am with you alway, even unto the end of the world." A divided heart God will not accept. Put your whole soul into your work, and never leave your work half done because you wish to go to another place. God will accept only faithful work. Reprove, rebuke, exhort, with all long-suffering and doctrine. Bind off your work thoroughly. Leave no dropped stitches for someone else to pick up. Do not disappoint Christ. Determine that you will succeed, and in the strength of Christ you may give full proof of your ministry.

A minister is one who ministers. If you confine your work to sermonizing, the flock of God will suffer; for they need personal effort. Let your discourses be short. Long sermons wear out both you and the people. If ministers would make their sermons only half as long, they would do more good and would have strength left for personal work. Visit families, pray with them, converse with them, search the Scriptures with them, and you will do them good. Give them evidence that you seek their prosperity, and want them to be healthy Christians. If you are staying in a family, do not allow yourself to be waited on. Show that you wish to be helpful. If possible, use the ax or the hoe. Bring in water and wood. Show that you regard work as a blessing. Physical exercise will be a blessing to you, and will increase your influence for good. Remember that to minister means far more than merely preaching.

Nothing is so discouraging to the advancement of present truth as the haphazard work done by some of the ministers for the churches. Faithful labor is needed. The churches are ready to die, because they are not strengthened in Christlikeness. The Lord is not pleased with the loose way in which the churches are left because men are not faithful stewards of God's grace. They do not receive His grace, and therefore cannot impart it. The churches are weak and sickly because of the unfaithfulness of those who are supposed to labor among them, whose duty it is to have an oversight over them, watching for souls as they that must give an account. Be thorough and determined in your efforts to serve God. Keep the eye fixed on Christ. Do not fix your attention on some favorite minister, copying his example and imitating his gestures; in short, becoming his shadow. Let no man put his mold upon you. Let the hand of God mold and fashion you after the divine similitude. Cease from man, whose breath is in his nostrils. Hang your helpless soul on Jesus Christ. He is unchangeable, the same yesterday, today, and forever.

My heart was made glad as I heard the testimonies borne after the discourse on Sabbath. These testimonies made no reference to the speaker, but to the light and truth; and this is the way it should ever be. Praise no man; flatter no man; and permit no man to praise or flatter you. Satan will do enough of this work. Lose sight of the instrument, and think of Jesus. Praise the Lord. Give glory to God. Make melody to God in your hearts. Talk of the truth. Talk of the Christian's hope, the Christian's heaven.

If we neglect to walk in the light given, it becomes darkness to us; and the darkness is proportionate to the light and privileges which we have not improved. Christ says, "If therefore the light that is in thee be darkness, how great is that darkness!" If we walk in the knowledge of the truth, our light will shine to those around us in spirit, in words, in actions; we will be fruitful branches of the living vine. If we know God's requirements and claim to love Him, yet cherish sin, God will not hear us when we ask for His blessing; for He does not minister to sin. There are those whose conscience is hardened by habitual sin. They bear no rich clusters of precious fruit, because they are not branches of the true vine. Their prayers rise no higher than their heads, because they are in their prayers presenting only a form of words, whether offered in the church, in the family, or in secret. They receive no strength, because they ask amiss.

But when those who are striving with all their power to overcome, confess their sins, God is faithful and just to forgive their sins, and to cleanse them from all unrighteousness for Christ's sake. When brought into the sanctuary of the soul, the truth of God works by faith and purifies the soul, elevating, refining, ennobling it.

There was a time when Israel could not prevail against their enemies. This was because of Achan's sin. God declared, "Neither will I be with you any more, except ye destroy the accursed thing from among you." God is the same today. If defiling sins are cherished by those who claim to believe the truth, the displeasure of God rests upon the church, and He will not remove it until the members do all in their power to show their hatred for sin, and their determination to cast it out of the church. God is displeased with those who call evil good and good evil. If jealousy, evil surmising, and evil-speaking are allowed to have a place in the church, that church is under the frown of God. It will be spiritually unhealthy until it is cleansed from these sins, for till then God cannot reveal His power to strengthen and elevate His people and give them victory.

God is not pleased with the slothful work done in the churches. He expects His stewards to be true and faithful in giving reproof and correction. They are to expel wrong after the rule God has given in His Word, not according to their own ideas and impulses. No harsh means must be used, no unfair, hasty, impulsive work done. The efforts made to cleanse the church from moral uncleanness must be made in God's way. There must be no partiality, no hypocrisy. There must be no favorites, whose sins are regarded as less sinful than those of others. Oh, how much we all need the baptism of the Holy Ghost. Then we shall always work with the mind of Christ, with kindness, compassion, and sympathy, showing love for the sinner while hating sin with a perfect hatred.

A work needs to be done for many who are assembled here. The door of the heart is blocked up with the rubbish of selfishness, questioning, criticism, judgment pronounced in accordance with the unsanctified heart. Now is the time to seek God, with earnest confession and contrition, that He may turn His face toward us, and light and blessing come into our midst. Then the enemy will be disappointed. The heavenly universe will rejoice, and souls who are now under temptation and the frown of God will be won to Christ. Shall we not clear away the darkness by doing the work God has given us to do? We are laborers together with God. Jesus is waiting to work in us and by us and through us to will and to do of His good pleasure. If we neglect the Lord's heritage and feel little burden for the church and souls perishing in their sins, we are condemned by God for not strengthening that which was ready to die. If, as Christ's overseers, we do our work with an eye single to the glory of God, there is no reason why the church should be weak, faithless, and corrupt. Let the watchmen on the walls of Zion awake! Let them do their duty with fidelity. They need so much the heavenly endowment, that they may be laborers together with God in the great plan of salvation. To those who have been true and faithful Christ will say, "Come, ye blessed of my Father, inherit the kingdom prepared for you from the foundation of the world." "Enter thou into the joy of thy Lord." All who enter the kingdom of heaven as conquerors will understand the meaning of this benediction, for they will have done the work Christ has given them to do. They have participated with Him in saving the souls of their fellow men. Through the grace of Christ they have brought sheaves to the Master, and with all the heavenly universe they rejoice as they see souls that have been saved through their earnest efforts, given abundant entrance into heaven, made heirs of God and joint heirs with Christ. How foolish then will appear all fear and distrust of Christ, as the redeemed see that He was waiting to give them freely the richest blessings of heaven.

Let none here shut themselves away from God by their perversity of spirit, and then keep complaining that they have no light. Arise, dear souls; arise by faith, and do what you ought to do. Christ says, Follow Me, and you shall not walk in darkness. Let go your human wisdom, and ask God for that wisdom which is pure, elevating, and ennobling, and it shall be given you. Come up out of the cellar of doubt, of unbelief, of jealousy, and evil surmising, into the upper chamber of faith, hope, courage, and thankfulness. Make melody to God in the heart. The garden of the Lord is strewn with precious flowers. Gather the roses and the lilies and the pinks from God's spiritual garden. Rejoice in the Lord always, and again I say, Rejoice. Let not the world receive the impression that there is no peace nor joy nor happiness in serving the Lord.

It is Satan's work to misrepresent the Father and His Son, to misrepresent truth and gloss over error, making it appear as truth. But connected with God, we may distinguish between the genuine and the spurious. Light will dispel darkness. Why should we not avail ourselves of God's gracious promises, returning the glory to Him in heartfelt thanksgiving? Christ died for us that we might enter into possession of eternal riches. With hearts filled with gratitude to God, let us use the opportunities He has placed within our reach, that we may be fitted and prepared for the mansions Jesus has gone to prepare for those who love Him. If we fail through indolence, unbelief, worldliness, or covetousness, we shall suffer irreparable loss, for we shall lose an eternity of bliss. I tell you in the fear of God that day by day we are forming characters that will decide our destiny for weal or for woe.

Heaven is a holy place, and there entereth into it nothing that defileth. We cannot be truly happy here unless God's will is our will, unless we are sanctified to God, body, soul, and spirit. The more we think of heaven, the more happiness we shall have.—Manuscript 8a, 1888.

✦✦✦

Remarks by Ellen G. White on Missionary Work

Minneapolis, Minnesota, October 23, 1888

OUR SAVIOUR has given to everyone his work, and no one of us can plead any excuse to God why he has not done the very work which God has given him to do. He does not require of the men to whom He has entrusted two talents the use of five talents; but He expects us to do our very best according to the capability and the powers which He has given us. And while we seek to put to use the talents He has given us, these talents will improve.

The plans which have been suggested by our brother we believe to be sound, and if we will practice something in this line in the several churches, we shall find that those churches which carry out a system of labor will be living churches; for a working church is a living church. But here comes in the difficulty. There needs to be ability to educate properly, to teach how the different members shall have their part in the work; and every one who is set as a leader in the church, or a minister who has charge in the churches should consider this a part of his work. Now how is it possible for them to neglect this part of the work, and yet to be able to fulfill the direction that is given in the Bible by Paul, to "present every man perfect in Christ Jesus"? This is the very work that is devolving on the teacher. It is to try to educate, educate, educate, by precept and example; and if we can get a church in working order, and if we can teach them how to work in this very line, you will find that these workers will have a special interest. "Why, yes," they will say, "I have acted a part in that work; I have done something in that, and I have an interest to do more." Just according to the several ability which God has committed to them can they work intelligently, and work in Christ.

Now here is the great essential point, to be sure that these workers have the spirit of Jesus Christ. If they are filled with the love of God, which should be in the heart of every worker, and if they seek wisdom from above, they will become more and more intelligent in regard to their work, and they will become more efficient in their work and will come up to be useful workers. Now, the very first thing is to have our hearts and minds and ways and manners so that they will not offend. We want to be such excellent representatives of the missionary cause that it shall stand as high as possible. Our brother was speaking in regard to commencing on the bottom round of the ladder. I believe this is the best way. It is not best for those uneducated to grasp at the top round of the ladder and think that they can do the work; but if they will be humble they will begin to gain an experience and have an aptitude for the work.

I want to know why, as Christians who profess to believe the most solemn truths that God ever gave to mortals, we should not have works to correspond to our faith. Christ has said, "Let your light so shine before men, that they may see your good works, and glorify your Father which is in heaven." That is the work we are to do, and God will help us by letting His light shine through us. We want to be the very best and most intelligent workers that there are anywhere.

We can see many of our sisters who know how to crochet fine articles for their houses. Now, what if they would spend their time in earnest prayer to God and the study of His Word that He would help them to have heavenly wisdom to know how to save the souls of those around them? It looks to me as though this kind of work is hay, wood, and stubble, of substances that are consumable and perishable; but the work that they might do in cleansing their own household and working for their neighbors would present lasting results of good. And if they were interested in this work they might be sowing seeds of truth. We must sow beside all waters, and we do not know which shall prosper, this or that. But the first work is a personal consecration to God.

I have seen ladies in England who would be riding in their carriages with their little dogs in their arms and the little blanket to put over them, and the houses that were built, beautiful and expensive. You ask what these houses are for, and the answer is, "For the hounds and dogs." But you can see the little children and women, miserable and poor, in the streets, destitute of clothing. Now, what sense is there in that? Do you think that work will be as far reaching as eternity? We do not want to misuse any of God's creatures, but we want to give our first attention to those souls for whom Christ died, and we do not want to devote our means in such foolish channels. We do not want our means to flow out for our own selfish interests; but we want to use it in gaining that experience that will help us to advance the missionary work; and in doing this we are laying up a treasure in heaven. God Himself will connect with every self-sacrificing work and effort that shall be made to educate and train ourselves for labor, and will put His seal and mold on it. It may look to us very feeble, and we may never understand the results of our labor, but God knows all about it, and we sow beside all waters, not knowing which will prosper, this or that.

There are churches in different places which we may find that are ready to die. If they were ready to die to self and sin, if covetousness and the love of pleasure would die, they would not be so bad; they would be led to bring all their powers into exercise for doing the work of the Master, and then it would be a good death. But it is a spiritual death that pervades our churches. There are not those who feel the importance of teaching the members of the church and trying to get workers for the cause of God, to educate them that they may see the importance of putting to the stretch every power and talent that God has given them.

Our sisters can do a good work for the Master. They can work for the sisters in their homes. Our brethren can reach the men. Those who have a little time, in the place of smoking the cigar and enjoying themselves at the saloon, can not only save their money, but their time, and can do a good work for the Master.

I remember that when the converting power of God came upon me in my childhood I wanted everyone else to get the blessing that I had, and I could not rest till I had told them of it. I began to visit with my young companions and went to their houses to talk with them and tell them my experience, how precious the Saviour was to me, and how I wanted to serve Him, and how I wanted them to serve Him also. So I would talk of the preciousness of Christ, and I would say, Won't you kneel down and pray with me? Some would kneel and some would sit in their chairs, but before we gave up, every one would be on their knees and we would pray together for hours, till the last one would say, "I believe that Jesus has forgiven my sins." Sometimes the sun would begin to make its appearance in the heavens before I would give up the struggle.

There is a great power in Jesus. Now when we go into the house we should not begin to talk of frivolous things, but come right to the point and say, I want you to love Jesus for He has first loved you. And as Brother Starr has said, take along the publications and ask them to read. When they see that you are sincere they will not despise any of your efforts. There is a way to reach the hardest hearts. Approach in the simplicity, sincerity, and humility that will help us to reach the souls of those for whom Christ died. We do not want to be negligent in this work.

The plan now under consideration I believe to be one that God will be pleased with. Churches that are now ready to die want someone to devise and plan for them who has the power to set things in operation. But who will do it? There are enough who want to be Christians, and if we will let the leaven begin to work, it will take one and then another, just as the Spirit of God will work with us, and we will see that we can reach the people, not by our own smartness, but by the Spirit of God. Yet we want the ability and power that God has given us to be brought into use. We do not want to be novices forever; we want to know how to conduct ourselves properly; we want Christian politeness. And we want to carry it with us in all our work. We do not want any of the sharp corners which may be in our character to be made prominent, but we want to work in humility, so we will forget them, and better characteristics will come in. We want cheerfulness in our work. A great deal depends on the way you meet those whom you go to visit. You can take hold of the hand in such a way as at once to gain the confidence. If you take hold of it with a cold, unimpressive manner, as though you were an iceberg and did not want to be melted, you will find no warmth in return.

When we were on the boat on our way to Europe I met a physician who said, "I want to give you a little advice. You will find a cold, stiff-necked people, and if you will be as stiff you will never do them any good; but if you will go right to them and talk with them no matter how diffident they seem to be, they will meet you all right; talk to them just as you did to me. They will see that you have a heart and will love to talk with you. I love to talk with you about these things; do the same way in England."

You don't want to hold yourselves as though it were a condescension to come in contact with poor families. Talk as though they were as good a piece of humanity as you are. They have little enough light and joy, and why not carry additional joy and light to shine in upon them and fill their hearts? What we want is the tender sympathy of Jesus Christ, and then we can melt our way right into their hearts. We want to clothe ourselves, not with pomposity, but with plain, simple dress, so that they will feel that we are an equal with them, and as though we considered that they were worth saving, and we can melt our way into their hearts.

Now, brethren and sisters, we want the iron taken out of our souls, and we want it taken out of our manner of work. We can educate workers in every church. Don't let the ministers feel that they must do all the talking, and all the laboring; but call on others to lead the meetings occasionally. In doing this they are being educated. Let them take turns in giving Bible readings. This is calling into use the talent which God has given them.

I read of a man who had a corps of workmen over whom he placed an overseer. He had charge of twelve men and they were to dig a trench, and the man came along one day where they were at work, and there was the overseer down in the trench, and the sweat was rolling off from his brow, but the twelve men were looking down into the trench watching him in his labor. The overseer was called up and asked what he was doing down there. "I ordered you to keep twelve men at work. Why have you not done it? Here are your wages."

Now, God has made us teachers of the flock, and He wants us to educate them in every branch of the work, that we may bring in all the talents. Our ministers do the labor instead of educating others to take the responsibility of the cause. The minister's work should be the work of a teacher. One laborer might set twenty to work in less time than it would take him to do the work himself. Let them blunder and make mistakes, and then kindly show them how they can do it better, and then you can be educating, educating, educating, until you have men and women who have experience in the things of God and can carry responsibility, and that is what we have been suffering for. We need men who can bear responsibility, and the best way to gain the experience they need is to engage in this work.

Then if we work for others we will not lack for something to talk about when we assemble together. We will not have to talk about our brethren and think of our self-sufficiency, for we will be working out of those things and getting to be workers for Jesus Christ. If this branch of the work could be taken up in every conference and church, I believe we should see in the year to come an elevation, a healthfulness, a different atmosphere in the church. There would not be so many tattlers and gossipers. There would not be so much time for idle tales, and we would see many souls converted to Christ. Why should we not feel an interest for those around us when Christ has given us such an evidence of His love? Why, brethren, God will not leave us. He will let His converting power be upon us. These things will enlarge as the waves from a pebble thrown in the water; the first are small, but they grow larger and larger till they reach the bank.

Brethren, we want to do something to set things in operation for God. We want to do something that will save souls, that at last we may enter into the joy of our Lord, that we may give praises to our Lord that we have been the means of saving some through Him. That some may say, It is through your instrumentality, it is you who saved me through Jesus Christ. That is the way we shall enter into the joy of our Lord. This is the way we want to work. We cannot know here what the effect of our work has been, but we shall see in eternity what we have done for the Master. Shall we plan and devise to carry out these plans to the letter? Then the blessings of the Lord will attend all our labors.—Manuscript 10, 1888.

✦ ✦ ✦

Morning Talk by Ellen G. White

Minneapolis, Minnesota, October 24, 1888

NOW OUR meeting is drawing to a close, and not one confession has been made; there has not been a single break so as to let the Spirit of God in.

Now I was saying what was the use of our assembling here together and for our ministering brethren to come in if they are here only to shut out the Spirit of God from the people? We did hope that there would be a turning to the Lord here. Perhaps you feel that you have all you want.

I have been awake since two o'clock and I have been praying, but I cannot see the work making the advancement that I wish I could. I have been talking and pleading with you, but it does not seem to make any difference with you. As I have told my children, although they are thousands of miles away, when I go to God in prayer for them I know where they are standing in the Christian life, and if they are not living close to God I am alarmed.

Had Brother Kilgore been walking closely with God he never would have walked onto the ground as he did yesterday and made the statement he did in regard to the investigation that is going on. That is, they must not bring in any new light or present any new argument notwithstanding they have been constantly handling the Word of God for years, yet they are not prepared to give a reason of the hope they have because one man is not here. Have we not all been looking into this subject?

I never was more alarmed than at the present time. Now, I have been taken down through the first rebellion, and I saw the workings of Satan and I know something about this matter that God has opened before me, and should not I be alarmed? And then to take the position that because Elder Butler was not here that that subject should not be taken up. I know this is not of God and I shall not feel free until I have told you.

Here was the enemy inculcating his ideas in the hearts of the angels, and they express these ideas that he has inculcated as their own, and Satan takes them and tells them to the other angels as the sentiments of the angels he has been working with, and thus he inculcates his ideas into their minds, and then draws them out of the angels as their own ideas.

Now I am full of pain as I view these things, and how can I help it? Do you think that when I see these things transpiring that I can keep still and say nothing when these things have been shown me? I want to tell you, my brethren, that it is not right to fasten ourselves upon the ideas of any one man.

Now I want to tell you what a good brother said to me as he was about to leave the meeting. He came to me with such a feeling of relief that everything was settled and our old position was all right.

Well, one says, "Your prayers and your talk run in the channel with Dr. Waggoner." I want to tell you, my brethren, that I have not taken any position; I have had no talk with the doctor nor with anyone on this subject, and am not prepared to take a position yet. By their fruits ye shall know them. I took my brethren and told them just where they were, but they did not believe me, they did not believe they were in any danger.

If Elder Waggoner's views were wrong, what business has anyone to get up and say what they did here yesterday? If we have the truth it will stand. These truths that we have been handling for years—must Elder Butler come and tell us what they are? Now, do let us have common sense. Don't let us leave such an impression on this people. One brother asked me if I thought there was any new light that we should have or any new truths for us? Well, shall we stop searching the Scriptures because we have the light on the law of God and the testimony of His Spirit? No, brethren. I tell you in the fear of God, "Cease ye from man, whose breath is in his nostrils." How can you listen to all that I have been telling you all through these meetings and not know for yourself what is truth? If you will search the Scriptures on your knees, then you will know them and you will be able to give to every man that asketh you a reason of the hope that is within you.

Let us come to God as reasonable beings to know for ourselves what is truth. But if you want to take a position that only one man can explain the truth, I want to tell you that this is not as God would have it. Now, I want harmony. The truth is a unit. But if we fasten to any man we are not taking the position that God would have us take. We want to investigate every line of truth, especially if it bears the signet of God. Can you tell in what way God is going to give us new truth?

When I have been made to pass over the history of the Jewish nation and have seen where they stumbled because they did not walk in the light, I have been led to realize where we as a people would be led if we refuse the light God would give us. Eyes have ye but ye see not; ears, but ye hear not. Now, brethren, light has come to us and we want to be where we can grasp it, and God will lead us out one by one to Him. I see your danger and I want to warn you.

Now, this is the last ministers' meeting we will have unless you wish to meet together yourselves. If the ministers will not receive the light, I want to give the people a chance; perhaps they may receive it. God did not raise me up to come across the plains to speak to you and you sit here to question His message and question whether Sister White is the same as she used to be in years gone by. I have in many things gone way back and given you that which was given me in years past, because then you acknowledged that Sister White was right. But somehow it has changed now, and Sister White is different. Just like the Jewish nation.

Now, we did not intimate one word that we did not want that subject taken up. We did want an investigation, but I cannot take my position on either side until I have studied the question. There is the danger God has shown me that there would be a deceitful handling of the Word of God. I have been shown that when debaters handle these truths, unless they have the Spirit of God, they handle them with their own efforts. They will, by making false theories and false statements, build up a structure that will not stand the test of God. This is what the Lord has shown me.

Now, brethren, we want the truth as it is in Jesus. But when anything shall come in to shut down the gate that the waves of truth shall not come in, you will hear my voice wherever it is, if it is in California or in Europe, or wherever I am, because God has given me light and I mean to let it shine. And I have seen that precious souls who would have embraced the truth have been turned away from it because of the manner in which the truth has been handled, because Jesus was not in it. And this is what I have been pleading with you for all the time—we want Jesus. What is the reason the Spirit of God does not come into our meetings? Is it because we have built a barrier around us? I speak decidedly because I want you to realize where you are standing. I want our young men to take a position, not because someone else takes it, but because they understand the truth for themselves.

Here is Elder Smith and Elder Van Horn, who have been handling the truth for years, and yet we must not touch this subject because Elder Butler was not here. Elder Kilgore, I was grieved more than I can express to you when I heard you make that remark, because I have lost confidence in you. Now, we want to get right at what God says; all this terrible feeling I don't believe in. Let us go to the Lord for the truth instead of our showing this spirit of combativeness. God has given me light, and you have acknowledged it in times past.

Now, the words that were spoken here were that Elder Waggoner was running this meeting. Has he not presented to you the words of the Bible? Why was it that I lost the manuscript and for two years could not find it? God has a purpose in this. He wants us to go to the Bible and get the Scripture evidence. I shall find it again and present it to you. But this investigation must go forward. All the object I had was that the light should be gathered up, and let the Saviour come in.

I don't expect my testimony is pleasing, yet I shall bear it in God's fear. God knows there is a preparation going on here to fit these ministers for the work, and unless we are converted God does not want us. I hope Brother Morrison will be converted and handle the Word of God with meekness and the Spirit of God. These truths will stand just as long as time shall last. You want the eyesalve that you can see, and Jesus will help you if you will come to Him as little children. May God help us to seek Him with all our hearts.—Manuscript 9, 1888.

✦ ✦ ✦

A Call to a Deeper Study of the Word

Minneapolis, Minnesota, November 1, 1888

Dear Brethren Assembled at General Conference:

I entreat you to exercise the spirit of Christians. Do not let strong feelings of prejudice arise, for we should be prepared to investigate the Scriptures with unbiased minds, with reverence and candor. It becomes us to pray over matters of difference in views of Scripture. Personal feelings should not be allowed to influence our words or our judgment. It will grieve the Spirit of God if you close your understanding to the light which God sends you.

Dr. Waggoner has spoken to us in a straightforward manner. There is precious light in what he has said. Some things presented in reference to the law in Galatians, if I fully understand his position, do not harmonize with the understanding I have had of this subject; but truth will lose nothing by investigation, therefore I plead for Christ's sake that you come to the living Oracles, and with prayer and humiliation seek God. Everyone should feel that he has the privilege of searching the Scriptures for himself, and he should do this with earnest prayer that God will give him a right understanding of His Word, that he may know from positive evidence that he does know what is truth.

I would have humility of mind, and be willing to be instructed as a child. The Lord has been pleased to give me great light, yet I know that He leads other minds, and opens to them the mysteries of His Word, and I want to receive every ray of light that God shall send me, though it should come through the humblest of His servants.

Of one thing I am certain, as Christians you have no right to entertain feelings of enmity, unkindness, and prejudice toward Dr. Waggoner, who has presented his views in a plain, straightforward manner, as a Christian should. If he is in error, you should, in a calm, rational,

303

Christlike manner, seek to show him from the Word of God where he is out of harmony with its teachings. If you cannot do this you have no right as Christians to pick flaws, to criticize, to work in the dark, to prejudice minds with your objections. This is Satan's way of working.

Some interpretations of Scripture given by Dr. Waggoner I do not regard as correct. But I believe him to be perfectly honest in his views, and I would respect his feelings and treat him as a Christian gentleman. I have no reason to think that he is not as much esteemed of God as are any of my brethren, and I shall regard him as a Christian brother, so long as there is no evidence that he is unworthy. The fact that he honestly holds some views of Scripture differing from yours or mine is no reason why we should treat him as an offender, or as a dangerous man, and make him the subject of unjust criticism. We should not raise a voice of censure against him or his teachings unless we can present weighty reasons for so doing and show him that he is in error. No one should feel at liberty to give loose rein to the combative spirit.

There are some who desire to have a decision made at once as to what is the correct view on the point under discussion. As this would please Elder B., it is advised that this question be settled at once. But are minds prepared for such a decision? I could not sanction this course, because our brethren are exercised by a spirit which moves their feelings, and stirs their impulses, so as to control their judgment. While under so much excitement as now exists, they are not prepared to make safe decisions.

I know it would be dangerous to denounce Dr. Waggoner's position as wholly erroneous. This would please the enemy. I see the beauty of truth in the presentation of the righteousness of Christ in relation to the law as the doctor has placed it before us. You say, many of you, it is light and truth. Yet you have not presented it in this light heretofore. Is it not possible that through earnest, prayerful searching of the Scriptures he has seen still greater light on some points? That which has been presented harmonizes perfectly with the light which God has been pleased to give me during all the years of my experience. If our ministering brethren would accept the doctrine which has been presented so clearly—the righteousness of Christ in connection with the law—and I know they need to accept this, their prejudices would not have a controlling power, and the people would be fed with their portion of meat in due season. Let us take our Bibles, and with humble prayer and a teachable spirit, come to the great Teacher of the world; let us pray as did David, "Open thou mine eyes, that I may behold wondrous things out of thy law" (Ps. 119:18).

I see no excuse for the wrought-up state of feeling that has been created at this meeting. This is the first time I have had opportunity to listen to anything in reference to this subject. I have had no conversation in regard to it with my son W. C. White, with Dr. Waggoner, or with Elder A. T. Jones. At this meeting I have heard for the first time Dr. Waggoner's reasons for his position. The messages coming from your president at Battle Creek are calculated to stir you up to make hasty decisions and to take decided positions; but I warn you against doing this. You are not now calm; there are many who do not know what they believe. It is perilous to make decisions upon any controverted point without dispassionately considering all sides of the question. Excited feelings will lead to rash movements. It is certain that many have come to this meeting with false impressions and perverted opinions. They have imaginings that have no foundation in truth. Even if the position which we have held upon the two laws is truth, the Spirit of truth will not countenance any such measures to defend it as many of you would take. The spirit that attends the truth should be such as will represent the Author of truth.

Says the apostle James: "Who is a wise man and endued with knowledge among you? let him shew out of a good conversation his works with meekness of wisdom. But if ye have bitter envying and strife in your hearts, glory not, and lie not against the truth. This wisdom descendeth not from above, but is earthly, sensual, devilish. For where envying and strife is, there is confusion and every evil work. But the wisdom that is from above is first pure, then peaceable, gentle, and easy to be intreated, full of mercy and good fruits, without partiality, and without hypocrisy. And the fruit of righteousness is sown in peace of them that make peace" (James 3:13-18).

The truth must be presented as it is in Jesus; if there are any among us who become stirred up because ideas contrary from what they have believed are presented in this meeting, then stop your unsanctified criticisms and candidly investigate the subject, and it will sanctify the soul.

Two years ago, while in Switzerland, I was addressed in the night season by a voice which said, "Follow me." I thought I arose, and followed my guide. I seemed to be in the Tabernacle at Battle Creek, and my guide gave instructions in regard to many things at the conference. I will give in substance a few things that were said: "The Spirit of God has not had a controlling influence in this meeting. The spirit that controlled the Pharisees is coming in among this people, who have been greatly favored of God."

Many things were spoken which I will not now present to you. I was told that there was need of great spiritual revival among the men who bear responsibilities in the cause of God. There was not perfection in all points on either side of the question under discussion. We must search the Scriptures for evidences of truth. "There are but few, even of those who claim to believe it, that comprehend the third angel's message, and yet this is the message for this time. It is present truth. But how few take up this message in its true bearing, and present it to the people in its power! With many it has but little force."

Said my guide, "There is much light yet to shine forth from the law of God and the gospel of righteousness. This message, understood in its true character, and proclaimed in the Spirit, will lighten the earth with its glory. The great decisive question is to be brought before all nations, tongues, and peoples. The closing work of the third angel's message will be attended with a power that will send the rays of the Sun of Righteousness into all the highways and byways of life, and decisions will be made for God as supreme Governor; His law will be looked upon as the rule of His government."

Many who claim to believe the truth will change their opinions in times of peril, and will take the side of the transgressors of God's law in order to escape persecution. There will be great humbling of hearts before God on the part of every one who remains faithful and true to the end. But Satan will so work upon the unconsecrated elements of the human mind that many will not accept the light in God's appointed way.

I entreat you, brethren, be not like the Pharisees, who were blinded with spiritual pride, self-righteousness, and self-sufficiency, and who because of this were forsaken of God. For years I have been receiving instructions and warnings that this was the danger to our people. Says the Scripture: "Nevertheless among the chief rulers also many believed on him; but because of the Pharisees they did not confess him, lest they should be put out of the synagogue: for they loved the praise of men more than the praise of God" (John 12:42, 43).

There is positive danger that some who profess to believe the truth will be found in a position similar to that of the Jews. They take the ideas of the men they are associated with, not because by searching the Scriptures they conscientiously accept the teachings in doctrine as truth. I entreat you to make God your trust; idolize no man, depend upon no man. Let not your love of man hold them in places of trust that they are not qualified to fill to the glory of God; for man is finite and erring, liable to be controlled by his own opinions and feelings. Self-esteem and self-righteousness are coming in upon us, and many will fall because of unbelief and unrighteousness, for the grace of Christ is not ruling in the hearts of many.

We are to be ever searching for the truth as for hidden treasures. I entreat you, close not the door of the heart for fear some ray of light shall come to you. You need greater light, you need a clearer understanding of the truth which you carry to the people. If you do not see light yourselves, you will close the door; if you can you will prevent the rays of light from coming to the people. Let it not be said of this highly favored people, "Ye entered not in yourselves, and them that were entering in ye hindered" (Luke 11:52). All these lessons are given for the

306

benefit of those upon whom the ends of the world are come.

I have been shown that Jesus will reveal to us precious old truths in a new light, if we are ready to receive them; but they must be received in the very way in which the Lord shall choose to send them. With humble, softened hearts, with respect and love for one another, search your Bibles. The light may not come in accordance with plans that men may devise. But all who reverence the Word of God just as it reads, all who do His will to the best of their ability, will know of the doctrine, whether it be of God, notwithstanding the efforts of the enemy to confuse minds and to make uncertain the Word of God. God calls every man's attention to His living Oracles. Let no one quench the Spirit of God by wresting the Scriptures, by putting human interpretations upon His inspired Word; and let no one pursue an unfair course, keep in the dark, not willing to open their ears to hear and yet free to comment and quibble and sow their doubts of that which they will not candidly take time to hear.

Let men be careful how they handle the Word of inspiration, which has been preserved for ages through the power of God. If men were themselves controlled by the Holy Spirit they would bring heart and soul to the task, searching and digging in the mines of God for precious ore. They would be eager to come into harmony with the writings of inspired men. If they are not controlled by the Spirit of God, they will give evidence of this by caviling over His Word and by sitting in judgment upon its teachings just as did the Jews.

We should guard against the influence of men who have trained themselves as debaters, for they are in continual danger of handling the Word of God deceitfully. There are men in our churches all through the land who will pervert the meaning of the Scripture to make a sharp point and overcome an opponent. They do not reverence the Sacred Word. They put their own construction upon its utterances. Christ is not formed within, the hope of glory. They are educated critics, but spiritual truths can only be spiritually discerned. These men are ever ready and equipped to oppose at a moment's notice anything that is contrary to their own opinions. They handle the Scriptures in an unwise way, and bring self into everything they do.

"And the servant of the Lord must not strive; but be gentle unto all men, apt to teach, patient, in meekness instructing those that oppose themselves; if God peradventure will give them repentance to the acknowledging of the truth; and that they may recover themselves out of the snare of the devil, who are taken captive by him at his will" (2 Tim. 2:24-26). The servant of the Lord must not strive, but must teach the Word of God in the manner that God has ordained. Any other way is not God's way, and will create confusion.

Brother Morrison is a debater; he is a man who has not had a daily, living experience in the meekness and lowliness of Christ. He is in danger of making false issues, and of treating them as realities. He will create strife, and the result will be dissensions and bickerings. He has many things to overcome, and if he fails to overcome them, he will make shipwreck of faith, as did Elder Canright. It is dangerous to cherish feelings of self-sufficiency. He must have the meekness of Christ; the sanctifying power of the truth must be brought into the sanctuary of his soul; then he will be a polished instrument in the hands of God to do His work.

It is a matter of deep concern to us whether or not we are perfecting a Christian character, growing in grace and in the knowledge of our Lord Jesus Christ. If we are daily learners in the school of Christ we shall be daily obtaining an experience in Christian life, and we shall not be self-sufficient and self-exalted. We shall be as humble as little children, and there will be a nourishing power in our words which will drop as the dew. The fruits of righteousness, sown in peace of them that make peace, will then appear.

Growth in grace will give Brother Morrison increased ability to comprehend the deep mysteries of the gospel. Those who are in so great a degree unacquainted with Christ are ignorant of the spirit they cherish. They will be dry and Christless. The knowledge of Christ and His Word is the foundation and fullness of all knowledge. Many workers are not now fitted for the position of trust they occupy. They must be transformed by the grace of Christ. God wants to give our brethren another spirit. Without this change they will carry the spirit of irreverence for God and His living Oracles into their work; and if this mold is put upon the work, it will dishonor God. The subduing, softening influence of the grace of Christ must fashion and mold character; then it will be a pleasure to deal justly, to love mercy, and to walk humbly with God.

The debating spirit has come into the ranks of Sabbathkeepers to take the place of the Spirit of God. They have placed finite men where God should be, but nothing can suffice for us but to have Christ dwell in our hearts by faith. The truth must become ours. Christ must be our Saviour by an experimental knowledge. We should know by faith what it is to have our sins pardoned, and to be born again. We must have a higher, deeper wisdom than man's to guide us amid the perils surrounding our pathway. The Spirit of Christ must be in us just as the blood is in the body, circulating through it as a vitalizing power.

Our greatest fear should be that we may be found rebelling against God's Word, which is to be our guide amid all the perils of the last days. We must be sure that we are on the Lord's side, that we have the truth as it is in Jesus. With the grace of God in the soul, we may be secure anywhere, strong in the Lord, and in the power of His might.

We would discourage the discipline that tends to make persons debaters. We urge you not to connect young men who are learning to be teachers of Bible truth with one who has a debating spirit, for they will surely receive the wrong mold of character. The habitual debater is so accustomed to beclouding and turning aside evidence, and even the Scriptures, from the true meaning to win his point, that everything that does not strike him favorably and is not in harmony with his ideas he will combat, caviling at God's inspired Word.

There is too little dependence upon God. When God would have a special work done for the advancement of the truth, He will impress men to work in the mines of truth with prayerful earnestness to discover the precious ore. These men will have Christlike perseverance. They will not fail or be discouraged. They will sink self out of sight in Jesus. Men will go forth in the spirit and power of Elijah to prepare the way for the second advent of the Lord Jesus Christ. It is their work to make crooked things straight. Some things must be torn down, some things must be built up. The old treasures must be reset in a framework of truth. They are to preach God's Word; their testimony must not be molded by the opinions and ideas that have been regarded as sound, but by the Word of God, which liveth and abideth forever. They are to lift up Christ and call sinners to repentance. They are to practice the graces of Christ, to pursue a straightforward course, breaking down skepticism and urging upon all their personal responsibility to be kind and courteous, to do good and to win souls to Jesus.

The Scripture should not be treated in a debating style. Those who have educated themselves as debaters have so increased their spirit of combativeness that they are ready to cavil over the Word of God, to resist and oppose everything that disagrees with their ideas or opinions. They are in their element when an opportunity is offered for them to question and criticize, for it is natural for them to be ready for battle at any time. They will play upon words, misinterpret and misstate, because this has become a settled habit with them, a second nature. Nothing is safe in their hands. Now, the Lord desires that those who are in this condition should be converted, that they become as little children—simple, meek, teachable, and Christlike.

We must have the power of God to soften and change the rugged traits of our character, that we may be susceptible to the influence of truth. We should look upon the Word of God with reverence, as something sacred. Christ is true, and without Him we know nothing as we ought to know it. We are lacking in the spirituality of true religion.

When the Jews took the first step in the rejection of Christ, they took a dangerous step. When afterward evidence accumulated that Jesus of Nazareth was the Messiah, they were too proud to acknowledge that they had erred. So with the people of our day who reject the truth. They do not take time to investigate candidly, with earnest prayer, the evidences of the truth, and they oppose that which they do not understand. Just like the Jews, they take it for granted they have all the truth, and feel a sort of contempt for anyone who should suppose they had more correct ideas than themselves of what is truth. All the evidence produced they decide shall not weigh a straw with them, and they tell others that the doctrine is not true, and afterward, when they see as light evidence they were so forward to condemn, they have too much pride to say "I was wrong"; they still cherish doubt and unbelief, and are too proud to acknowledge their convictions. Because of this, they take steps that lead to results of which they have never dreamed.

Those who have not been in the habit of thinking and investigating for themselves, believe certain doctrines because their associates with them in the work believe them. They resist the truth without going to the Scriptures for themselves to learn what is truth. Because those in whom they have had confidence oppose the light, they oppose it, not knowing they are rejecting the counsel of God against themselves.

God has a work to do in our world that many finite minds do not see or understand, and when God unfolds truth to His people, and it does not come in harmony with their ideas, many are ready to despise and reject it. I entreat you, brethren, reverence your Bible. Plead with God for light. Fast and pray in your closet upon your knees. Ask God to lead you into all truth. Tell Him that you want the truth as it is in Jesus. It is not wise for one of these young men to commit himself to a decision at this meeting, where opposition, rather than investigation, is the order of the day. The Scriptures must be your study, then you will know that you have the truth. Open your heart that God might write the truth upon its tablets.

One who would be a teacher of sacred things should not go forth to work with the people without a full assurance that he has the truth. He should not go forth feeling that perhaps the doctrines which he advocates may not all be substantiated by the Bible. Anything short of a full conviction that what he presents is truth will make his preaching powerless, unless he has the presumption to put forth mere assertions as conclusive evidence. This is unfair, and yet this has often been done by sharp debaters. You should give your authority to the people from God's Word. You should not believe any doctrine simply because another says it is truth. You should not believe it because Elder Smith, or Elder Kilgore, or Elder Van Horn, or Elder Haskell says it is truth, but because God's voice has declared it in His living Oracles.

Truth will triumph gloriously, and those who have received the truth because God has revealed it in His Word will triumph with it. Those who neglect to search for evidence for themselves, and rely upon what someone else says, will not have root in themselves, and will not be able to give a reason of the hope that is within them. God's commands must be heard. He says, "Go forward." There are large fields to be explored. There are mines to be discovered in which are precious

310

jewels of truth. Let no one close these mines, and cease to dig for the truth lest they should have to cast aside some preconceived idea or opinion. No, brethren, we want to know the truth; and God forbid that any of you should turn from precious truths simply because you do not want to believe them.

No one must be permitted to close the avenues whereby the light of truth shall come to the people. As soon as this shall be attempted, God's Spirit will be quenched, for that Spirit is constantly at work to give fresh and increased light to His people through His Word. Let the love of Christ reign in hearts here. Let all yield themselves to that heavenly power which alone can create unity by quelling selfish ambitions and human pride. When the Spirit of God comes in, love will take the place of variance, because Jesus is love; if His spirit were cherished here our meeting would be like a stream in the desert.

Has the truth as it is in Jesus been received into the heart? Have the mind of God and His ways become our mind and our ways? Is the law of God our standard? If it is, its principles will be wrought out in our life. Wherever the love of Jesus reigns there is peace with God, joy in God; and the love and joy are reflected to others. We cannot afford to be deceived by a semblance, a form. The truth of the Bible may be read, and we may think that a form of words will accomplish that which only the Spirit of God can accomplish by its converting, transforming power. We may hold certain points of truth firmly and yet refuse to let in any fresh rays of light which God may send to show us the beauty of the truth. It is dangerous for us to take a step in uncertainty. We should not reject or oppose the views of our fellow laborers because they do not agree with our ideas until we have used every means in our power to find out whether or not they are truth, comparing scripture with scripture.—Manuscript 15, 1888.

✢ ✢ ✢

APPENDIX B

What Became of A. T. Jones
and E. J. Waggoner?

Statement Prepared by Arthur L. White
Secretary of the Ellen G. White Estate

ELDER A. T. JONES was born April 26, 1850, in Ohio, and from 1870 to 1873 served in the United States Army. While stationed near Walla Walla in the Territory of Washington in 1873 he was led to the Seventh-day Adventist Church. Jones was a studious man, interested especially in history; and after becoming a Seventh-day Adventist, in due time he entered the ministry. His name appeared in ministerial lists of the denomination in 1885, when it is noted that he became an associate editor of the *Signs of the Times,* published in Oakland, California.

Elder E. J. Waggoner was born in Wisconsin, January 12, 1855. He attended Battle Creek College in its earliest days and received a classical education. After completing his college work, he was persuaded to take the medical course. He completed his work at Bellevue Medical College, New York. From there he went to the Battle Creek Sanitarium, where he served as staff physician for some time. Waggoner's heart was in evangelism, and in 1883 he was called to assist his father, J. H. Waggoner, editor of the *Signs of the Times.* The May 6, 1886, issue lists E. J. Waggoner and A. T. Jones as associate editors.

The two men were quite different in build, manner, temperament, and delivery. Of this a personal acquaintance, A. W. Spalding, wrote:

"Unlike as garden fruit and apples of the desert were these two, yet they teamed together in close fellowship and cooperation. Young Waggoner was not even like his father, tall and massive; he was short, stocky, somewhat diffident. Jones was a towering, angular man, with a loping gait and uncouth posturings and gestures. Waggoner was a product of the schools, with a leonine head well packed with learning, and with a silver tongue. Jones was largely self-taught, a convert found as a private in the United States Army, who had studied day and night to amass a great store of historical and Biblical knowledge. Not only was he naturally abrupt, but he cultivated singularity of speech and manner, early discovering that it was an asset with his audiences."—*Origin and History of Seventh-day Adventists,* vol. 2, pp. 289-291.

The Minneapolis Conference and its aftermath drew both Elder Jones and Elder Waggoner into increasing prominence in the work of the church. God blessed their ministry, and it was their privilege to lead in a renewed emphasis on the basic Protestant doctrine, righteousness by faith. For many years they were held in high esteem.

Knowing well the peril of those who are used mightily of God, and with a seeming premonition, Ellen White wrote in 1892:

"It is quite possible that Elder Jones or Waggoner may be overthrown by the temptations of the enemy; but if they should be, this would not prove that they had had no message from God, or that the work that they had done was all a mistake. But should this happen, how many would take this position, and enter into a fatal delusion because they are not under the control of the Spirit of God. They walk in the sparks of their own kindling, and cannot distinguish between the fire they have kindled, and the light which God has given, and they walk in blindness as did the Jews.

"I know that this is the very position many would take if either of these men were to fall, and I pray that these men upon whom God has laid the burden of a solemn work, may be able to give the trumpet a certain sound, and honor God at every step, and that their path at every step may grow brighter and brighter until the close of time."—Letter 24, 1892.

Jones and Waggoner, so highly honored of God, because of their wide influence for good, became the special point of attack of the great adversary. The Ellen G. White communications to both men through a fifteen-year period following 1888 reveal that each had weaknesses in his experience and each made mistakes. This, however, did not disqualify them to do God's service. It is with regret that we record that both men lost their way. We shall review rather briefly the experience of the two men, and then deal first in detail with Elder A. T. Jones. All that appears here is presented in kindness, but it is appropriate that a record of the facts be made available to all interested in the work of the church, and in the experience of these two men at one time so influential in its work.

In 1884 Elders Waggoner and Jones met. On April 26, 1886, as Elder J. H. Waggoner, the father of E. J. Waggoner, was released from his responsibilities as editor of the *Signs of the Times*, E. J. Waggoner and A. T. Jones were selected to serve jointly, and their names appeared jointly as editors for three years, from May 13, 1886, to May 6, 1889. The issue of May 6, 1889, lists E. J. Waggoner as editor and A. T. Jones as special contributor.

Elder Waggoner then carried the work of editor until May 11, 1891, when the name of Elder M. C. Wilcox appears on the masthead. It will be observed that the two men held editorial responsibilities through the Minneapolis conference and E. J. Waggoner for two and a half years beyond.

313

THIRTEEN CRISIS YEARS

Elder A. T. Jones

Through the 1890's Elder A. T. Jones was much in Battle Creek. He attended all sessions of the General Conference from 1888 to 1905, and often presented important addresses. Ellen White had occasion in April, 1893, to caution Elder Jones regarding extreme views in his presentations of the relation of faith and works (1 SM 377-380), and a few months later to reprove him for giving wholehearted support to Anna Rice Phillips who claimed the gift of prophecy (2 SM 85-95). From time to time Ellen White counseled him to exercise caution in his manner of speaking and writing so as to avoid giving offense.

On October 5, 1897, he was elevated to the position of leading editor of the *Review and Herald*. It was announced that with this arrangement Elder Jones "instead of speaking to comparatively few of our people at annual gatherings, he will address all of them every week. This will give to our churches and scattered brethren everywhere, the privilege of receiving, each week, the words of faith, hope, courage, and good cheer that have been a means of so much blessing to many all over both America and Europe."—*Review and Herald,* Oct. 5, 1897, p. 640. Uriah Smith served as an associate editor.

This arrangement continued until May 14, 1901, when an adjustment was made, and Elder Uriah Smith was returned to the position as editor in chief of the *Review and Herald* and Brother Jones was freed for evangelistic work in the field.

At the General Conference session held February 19 to March 8, 1897, at College View, Nebraska, Jones was elected a member of the General Conference Committee. He served in this capacity until, in a most unusual action, he resigned some time prior to the General Conference of 1901. Concerning this it should be noted that subsequent to the General Conference session held in February, 1899, efforts were made to right certain wrongs pointed out by the testimonies, and it is reported:

"The efforts of the Committee in this direction did not in every instance meet with that hearty co-operation that might be expected. This caused Elder Jones to lose sight of the dignity of his position to the extent of allowing, as the Testimony says, 'an evil spirit to cast drops of gall into his words,' and, forgetting the warning given him of God, 'he pressed his brethren into hard places.' When mildly reproved by the president of the General Conference for his course, and counseled to make the matter right with the brethren by apology, he resigned from the Committee."—*A Statement Refuting Charges Made by A. T. Jones Against the Spirit of Prophecy and the Plan of Organization of the Seventh-day Adventist Denomination,* pp. 15, 16 (96-page pamphlet published in May, 1906, by the General Conference Committee).

At the General Conference session held in Battle Creek in April,

1901, as presented in chapters 17 and 18, the work of the church was reorganized, which reorganization resulted in the drawing in of a number of men to carry responsibilities. The field was divided into union conferences and provision was made for the organization of General Conference departments. Jones was again elected to the General Conference Committee, a position which he held until the session of 1905. In the summer of 1901 he was assigned to general work in the field, and attended certain camp meetings.

He took the position that we should have no "kings," that is, we should not have conference presidents. This sentiment prevailed in the writing up of a new constitution at the General Conference of 1901. The result was that a General Conference Committee was elected, with the committee authorized to appoint a chairman and other officers. A. T. Jones gave strong support to this plan. As he entered the field, attending camp meetings in 1901, his work took him to the West Coast, first to the Pacific Northwest and then to California. At the California Conference session in June he was elected president, and oddly enough, accepted the office. His harsh and domineering spirit soon cost him the confidence of many of those with whom he worked.

In the summer of 1903, at a time when affairs at the conference were most uncomfortable, he had an interview at Elmshaven with Ellen White, in which he told her that at the request of Dr. J. H. Kellogg he was planning to go to Battle Creek to teach Bible in the American Medical Missionary College. He hoped to be able to help Dr. Kellogg. She counseled him not to go. He promised Sister White that he would be guarded. She had been warned in vision that such a move on his part would lead to his downfall. She wrote of it thus:

"In vision I had seen him [A. T. Jones] under the influence of Dr. Kellogg. Fine threads were being woven around him, till he was being bound hand and foot, and his mind and his senses were becoming captivated."—Letter 116, 1906.

Then, comments Ellen White, as she reported this to Brother Jones just before he went to Battle Creek, she could see "that his perceptions were becoming confused, and that he did not believe the warning given. The enemy works in a strange, wonderful way to influence human minds."—*Ibid.* But Jones was sure that he would not fall away. He was a man with too much self-confidence.

In 1905, still a member of the General Conference Committee, he was invited to assist in meeting some religious liberty crises in Washington, D.C. But in two months he was back in Battle Creek. Ellen White endeavored to draw Elder Jones away from Battle Creek into evangelistic work, and this would doubtless have saved the man. On February 26, 1905, she wrote:

"Elder A. T. Jones, God calls upon you to go out into the cities, and give the last message of warning. Look to God for your support as you

315

go. Call the people together, and you will certainly not work in vain. Let the truth go forth as a lamp that burneth. No longer confine your efforts to one place. Let there be held, right where you are, a solemn convocation. Let there be a renunciation of self to God. Hold fast the beginning of your faith unto the end. Let not your faith waver. Go forth in faith. . . .

"There are those who have never heard the message of mercy and warning. In the name of the Lord I say, Delay not. Proclaim the gospel message in the cities of America. Scatter the seeds of truth throughout these cities. Take with you reliable men, who with pen and voice will act their part in proclaiming the message of present truth to the world."— Letter 187, 1905.

But he continued in Battle Creek under influences he was no match for. He was soon in bitter opposition to his brethren and to the Spirit of prophecy. He issued a number of tracts and pamphlets in defending his course.

A number of enlightening statements made by Ellen White in communications to him or in which reference is made to him between the time he joined Dr. Kellogg in Battle Creek until her last message to him in 1911 are most revealing. There unfolds the picture of the progressive steps in the experience of a man, self-confident, flaunting warning messages, and deliberately placing himself under influences that finally captivated him and led to his spiritual destruction. There follows in chronological order excerpts from several Ellen G. White documents:

July 23, 1904, "Inharmonious Note" at the Berrien Springs Meeting.—"The words and attitude of Brother ——— and Brother A. T. Jones at the Berrien Springs meeting [1904] struck an inharmonious note,—a note that was not inspired of God. It created a state of things which resulted in harm that they did not anticipate. It made the work of the meeting very much harder than it would otherwise have been. Had it not been for their injudicious course, the Berrien Springs Conference would have shown very different results."—*Special Testimonies, Series B, No. 2, p. 42.*

December 29, 1905, Lost Spiritual Eyesight and Repudiated God's Warnings.—"I send no more [testimonies to be read to the Battle Creek church] to A. T. Jones, for I have evidence that a work will have to be done for him before the Lord will accept his service. God has given him warnings which he has repudiated, and I am deeply grieved that he has so little spiritual eyesight."—Letter 345, 1905 (written to G. W. Amadon, first elder of the Battle Creek church).

March 12, 1906, The Wrong Spirit and Demonstrations of Bitterness. —"You may be surprised to hear the words that you have heard from Elder A. T. Jones; but I am not at all surprised. This is the development of the man when the spirit that is counter to the Spirit of God

APPENDIX B

comes upon him. In him as he is at the present time, you have a representation of a man who is not under the molding influence of the Spirit of God. The Lord accepts no such demonstrations of bitterness. . . .

"Read in my books, *Patriarchs and Prophets* and *Great Controversy,* the story of the first great apostasy. History is being repeated and will be repeated. Read then, and understand."—Letter 98, 1906.

April 2, 1906, Captivated, Deluded, and Deceived.—"During the General Conference at Takoma Park [May, 1905], Elder Jones's case was again presented to me. After this, I had a long conversation with him in which I pointed out his danger. But he was self-confident, and declared to me that Dr. Kellogg believed the truth and the testimonies just as firmly as the rest of us believed and advocated them. In this conversation Elder Jones manifested that which had been revealed to me regarding him, that in the place of receiving the warnings he was full of self-confidence; that he had exalted himself, and in the place of being prepared to help Dr. Kellogg, he had united with him to disbelieve and distrust, and falsely to accuse the ministers and others who were trying to save Dr. Kellogg and other physicians who were in peril. . . .

"I warned Elder Jones, but he felt that he was not in the least danger. But the fine threads have been woven about him, and he is now a man deluded and deceived. Though claiming to believe the testimonies, he does not believe them."—Letter 116, 1906 (to Dr. David Paulson).

May 1, 1906, Chose Darkness Rather Than Light.—"I am sorry for A. T. Jones, who has been warned over and over again. Notwithstanding these warnings, he has allowed the enemy to fill his mind with thoughts of self-importance. Heed not his words, for he has rejected the plainest light and has chosen darkness instead. The Holy One hath given us messages clear and distinct, but some poor souls have been blinded by the falsehoods and the deceptive influences of satanic agencies, and have turned from truth and righteousness to follow these fallacies of satanic origin."—Manuscript 39, 1906.

June 15, 1906, Voice Controlled by Dr. Kellogg.—"Dr. Kellogg controls the voice of Elder A. T. Jones, and will use him as his mouthpiece. My prayer is, O God, open Thou the blind eyes, that they may see; and the ears of the deaf that they may hear, and become humble."—Letter 182, 1906.

July 5, 1906, Grieved the Holy Spirit.—"Elder A. T. Jones, Dear Brother,—Again and again your case has been presented before me. I am now instructed to say to you, You have had a large knowledge of truth, and less, far less, spiritual understanding. When you were called to the important work at Washington, you had need of far more of the humble grace that becometh a Christian. Since the Berrien Springs meeting, your attitude and the attitude of several others has grieved the Spirit of God. You have been weighed in the balance and found wanting. . . .

317

THIRTEEN CRISIS YEARS

"Self-exaltation is your great danger. It causes you to swell to large proportions. You trust in your own wisdom, and that is often foolishness. Do you remember the counsel which I gave you in my letter of April, 1894? This was in answer to your letter expressing deep regret over the part you had taken in an unwise movement [Anna Phillips, see *Selected Messages*, book 2, pp. 85-95] and you appealed to me for instruction, that you might ever avoid such mistakes. . . .

"When at the General Conference at Washington I had a conversation with you, but it seemed to have no influence upon you. You appeared to feel fully capable of managing yourself. After that conversation, scene after scene passed before me in the night season, and I was then instructed that you neither had been nor would be a help to Dr. Kellogg: for you were blind in regard to his dangers and his real standing. You can not be a help to him; for you entirely misjudge his case. You consider the light given me of God regarding his position as of less value than your own judgment. . . .

"Brother Jones, I have a message for you. In many respects you are a weak man. If I were to write out all that has been revealed to me of your weakness, and of the developments of your work that have not been in accordance with the course of a true Christian, the representation would not be pleasing. This may have to be done if you continue to justify yourself in a course of apostasy. Until your mind is cleared of the mist of perplexity, silence is eloquence on your part.

"I am so sorry that you are spoiling your record. . . .

"Brother Jones, will you not earnestly seek the Lord, that in your life there may be a humbling of self, and an exaltation of the principles of righteousness? The success and prosperity of your work will depend upon your following strictly where Jesus leads the way. God would have you stand as a faithful watchman, laboring earnestly for souls ready to perish. If you will consent to be a worker together with God, you may manifest in earnest words and works, the gracious influence of the Holy Spirit. True repentance will bring newness of life."—Letter 242, 1906.

July 27, 1906, A Revival of the First Great Apostasy.—"My heart was filled with sorrow because of the course that J. H. Kellogg is following. And A. T. Jones is following the same course and voicing the same sentiments, with a most determined spirit. When a realization of this comes over me, with such force, great sorrow fills my soul.

"I have before me such a revival of the first great apostasy in the heavenly courts, that I am bowed down with an agony that cannot be expressed. It is in Battle Creek that the warnings that are given are entirely disregarded."—Letter 248, 1906 (to D. H. Kress).

August 1, 1906, Under Hypnotic Power.—"God showed me what He would do for Dr. Kellogg if he would take hold of His hand. But he wrenched himself away. At the Berrien Springs meetings [1904] the most precious offers were given him, and when he wrenched himself away I had such agony of heart that it seemed as if soul and body were being rent asunder.

"I have seen Dr. Kellogg exerting a hypnotic influence upon persons, and at such times the arch deceiver was his helper. Those who sustain him are guilty with him. This blindness of understanding is a strange thing in our ranks. In regard to A. T. Jones, he has a theory of truth, which his books express, and he dares not tear up his past experience, which has been published. But he virtually turns away from his former experience by his present course of action. . . .

"Dr. Kellogg has had every advantage to make impressions on human minds, and he will improve this to the best of his ability in an effort to destroy confidence in the testimonies. Those associated with him who have upheld him, will have to answer before God for their course of action."—Letter 258, 1906.

September 30, 1907, Giving Heed to Doctrines of Devils.—"A. T. Jones, Dr. Kellogg, and Elder Tenney are all working under the same leadership. They are classing themselves with those of whom the apostle writes, 'Some shall depart from the faith, giving heed to seducing spirits and doctrines of devils.' In the case of A. T. Jones I can see the fulfillment of the warnings that were given me regarding him."—Letter 306, 1907.

October 1, 1907, Now in Apostasy.—"I want to say to you, Brother and Sister Starr, that the time we have so long anticipated has come. A. T. Jones has come to the place where he voices the mind and faith of Dr. Kellogg. They have now taken a decided stand against the truth, and special efforts will be made to lead souls away. This apostasy has cost us dearly. . . . Warning after warning has been given to these men, but they have set themselves first to deny the messages, and then to declare that they did not believe the testimonies. Their work against the truth has been as marked by deception as was the course of Canright. Many whose sympathies were with Dr. Kellogg, have united with him, and have departed from the faith."—Letter 316, 1907.

Nov. 11, 1908, Departed From the Faith.—"I must warn our people against laboring in any line in connection with A. T. Jones. He is one who has departed from the faith, and has given heed to seducing spirits. He knows not what manner of spirit he is of."—Letter 330, 1908.

November 10, 1911, Confession and Rebaptism the Only Way Back.—"Elder A. T. Jones, I have given you instruction in straight, clear lines in regard to the perverting influence under which you have placed yourself. Your lips have uttered perverse things. You have denied the clear light of truth, and have linked up with strange elements. I gave you a correct statement in regard to your position, but you went on doing the very things the Lord had warned you not to do. It has been a strange course for one who has been enlightened by the Lord as you have been, but you have acted very much like a man who has lost his bearings. The question is, Do you think you can still hold your membership in the Seventh-day Adventist Church and go on hurting the influence of this people by the tracts that you publish? You have done a cruel work.

"I have warned you in regard to these things. I presented the case as the Lord presented it to me. When your blind eyes are opened, when your spiritual eyesight is restored by the heavenly anointing, you will see that you have a work to do for your own soul, and to undo what you have done to confirm others in unbelief. . . .

"We should rejoice greatly if you would be really converted. The Lord will not receive you as a faithful minister, to be trusted with His flock, unless you throw your lot in with His people, to confirm them in the faith—not to rule them according to human ideas. . . .

"If you wish to renew your covenant with God by confession and repentance and rebaptism, we shall rejoice with you. When you are converted, your self-sufficiency will disappear, and you will become meek and lowly in heart. When you see and repent of your mistakes, you will be a great blessing in helping others. The destroyer now takes advantage of your self-righteousness to weave into your experience his own ideas and theories. When you are really desirous of uniting with those from whom you have withdrawn yourself, the testimony will be borne that you looked up after you had stepped off the platform on which you had previously stood, and that hands were put beneath your arms, and you and Elder Waggoner were lifted once more on to the platform, standing there with shining countenances and uplifted hands. Has this time come?"—Letter 104, 1911.

In mid-1907, because of his warfare against the church and its leaders, the ministerial credentials of A. T. Jones were withdrawn. In July, 1908, he had an interview with Ellen White, which was not at all satisfactory.

He asked for a hearing at the General Conference session of 1909 held in Washington. The request was granted, and these meetings were held, at which he stated his case. Elder A. V. Olson, who was present, reports:

"Though not a delegate I was invited to attend the last meeting. Seated on the platform were Brethren C. W. Flaiz, acting chairman, and W. T. Bartlett, of England, acting secretary. At a table below the pulpit sat Brother A. G. Daniells, the General Conference president, at one end and A. T. Jones at the other end. Before final action was taken Brother Daniells arose and made a statement in which he said how much he personally had appreciated the fine, faithful, and efficient services that Brother Jones had rendered the cause during many years of association with us, how we had esteemed and loved him, and how our hearts had been filled with sorrow because of the misunderstanding and conflict that had come in to mar our sweet fellowship, and to separate him from his brethren.

"Then turning to Brother Jones, he made a very tender and touching appeal for him to forget the past and to come back to stand shoulder to shoulder with his brethren in the service of the Lord. He assured him that we all loved him and that we wanted him to go with us in the march toward the kingdom of God. Extending his hand across the table, he said, in a choking voice, 'Come, Brother Jones, come.' At this, Brother Jones arose, started to reach his hand across the table, only to draw it back. Several times, as Brother Daniells continued to plead, saying, with tears in his voice, 'Come, Brother Jones, come!' Brother Jones would hesitatingly reach out his hand part way across the table, and pull it back again. The last time he almost clasped the hand outstretched from the other side, then, suddenly, pulled it back, and cried out, 'No! No!' and sat down. That was one of the saddest scenes that I have ever witnessed. There were not many dry eyes in the Seminary chapel that afternoon. We all loved Brother Jones, and it grieved us to see him go out into the dark."—E. G. White Estate Document File No. 53.

Shortly after this, by formal action, he was dropped from the membership roll of the Seventh-day Adventist Church of which for years he had been a member.

Subsequent to working with Dr. Kellogg, A. T. Jones entered upon the publication of *The American Sentinel of Religious Liberty,* a monthly journal which he issued over a period of several years. In November, 1915, he moved to Washington, D.C., and devoted his time to publishing this paper. He began to attend The People's Church, a colored Seventh-day Adventist church that had broken away from the conference and was pastored by F. H. Seeney. On the invitation of the officers of this church, A. T. Jones participated in the work of the church and then joined the group. He was granted membership on April 15, 1916.

In February, 1923, Jones returned to Battle Creek for rest and treatment, and was making satisfactory progress until in early May, when he suffered a stroke of apoplexy that caused his death a few days later. Funeral service was conducted in Battle Creek at a funeral home by the Reverend G. E. Fifield. He was buried at Kalamazoo, Michigan. A brief obituary copied from the Battle Creek *Enquirer* appeared in the *Review and Herald* of June 28, 1923. Mrs. Jones ever remained true to the message.

Elder E. J. Waggoner

Elder E. J. Waggoner continued his editorial work at the *Signs of the Times* until May, 1891. In 1892 he was called to England to lead out in the editorial work there. He was stationed there until the General Conference session of 1903. During the last few years of his European sojourn, Elder W. W. Prescott was in the field laboring closely with him.

In 1894 Ellen White expressed fears concerning certain views held by Elder Waggoner in regard to organization. The communication is addressed to A. T. Jones and we quote in part:

"God has in a special manner used you and Brother Waggoner to do a special work, and I have known this. I have given all my influence in with yours, because you were doing the work of God for this time. I have done all that it was possible for me to do in Jesus Christ to stand close to you, and help you in every way; but I am very sorrowful when I see things that I cannot endorse, and I feel pained over the matter. I begin to be afraid.

"Elder Waggoner has entertained ideas, and without waiting to bring his ideas before a counsel of brethren, has agitated strange theories. He has brought before some of the people, ideas in regard to organization that ought never to have had expression. I supposed that the question of organization was settled forever with those who believed the testimonies given through Sister White. Now if they believe the testimonies why do they work contrary to them? Why should not my brethren be prudent enough to place these matters before me, or at least to enquire if I had any light upon these subjects? Why is it that these things start up at this time when we have canvassed the matter in our previous history, and God has spoken upon these subjects? Should not that be enough?

"Why not keep steadily at work in the lines that God has given us? Why not walk in the clear light He has revealed and in place of tearing to pieces that which God has built up, work on the side of Jesus Christ? O how Satan would rejoice to get in among this people, and disorganize the work at a time when thorough organization is essential, and will be the greatest power to keep out spurious uprisings, and to refute claims not endorsed by the word of God. We want to hold the lines evenly, that there shall be no breaking down of the system of regulation and order. In this way license shall not be given to disorderly elements to control the work at this time. We are living in a time when order, system, and unity of action is most essential."—Letter 37, 1894 (to A. T. Jones, Jan. 14, 1894).

Elder Waggoner, representing the British field, attended the General Conference session of 1897 and gave a series of eighteen studies on the book of Hebrews. He also presented the sermon on the last Sabbath of the conference. Dr. Kellogg was also at this session and spoke frequently, and there introduced his pantheistic views—views which were to have a far-reaching influence on Elder Waggoner.

Within the next few years, while laboring in Great Britain, Waggoner began to espouse and promulgate views of spiritual affinity—that is, that one not rightfully a marriage partner here might be one in the life to come, and this allows a present spiritual union. This was to lead to his downfall. He came to the 1901 General Conference session "enthused with what" he "supposed to be precious spiritual light" (Letter 224, 1908). Ellen White was shown that, instead, the views he was then espousing were "dangerous, misleading fables," similar to the fanaticism she had been called to meet following 1844. Of this she later wrote: "Dr. Waggoner was then departing from the faith in the doctrine he held regarding spiritual affinities."—*Ibid.*

She also stated: "In the European field for a long time he has sown seeds that have [borne] and will bear evil fruit, leading some to depart from the faith, and to give heed to seducing spirits, doctrines of satanic origin."—Letter 121, 1906.

After the 1903 General Conference session, Elder Waggoner remained in the United States. O how earnestly Ellen White labored for him! She urged that he be placed on the faculty of the newly established Emmanual Missionary College, on a probationary basis, in the fervent hope that he could clear himself of subtle deceptive theories. Message after message was sent to him in warning and appeal.

To him she wrote on October 2, 1903: "It is those who have had the most light that Satan seeks the most assiduously to ensnare. He knows that if he can deceive them, they can, under his control, clothe sin with the garments of righteousness, and lead many astray. God grant that our teachers may see and understand this, their great danger, and that they may recover themselves from the snare of Satan, and put forth redoubled efforts to save others who are exposed."—Letter 230, 1903.

Then two days later she wrote again, speaking very plainly: "You have been represented to me as being in great peril. Satan is on your track, and at times he has whispered to you pleasing fables, and has shown you charming pictures of one whom he represents as a more suitable companion for you than the wife of your youth, the mother of your children.

"Satan is working stealthily, untiringly, to effect your downfall through his specious temptations. He is determined to become your teacher, and you need now to place yourself where you can get strength to resist him. He hopes to lead you into the mazes of spiritualism. He hopes to wean your affections from your wife, and to fix them upon another woman. He desires that you shall allow your mind to dwell upon this woman, until through unholy affection she becomes your god.

"The enemy of souls has gained much when he can lead the imagination of one of Jehovah's chosen watchmen to dwell upon the possibilities of association, in the world to come, with some woman whom he loves, and there raising up a family."—Letter 231, 1903. Published in *Medical Ministry*, pp. 100, 101.

After a winter term of teaching at Berrien Springs, Elder Waggoner, still in the fog, went to Battle Creek to join A. T. Jones and Dr. J. H. Kellogg, and in so doing placed himself in the midst of pantheistic teachings and skepticism concerning the Spirit of prophecy.

On August 1, 1904, Ellen White addressed a solemn message to Brethren Paulson, Sadler, Jones, and Waggoner in which she presented what God had presented to her "in the night season." The last part of the nine-page appeal is directed specifically to Brethren Jones and Waggoner:

"Our Counselor then laid his hands on the shoulders of Elder A. T. Jones and Elder E. J. Waggoner, and said, 'You are confused. You are in the mist and fog. You have need of the heavenly anointing.' To Brother Jones He said, 'Why have you permitted your mind to be worked as it has been? I warned you not to permit this.' He said to Brother Waggoner, 'Leave the place where you now are, and walk in the path that I have pointed out. *Living Temple* is full of seductive sentiments, which if received, will tear down the foundations of your faith, and weaken your perceptions of truth and righteousness.'

"Addressing them both, He said, 'There is a work for both of you to do. Your minds need to be thoroughly renewed. Your faith is to rest on a high, holy, substantial foundation. God has a work for you to do in sounding the last message of warning to the world. Turn away from scientific theories. What is the chaff to the wheat?'

"The Speaker was represented to me as standing on a high platform. To this platform He raised both men, and placed one at His right hand and the other at His left. Then He said: 'The sentiments that you have received in harmony with the special theories presented in the book *Living Temple* are not pure truth. There is a commingling of truth and error, and it will be difficult for you to single out the true from the false, to distinguish between the threads of truth and the threads of error. My word is spirit and life. I am the bread of life. . . .

" 'Cast out of your minds the sophistries that you have been receiving. God would have your minds cleansed from these theories. Hold fast the beginning of your confidence firm unto the end. Warn others to let spiritualistic sophistries alone. Preach the word as you have done in the past, and My Spirit will be with you. Holy angels will accompany you if you will follow the way that God has marked out.

" 'Separate entirely from the bewitching, misleading sentiments that run through *Living Temple*. You are to be My witnesses. You are to declare My word.' . . .

"My brethren, I am so glad, so thankful, for this message that the Lord has given me for you. He said, 'I will make you both free if you will take hold of My strength. You each have a work to do in proclaiming the message that Christ came to give John, telling him to write it in a book, and send it to the churches.' "—Letter 279, 1904.

Then Ellen White turns to what might be if the two men, believing the testimony, responded wholeheartedly. But Heaven's appeal fell on dull ears. The steps that might have been taken were not taken. In 1905, Ellen White appealed to Elder Waggoner as she did to A. T. Jones, to enter the field of evangelism. She well knew that in saving others they might save themselves. Both men preferred to remain in Battle Creek.

In 1906 Elder Waggoner, after his wife had divorced him because of his attentions to a nurse with whom he had become acquainted in England, married the lady. This, of course, terminated his connection with the church. A few years later we find him at the Battle Creek Sanitarium working in medical and religious lines. There is no record that he ever opposed the church. On May 28, 1916, at the age of 61 years, he died at his home of a heart attack after a full day of activity. Word of his death was given to the church in a back-page note in the *Review and Herald* of June 29, 1916.

This has been a sad recital. How subtle is Satan in his attacks on those to whom God has given great light. We return to the words of Ellen White penned in 1892:

"It is quite possible that Elder Jones or Waggoner may be overthrown by the temptations of the enemy; but if they should be, this would not prove that they had had no message from God, or that the work that they had done was all a mistake. . . . I pray that these men upon whom God has laid the burden of a solemn work, may be able to give the trumpet a certain sound, and honor God at every step, and that their path at every step may grow brighter and brighter until the close of time."—Letter 24, 1892.

It could have been, but seeds of evil cherished in the hearts of Jones and Waggoner gave the victory to the great adversary.

It should be remembered that while God used the preaching and writings of these two men in a broad reform movement within the church at a time when they were living close to Heaven, there followed in the years associated with their apostasy from the truth, much fruitless preaching and hurtful influences. A man may be a servant of God at one time in his life and an instrument of evil at another. Thus it was with Jones and Waggoner, the story of whose later years clutches at our hearts and reminds us painfully of Paul's words: "Let him that thinketh he standeth take heed lest he fall" (1 Cor. 10:12).

✦ ✦ ✦

APPENDIX C

The President of the
General Conference

In the Light of the Constitution Adopted in 1901
Statement by A. G. Daniells in a letter to
Dr. C. C. Nicola, July 30, 1906

NOW with reference to my assumption of the title of president of the General Conference. In dealing with this question I shall state the facts bearing upon it just as I understand them.

The General Conference was organized in the year 1863. The constitution which was formed and adopted by those who organized the conference made provision for the office of president and the manner of filling the office. A president was elected at the time the conference was organized. From that time until 1901, a period of thirty-eight years, that part of the constitution relating to the presidency remained practically unchanged. At no time during that period was the General Conference without a president.

At the general session held in Battle Creek in 1901 this feature of the constitution was changed. The committee on organization brought before the delegates a recommendation which read as follows:

"That the General Conference Committee be empowered to organize itself, and to appoint all necessary agents and committees for the conduct of its work."

This recommendation was brought up for consideration in the thirteenth meeting of the session, and after a brief statement regarding its meaning, was adopted. Its intent was then worked into the constitution. It was expressed in section 1, article 4, in this language:

"The Executive Committee of this conference shall be twenty-five in number, and shall have power to organize itself by choosing a chairman, secretary, treasurer, and auditor, whose duties shall be such as usually pertain to their respective offices. It shall also have the power to appoint all necessary agents and committees for the conduct of its work."

The constitution as thus amended substituted the word "chairman" for the word "president." It placed the selection and appointment of this chairman in the hands of the Executive Committee, instead of the delegates to the conference; and it transferred from the delegates to the members of the Executive Committee the privilege of selecting and the power to elect the secretary and treasurer of the General Conference. This amended constitution was adopted as a whole without rereading or discussion. The silence of the delegates regarding this change was not because the meaning of this new arrangement was clear to them, and the change acceptable. Many were confused by what was being done, and thought best to keep silent.

I have since learned that it was generally supposed that this new arrangement was a part of the plan of reorganization some of us had brought from Australia. But it was not a part of our plan. We were advocating the organization of union conferences, also general departments, such as we had developed in Australia. My mind and my time were so fully devoted to those features of reorganization which I had tested, and felt that I understood, that I did not even stop to ask why it was proposed to transfer from the delegates to the Executive Committee the right to select and appoint the chief officers of the denomination. I wonder that this proposal was not boldly challenged and sternly rejected by the delegates.

Soon after the Executive Committee had been elected they met to organize themselves. They elected a chairman, a secretary, a treasurer, and an auditor. They also appointed some department committees and officers.

The Executive Committee elected me chairman. It was a very busy time. Everybody was pressed with the closing work of the conference. My term of office and my duties as chairman were not defined by the committee. As time passed on and I got into the real work of the conference, I found myself at a loss sometimes to know just how to apply the title "chairman." In doing business with the railway associations, in signing documents sent to our office by Government statisticians, and in other matters, I was supposed to sign the blanks as president, and I did so. Sometime during the year, I do not remember just when, in making up the letterhead for the General Conference stationery, I had the word "president" attached to my name. In calling the General Conference session to be held in Oakland in April, 1903, I attached the word "president" to my name.

I have never denied having assumed the title "president." I have never apologized for having done so. I have never known that I committed any great wrong in using that title. I did not see any great difference between the words "chairman" and "president."

Although the title "president" was attached to my name on the General Conference letterhead, and I was generally designated by that title at camp meetings and elsewhere, no member of the General Conference Committee ever reproved me for this, nor criticized me to my face for it. At the General Conference council held at Battle Creek in

THIRTEEN CRISIS YEARS

November, 1902, I heard some criticism from a certain quarter regarding my use of this title.

The fact is, it was at this council that I received the first full ray of light that ever came to me as to what was involved in the arrangements to place the appointment of a chairman in the hands of the Executive Committee instead of leaving it in the hands of the delegates to the conference, where it had been from the time the conference was organized thirty-eight years before.

The explanation of this arrangement came out in this way: In the early part of the summer of 1902, while in England, I took a firm stand against certain proposals made by Dr. Kellogg. This led to a break between us. Soon after returning to America in the fall, I learned from reliable sources that the doctor had expressed the opinion that there would have to be a change in the chairmanship of the General Conference. After our November council had gotten fairly under way, certain members of the committee who were special friends of the doctor's, formally proposed and seconded that A. G. Daniells be relieved of the office of chairman, and that A. T. Jones be appointed chairman. While this proposal did not prove to be acceptable to very many members of the committee, the discussions that followed, and the facts that were brought out, fully explained the reason for giving to the committee, instead of the delegates, the power to appoint the chairman.

For years there had been more or less conflict between the president of the General Conference and the recognized leader of the medical work of the denomination. No matter who the president was, the conflict continued in proportion to the firmness of the president. In 1900 this controversy reached such a crisis that it was generally supposed that a serious rupture of some sort would occur at the 1901 conference.

The break did not come. Another effort was made to unite the general body and the medical department. Advantage was taken of the situation to make an arrangement by which it might be possible to get rid quickly of a troublesome factor; namely, a president elected for a specified time. This officer had previously been selected by the people's delegates to take special watchcare over the varied interests of the cause. When he saw the medical branch taking advantages, to the injury of other branches of the cause, he endeavored to prevent it. This, of course, brought him into conflict, but it protected certain interests of the work. It was plain that the General Conference president was a menace to the free, unrestricted prosecution of the plans of the medical leaders.

Different men had been tried, with but little change in the situation. The stronger the medical branch grew, the more serious the conflict became. The only sure and safe remedy was to place in the hands of the General Committee the power to make and unmake the leading officer.

Then if the medical part of the committee could manage the rest of the committee, no man could long remain a menace to the plans and projects of the medical branch. The chairman who ventured to stand against the ever-increasing demands of the medical leaders might be removed at any meeting of the committee, and a better friend to the medical cause made chairman in his place.

This is the explanation of that change made in the constitution in 1901. This is the explanation as it was worked out up to the point of the actual proposal to remove me from the chairmanship and to put A. T. Jones in my place. That the proposal did not carry was not the fault of the plan.

When a number of the members of the Executive Committee got their first clear understanding of what was involved in the new arrangement, they determined that they would test the situation and see whether this denomination had come to the place where its affairs were to be managed in this way. They proposed to know whether the chairman or president—whatever his title might be—would be supported by the committee when discharging the duties of his office conscientiously, even if he displeased some prominent member of the committee, or whether he would be abandoned and turned out for refusing to follow the dictation of another.

This was the issue to which we were brought by the application of this new feature of the constitution. I need not state the outcome of this conflict.

After this experience at the Fall Council of 1902, some of the members of the committee felt perfectly clear in their minds as to the course to be taken at the next session of the conference. In fact, all over the field the brethren had been reaching conclusions regarding the meaning of the new arrangement, and they came to the [1903] conference with their minds made up to express their convictions. They did so, and by an overwhelming majority repudiated the arrangement made in the 1901 conference regarding the selection and appointment of the General Conference officers.*

There was a good opportunity for the delegates of the conference and for the people to set me aside for having assumed the title of president. I was perfectly willing to be judged and dealt with by the delegates. In fact, I was willing all along to be dealt with by the whole

---

* A few months after the 1903 General Conference session, Ellen G. White wrote, on Nov. 17, 1903, concerning the election of denominational officers:

"Every member of the church has a voice in choosing officers of the church. The church chooses the officers of the state conferences. Delegates chosen by the state conferences choose the officers of the union conferences, and delegates chosen by the union conferences choose the officers of the General Conference By this arrangement every conference, every institution, every church, and every individual, either directly or through representatives, has a voice in the election of the men who bear the chief responsibilities in the General Conference."—*Testimonies,* vol. 8, pp. 236, 237.

committee, but I did object to being treated as a football by a faction whom I ventured to displease. We all know the verdict of the delegates. And, by the way, it was their own hearty, free action. They were not forced to elect me president. . . .

At the Washington conference in 1905 there was another opportunity to deal with me for assuming or usurping too much. Now it is very strange to me, and to many others, that after the delegates have twice reckoned with me, and expressed their views regarding my course, Elder Jones should make all this ado about my use of the title president. As already stated, I have never denied having used it. I have never apologized for using it. I have not boasted for having used it. I do not say it was right, and I do not know that it was wrong. I did the best I knew how at the time. Others might have been wiser.

We have been passing through a great crisis. I have desired to see and stand for true principles. The Lord has helped me in this terrible conflict. Others might have done better in dealing with the details of the controversy; but, notwithstanding all the mistakes I have made, the Lord has wrought a great victory. While there is some wreckage strewn along the way, there is nothing to what there would have been if the evil that was at work had been allowed to go on unopposed. —Ellen G. White Document File No. 53.

✦✦✦

APPENDIX D

Delegates at 1888 Session Bear Witness on Conjectures of Conference Rejection

IN THE fall of 1930 the author of the undated, privately published pamphlet, *Forty Years in the Wilderness in Type and Antitype,* was invited to conduct the fall Week of Prayer at Pacific Union College. The pamphlet carried the subtitle, "The Exodus and the Advent Movement," and contained repeated assertions of denominational rejection at Minneapolis of the message of righteousness by faith.

In his sermons the speaker followed the theme of his pamphlets, drawing a parallel between the Advent Movement and the experience of ancient Israel. The Kadesh-barnea rejection of divine leadership was set forth as a type of what the author termed a denominational rejection of the truths presented at Minneapolis in

330

1888. He predicted a Baal-peor type of experience that would involve Seventh-day Adventist leaders and thousands of church members in terrible and shocking immorality.

Three church leaders who had been delegates at the 1888 General Conference session and who in 1930 lived in the environs of Pacific Union College protested such a distortion of history and such a forecast. One of these three, Elder Cornell McReynolds, at a testimony meeting at the college during that Week of Prayer, reviewed what actually happened at Minneapolis. He pointed out that there were those who received great light and blessing at that session, he among them, and that they had not lost the experience they received there.

Within a few weeks all three of the delegates bore written testimony of facts with which they were familiar. They wrote of what they knew as eyewitnesses. All three recognized there had been a mixed reaction at Minneapolis. Some had accepted the message, some were undecided, and others had rejected it. In the interest of accuracy in reporting such an important point in denominational history, the eyewitness testimony of responsible church leaders in their prime, as they attended the Minneapolis Conference, may be contrasted with the unsupported conjecture from the pen and lips of one who was at the time a child of three, living far away.

The three from whom we have written statements are W. C. White, A. T. Robinson, and C. Cornell McReynolds. Elder W. C. White, who lived close to the Elmshaven office, where he served as secretary of the Ellen G. White Estate, presented his testimony in a written letter December 30, 1930, to the Week of Prayer speaker. We shall present his clear-cut testimony first. But before doing so, it may be well to look at the credentials of this man who was so very familiar with the General Conference session of 1888.

He was there as a member of the thirteen-man General Conference Committee, a position he had held for ten years. He was there as Ellen White's assistant. He was there as one of the five delegates from the California Conference. He was there as the secretary of the Foreign Mission Board and vice-president of the International Sabbath School Association, and the vice-president of the International Tract and Missionary Association, and also chairman of the General Conference Book Committee. During the Conference he was chosen as one of the two editors of the *General Conference Bulletin,* which covered the reports of the meeting to the field.

W. C. White was in his prime at 34 years of age, with a broad experience at home and overseas. When Elder O. A. Olsen, who was elected General Conference president, could not take office until he had closed up his work in Europe, W. C. White, as noted in the text, was pressed in to serve as acting president. He carried this responsibility for six months, one half of Elder Olsen's first term. If anyone was in a position to know what took place in 1888 and could be relied on to bear witness concerning the Minneapolis Conference, it was he. And his witness in 1930 is in full accord with what he wrote of the Conference just at its close.

In writing to the Week of Prayer speaker in 1930, W. C. White commented favorably on his strong points and on his effective ministry, and then called attention to his serious misrepresentation of the Minneapolis Conference. He wrote of the prejudice and feeling in 1888 against Elders Waggoner and Jones, and the spirit of the older workers at the Conference, and then said:

> But the most serious feature of the disaffection was the fact that, because Sister White urged the importance of the message of righteousness by faith, and because thereby she seemed to be upholding these brethren, contrary to their judgment, it grew into a spirit of rejection of the testimonies of Sister White. "Elder Waggoner was Sister White's pet" was a common remark. . . .
>
> Not all who were present, however, were among the class who rejected either the message or Sister White's testimony. Among them were some who can bear testimony, as did Elder McReynolds in a social meeting at the college [in 1930], that they received great light and blessing, and that they had not lost the experience that they received at that meeting. After the Conference they returned to their fields and carried the message to the churches in their conference, with most precious results.
>
> After the Conference, Sister White labored earnestly in various meetings, setting forth the rebellious course taken by some at the Conference, and emphasizing the great truth of righteousness by faith, with the result, not that the message was "rejected," but that it was more widely received. One by one, those who had been among the opposition at Minneapolis, made confessions, accepted and rejoiced in the new-found light, and preached it, at least theoretically. One of the last to yield was Uriah Smith, of whom Sister White writes in 1891, that he had "fallen on the Rock," and was "broken."
>
> Had the message been generally rejected, either at Minneapolis or soon after, as is inferred by some and as is stated in your book, would we find that Elder Jones and Sister White labored together in camp meetings and institutes, preaching this doctrine, of course with the sanction and endorsement of Conference officials?
>
> I think we may, however, grant that there was not that entering into the experience either by ministers or people, to the extent that God was calling for, and after a few years, without any open rejection or repudiation of the doctrine, a formalism and apathy prevailed.—W. C. White Letter, December 30, 1930, in White Estate Document File #331.

That the projections made by the Week of Prayer speaker were new and not a matter of accepted historical fact, is clear from the references W. C. White made in stating that:

> A number have come to me and others of our ministering brethren at the college since you asking us as to our opinions as to some of the new and minor points that you brought out in your It is evident that their minds have by these things been more or less diverted from the striking and vital truths that pertain to salvation, and that were so forcefully set forth by you.—*Ibid.*

These questions and those in his own mind led him over a period of some days, with the help of his aides at the Elmshaven office, to make a careful study of the records to see whether there was any documentary support for the position taken by the Week of Prayer speaker. He addressed himself to the point:

> You will remember that I handed you a copy of a letter that I had just found in the files, in which Sister White gave certain cautions to A. T. Jones regarding making extreme statements in preaching justification by faith [now published in *Selected Messages*, book 1, pp. 377-379]. Since then other similar statements have been found, and I have been making a study of this subject, based largely upon the manuscripts and *Review and Herald* articles. I am passing along with this to you, a few compilations I have made.—*Ibid.*

Then W. C. White discussed the time-setting potential of too close an analogy between Israel's experience and that of Seventh-day Adventists.

> Aside from the question of its being a correct statement of fact, your assertion that it was a few years after Minneapolis, that the message of righteousness by faith was "finally rejected," carries with it an inference that otherwise, 1928 would have marked the ending of the forty years of wilderness wandering and the entrance of Canaan. The extra "few years," that mark the

beginning of the wilderness wandering will naturally be added to 1928, and there will result an unfortunate speculation regarding the time either for the outpouring of the Spirit or of the second coming of Christ.

I am having copied for you from a *Review* of 1892 a report of one of Sister White's sermons at Lansing, Michigan [now in *Selected Messages*, book 1, pp. 185-191], in which she clearly sets forth that there is danger of this, and comes very close to a prediction that men would arise who would do this, thereby diverting the minds from the truths that would prepare them for Christ's coming. And this is not merely a theoretical possibility. . . .

I understand that you will be here again at the spring Week of Prayer. I venture to hope and to suggest to you that you may come a little early, and spend a day or two or more, if possible, here with us at the office. I should dearly love to study some of these things over with you, and I believe that, with what we are collecting from Sister White's manuscripts, it might be of value to you also.—*Ibid.*

The other two minister who were delegates at the 1888 General Conference and who resided close to Pacific Union College also denied in writing the allegations of the Week of Prayer speaker.

Elder A. T. Robinson, a minister and executive of long experience in North America and overseas, at the age of 38 attended the Minneapolis meeting as president of the New England Conference and consequently as a delegate. He had been in denominational work for six years first conducting evangelistic work in city missions and then as conference president. His caliber is shown in the fact that of the forty-five years he eventually gave to denominational work, twenty-six were in conference leadership, as president of conferences in South Africa, Australia, and in the East and West of the United States. The rest of his time was given to college Bible teaching and service as a sanitarium chaplain. At the Minneapolis General Conference he served on a number of important committees. He lived to the age of 98. On January 30, 1930, he set forth his testimony in writing:

I have heard, and seen in print, recent references to what is treated as a historical fact, that at the time of the Minneapolis General Conference in 1888, the doctrine of righteousness by faith was rejected by Seventh-day Adventists, as a denomination. Statements from the writings of Mrs. E. G. White are cited as proof of this alleged fact.

It is difficult for me to harmonize these statements with my own personal experience and observation in connection with the Minneapolis General Conference; also with my understanding of statements from the writings of Mrs. White, that are used in support of the view above referred to.

I was present at the Minneapolis meeting from the opening to the close. I listened to, and received a great blessing from, the studies presented on the subject of righteousness by faith.

I listened to many things that were said by our leading men concerning the attitude of the men who were leading out in the presentation of the theme of justification by faith. I heard no statements made that could rightly be construed as rejecting the doctrine of justification by faith. What was spoken of as an adverse attitude on the part of the men who were conducting the studies [particularly A. T. Jones] was criticized severely by some, and at times they were made the subject of ridicule. Perhaps I can best give one concrete illustration of what appeared to justify the attitude taken by some of our leading men toward the men who were prominent as teachers of righteousness by faith.

Elder U. Smith and A. T. Jones were discussing some features in connection with the ten kingdoms into which western Rome was divided. One day, Elder Smith, in his characteristic modesty, stated that he did not claim originality in the view he held on the subject, that he had taken statements of such men as Clark, Barnes, Scott, and others mentioned, and drawn his conclusion from such authorities. In opening his reply, Elder Jones, in his characteristic style, began by saying, "Elder Smith has told you he does not know anything about this matter. I do, and

THIRTEEN CRISIS YEARS

I don't want you to blame me for what he does not know."

This harsh statement called forth an open rebuke from Sister White who was present in the meeting.

I have read carefully the testimonies of reproof from the pen of Sister White, following that meeting, in which she charges our leading men with having stood in the way of light and blessing that God intended should have been cherished and accepted at that time. But that righteousness by faith, as a doctrine held by our leading men, and on which their belief has never changed, was rejected, at that time, is not a warranted conclusion.

I believe that some of our leading brethren, whom we all loved, and most of whom are now sleeping in the grave, stood in the way of great light and blessing being shed upon this movement at that time, by their attitude toward the men who were presenting the message for the time. But it appeals to me that so important a Bible doctrine as justification by faith, has never been set aside or rejected by this denomination.—Statement of A. T. Robinson in Ellen G. White Estate Document File #189.

The other witness to write on this point in early 1931 was a former local and union conference president, Elder Cornell McReynolds, who, at the age of 35, attended the Minneapolis Conference as a delegate from Kansas, where he was then serving as a licensed minister. He had been a year in denominational employ, having come from twelve years of teaching. His qualifications and potential were such that, even though not ordained, he was chosen as one of the five delegates from his conference, a field with more than a dozen ordained ministers. Four years later he was elected president of the Kansas Conference, and from then on much of his working life was spent in conference administrative work in both local and union levels. W. C. White, in his December 30, 1930, letter made reference to McReynolds' statement given at a testimony meeting at the college during the Week of Prayer.

Here is the written testimony of Cornell McReynolds:

In 1888 I was sent as a delegate from the Kansas Conference to the General Conference held that year in Minneapolis, Minnesota, that notable conference long to be remembered by many. . . .

We had heard that there would be an investigation of the teachings found in the Galatian letter at the Conference, and it was reported that there would be a debate. Certain articles in the *Review* during 1887 and all through 1888 had awakened some concern in my mind. Being decidedly prejudiced in favor of Elder Butler and against E. J. Waggoner, I went to that meeting with a prejudiced mind. On arriving there we learned that Elder Butler was sick and could not be present, which added to my disappointment.

Fortunately it was arranged for Elder Waggoner to give his studies first. With pencil and note-book in hand I listened for heresy and was ready to see flaws and find fault with whatever was presented. As Elder Waggoner started in it seemed very different from what I was looking for. By the close of his second lesson I was ready to concede that he was going to be fair and his manner did not show any spirit of controversy, nor did he even mention any opposition that he was anticipating. Very soon his manner and the pure gospel that he was setting forth had materially changed my mind and attitude, and I was an earnest listener for Truth. . . .

As Elder Waggoner proceeded with his studies the Spirit of God was working on my heart, and I was seeing where I had been all those years, living what some of us call (and very properly too) the "up and down" life. Getting into the dark, repenting, confessing, getting relief, and then for a while all going well; then relapsing into the same sad state again, and all because I did not feel happy and free. My faith was not constant. I had not learned how to hold on in the dark. At the close of Elder Waggoner's fourth or fifth lesson I was a subdued, repenting sinner. I felt that I must get away alone with the Lord. I went out of the city away into the woods; I did not want dinner; I spent the afternoon there on my knees and on my face before the Lord with my Bible. I had come to the point that I *did* believe the promises of God in His Word for forgiveness of my sins, and that it *did* mean *me* as well as any other sinner. His promise in 1 John 1:9; Isaiah 1:18;

334

Galatians 1:4; and Titus 2:14 and many of the promises were reviewed ⁓⁓⁓ ⁓⁓⁓ I saw Him as my own personal Saviour and there I was converted anew. All ⁓⁓⁓⁓⁓ that my sins were really forgiven were taken away, and from then till now, I have never doubted my acceptance as a pardoned child of God. . . .

We returned to our homes. Very soon some of our brethren came to us and began to inquire what about that debate. We heard that they had a debate and a lot of confusion and some bitter feelings were aroused, etc. We told them that that was all true but we got some things that were so much better to talk about that we had said nothing about that trouble.

By direction of the Conference Committee I went out to our churches, to one and two per week, and gave studies on the Truth so precious to me then, the subject of justification by faith, and rich blessings were found by many. My own soul was richly blessed, and real revival followed. . . .

Early in the spring, 1889, word began to come of some of those who had stood with the opposition at the Conference beginning to see light, and soon earnest confessions followed. Within two or three years most of the leading men who had refused the light at the Conference had come out with clear confessions. . . .

From the pen of the servant of God as published in the *Review and Herald*, August 13, 1889, I quote: "God has raised up men to meet the necessity of this time who will cry aloud and spare not, who will lift up their voice like a trumpet, and show my people their transgressions, and the house of Jacob their sins. Their work is not only to proclaim the law, but to preach the truth for this time—the Lord our righteousness. . . . But there are those who see no necessity for a special work at this time. While God is working to arouse the people, they seek to turn aside the message of warning, reproof, and entreaty. Their influence tends to quiet the fears of the people, and to prevent them from awaking to the solemnity of this time. Those who are doing this are giving the trumpet no certain sound. . . . They have become ensnared by the enemy."

For two, three, four, and more years following the Conference there came such appeals, admonitions and warnings almost weekly, and thank the Lord, they were not sent in vain. Many, both ministers and people, were aroused and sought the Lord with sincerity of soul, and found light and peace.—Statement of Cornell C. McReynolds, Ellen G. White Estate Document File #189.

A significant point that must not be overlooked is that what these three leaders wrote in 1930 when the rejection theory was brought to the front was in full accord with the eyewitness testimony of A. T. Jones in 1893, as noted in the text. It is in full accord with the consistent testimony of Ellen G. White, who was also there and deeply involved. It is also in full accord with the findings of such careful researchers (who were not present at Minneapolis) as A. G. Daniells, and A. W. Spalding. Neither J. N. Loughborough in his *Great Second Advent Movement,* published in 1905, nor the careful historian M. E. Olsen in his *A History of the Origin and Progress of Seventh-day Adventists,* published in 1925, suggests a denominational rejection. The witness supported by documentary evidence is consistent.